'The Olds Abroad'

With hand luggage only!

The diary and stories of a 60 year old husband & wife
travelling around the World.
One hundred & fifty three days. The trip of a lifetime!

Bob Cooke

 New Generation Publishing

Contents

Preface

How does a working class married couple with a combined age of one hundred and twenty two years reach a decision to travel around the world? Answer: A tangle of reasons and dreams.

In 2015 we made that 'one off' trip of a lifetime. A five month journey, visiting India, Australia, New Zealand, Fiji, Chile, Peru, Bolivia and Brazil. During which we celebrated our 40th wedding anniversary and my wife's 60th birthday. Throughout our adventure we kept diaries, making day to day entries. The main purpose was to record dates and places but notes of events and personal experiences were added.

On our return I decided to transcribe them and share the content with family and friends. A good way to avoid the glazed eye stare if a traveller's tale of over five minutes long is recounted! As I wrote, expanding jottings into full description, the more I remembered. Items that were amusing, scary, exciting and plainly informative.

There was a lot to tell and it seemed to me that much would be entertaining to a wider audience, along with knowledge that could forearm or help anyone thinking of a similar venture, especially folks of senior years that are being encouraged to explore the planet.

An idea for a book formed. To tell the story of the trip, the reasons it happened, the planning, our emotions and personal opinions. The biggest problem was what should be left out, a title came easy. 'The Olds Abroad,' from a WhatsApp group formed for us to keep in touch with home.

I'd like a reader to feel as if he or she was there from inception to journeys end and to know a little of our lives. For that I added a very brief biography. That apart, the book is presented in a day to day format. The layout gives a choice on how it's read, for example, skip 'About us' or 'planning' and go straight to the first day of the trip.

Before accepting my final draft as the best I could present, I reread and rewrote many of the paragraphs, took some of the mundane out, put other trivia in and while doing so questioned myself. Was I too critical of India? Did I overpraise Australia and New Zealand or say enough about Fiji? There can be no doubt that I love Latin America!

Destinations, accommodations and places of interest mentioned are easily researched using the internet, so any descriptions given are from a personal view. A few criticisms are made at the end.

For more pictures search and join the Facebook group. 'The Olds Abroad' book of the travel diary.

Acknowledgements and thanks are noted as and when they happened. The first is to Chris, who not only suffered my impatience, intolerance and moods during the journey, then had to tolerate them again as I wrote the story!

About us

Both of us Portsmouth born, me in 1952, the first of four children to newlywed young parents on Portsea Island. Formative years, infant and junior schooling at Paulsgrove, a post WW2 built, predominantly council housing estate. 1964 to 1968, secondary modern education in a craft based Technical High school. Early youth and teenage years, park football and youth club where in 1969 I met Christine. Graduated to pubs and nightclubs. Had the usual part time jobs dictated by age, paperboy, warehouse lad in a high street store and later, petrol pump attendant, which I continued even after obtaining a career start as an Assistant Technical Illustrator with the Ministry of Defence. By 1971 I'd become disillusioned in my civil service job and joined my father in his various business ventures, betting shop and car sales.

Christine, second of four sisters born 1955, again to working class parents. Early years growing up in one of the city's clearance and improvement areas. The changes Hitler and the Luftwaffe hadn't managed during the Blitz, the local corporation was.

In the 1960's, her family moved to a council house on a small estate in Milton. She attended a local secondary modern girls' school. In the 1970's, notwithstanding sibling rivalry and ambitions, prospects for females of her upbringing were limited. Until our marriage she'd follow a path that many trod. After leaving school her part time job became full time, a contribution to the household income being more important than a career path. Over the next few years our stories combine.

We married in 1975. The same year managing to get on the private housing ladder and our first child Charles arrived. 1976, first daughter Angela joined us. 1981 we moved to our present home. From then to 1994 the Cooke family experienced both tragedy and joy. The last business failed completely in 1986, Susanne was born the same year. Mary, two years later in 1988. Unfortunately during this period my sister, brother and both parents passed away.

By 1988 I'd given up hope of working within the motor trade. After a couple of periods of unemployment and by taking labouring jobs self-trained for the building trade. By 1994 I felt confident enough to start and offer a 'van and man' maintenance service. During all of these times, good or bad, I kept up my interest in football. Although only ever playing at Sunday league level, I later volunteered as an amateur coach, referee and manager, using my abilities as best I could for lad's, youth and men's teams.

Chris maintained the important positions of housewife and mother until our children were all in full time education, then she began to improve and test herself. Learned to drive, undertook voluntary work in school and studied for GCSE level Mathematics and English qualifications. Gaining these 'accidentally' led to a late start career and now has the status of Higher Level Teaching Assistant. Amazingly at the age of forty seven she began distance running, not so much now but her gym membership is well used to this day. During the 1990's our eldest children obtained university places, their attainments prompting the two youngest to seek the same in the 2000's. All achieved degrees, leading to differing career paths.

We both read when time allows. Chris enjoys novels and history. I have read many of Dicken's stories, my favourite being David Copperfield. I do prefer factual and have read many books concerning World War One.

With the development of the internet over the past twenty years one of my hobbies has been researching family history and I have compiled, sourced and documented ancestral trees for both of our families.

Neither of us had a sheltered upbringing, as children, world events were rarely kept from our gaze. Our parents were youngsters through the five years of World War Two. We, from the age of awareness to this date have

4

lived through the many conflicts that were never fully settled in 1945. The medium of television has not just been entertainment.

We both have a good sense of humour, having grown up with popular and alternative comedy from others that is now considered politically insensitive or racist. So it's not surprising that some jocular or dark comments made to each other would or could be perceived as either.

We're not easily shocked but that doesn't mean we can't be. Personally, only months before our trip, I was driving home and to my enjoyment the extended version of Baba O'Reilly (Teenage Wasteland) by the Who, had just been aired. The radio newscast that followed included the report of the infamous execution by burning to death of a captured Syrian pilot. I almost lost control of the car. By the time I'd arrived home the song and the vile murder had become inexorably linked. My mind was in turmoil.

Over many years I'd come to respect those who have faith in whatever religion. Maybe I could be described as a lapsed Christian, I'd certainly never been a practising one, unless bowing my head at an Armistice Day service or joining in a mumbled prayer at a funeral service counted.

In Brazil 2014 I'd seen reminders that charitable and Christian acts could be of great comfort. Many people there showed that in their kindness to me and my son. On occasions I'd taken time away from the hectic schedule to reflect in one or two of the ever open churches, joining ordinary folks doing the same.

That news broadcast became a tipping point. If the man upstairs had been looking out for me during difficult times, that day was the first time I actually acknowledged it. I consolidated my affirmation later in the year, by adding tattoos of St Christopher the patron saint of travellers and my birthday Saint, Mary Magdalen to the patriotic England and town inks.

Circumstances, reasons and dreams

When affordable, Chris and I have enjoyed the once a year, eight to ten day breaks in the usually guaranteed sunshine destinations, Greece, Spain, Canary Islands. We've made cultural trips to cities. As a family we travelled to Rome to celebrate my fiftieth birthday. History, food and drink, a grand combination. In recent years we'd had the pleasure of sharing holidays with our children and grandchildren.

Our eldest offspring have all travelled to one place or another, Asia, Australasia and South America. As proud parents we'd been privileged to share their experiences through letters and postcards pre internet, later by email.

2012, at my son Charles' home, family all present at the Christmas dinner table, we'd eaten, were enjoying drinks and talking amongst ourselves when 'out of the blue,' he suggested to me that we should consider going to the 2014 World Cup tournament in Brazil. I was slightly taken aback but knew this was a serious proposal, because we'd discussed this many times, had now both reached a period in our lives that it could actually happen and could afford it in time and finance. Crucially would the criteria be met again?

No great leap from agreement to planning and the stress of obtaining tickets. The probable payback to our wives considered, we travelled in June 2014, arriving the first day of the tournament. Stayed for just under five weeks. Followed the dismal England team and visited other cities. I fell in love with Brazil and its people, later having a tattoo as a reminder. 'Brasil, foi emociante.'

Prior to this my only proper adventure had been in 1970. Now a memory with about twenty surviving photographs. As a callow teenager of eighteen years old, with a work colleague and fourteen strangers I'd crossed 'old' Europe in a Ford mini-bus. To Greece, then back, a twelve day organised camping package with TransTrek, a

6

company born out of the hippy era that spawned today's almost compulsory gap year travel.

Two weeks before Charles and I went to Brazil, second daughter Susanne obtained a yearlong work permit and left England for Australia. I remember the sadness of taking her to the coach depot and recall the circumstances that prompted her to go, but that's her story. She being in Oz would be one of the reasons we would go there.

As many folks do, Chris and I had talked about undertaking an adventure. With envy we'd watch television programmes featuring famous people trekking mountains, making long railway journeys, visiting hard to get to places, forests, jungles, deserts, finding wildlife, exotic birds and fish.

On too many occasions lately my body had been telling me that the worn bits were getting even more worn. At sixty years old I started to reduce my physical work commitments. By 2014, my contribution to the household budget being limited to a small rental income, cash from part time building or decorating work and some very minor profit trading coins, watches and other items through ebay™.

Our Government in its bankruptcy of cash and reason has recently been adjusting and equalising retirement age for men and women. As a result Chris will not able draw a civil pension until she is sixty six years of age. Almost at a stroke, British administration has stolen six of her retirement years and nearly thirty thousand pounds. Not the only woman to suffer this outrage! I cannot grasp why there hasn't been a bigger outcry. If it had happened in France I'm sure another revolution would have taken place. I wonder now that as us old folks are still being milked is it only the expense of production and distribution that has prevented the wearing of cow bells?

Planning

So for the real deal. Where would we start? Where would we finish? I'd obviously extolled the virtues of Brazil, so South America obviously. Australia would be a definite as Susie was there. We'd need to get positively serious if this wasn't to remain a pipe dream. One evening, almost in jest I asked where Chris would like to be on or about her sixtieth birthday. "Fiji." Her blasé reply.

Over the next few weeks Atlas's were opened, possible destinations discussed, nothing was fixed, nowhere discounted. We were 'actually' formulating a travel plan, country by country, place by place.

Although important factors such as finance, time off work and leaving the house empty needed to be considered, a time frame for the venture was forming. Mother Nature would help. Some of the countries on our list best visited when she is kindest to humans. We'd decided that a circumnavigation of the globe was the best and most exciting plan, not just in and out of some far flung places.

The internet played a major part in planning. Websites, hundreds of them, some read for their advice, others for flight schedules. Those selling travel packages provided comparative information.

My experience of moving around a country the size of Brazil became invaluable. I don't claim to have done any planning for that trip, my son was travel manager. I'd watched, listened and learned. Attending the World Cup had been a perfect example of travelling in a set time frame. I'd need to do the same over a longer period, formulating entrance and exit strategies.

In August 2014 only we were privy to the very fluid plan. By September it was for a February 2015 start in India, onto Australia, then Fiji. Afterwards to cross South America and back home in June or July.

A big factor was baggage. For the Brazil trip Charles and I had taken hand luggage and full size trekking back packs, the latter as airline hold stowage. We both had bad experiences, my pack missing on arrival in Madrid for a connecting flight but fortunately located later that day. His had a bottle of sun tan lotion burst inside. On our return, his didn't arrive at London, although it was found and repatriated the next day. These events were uppermost in my mind, what if such a thing happened on a World trip? We decided to travel with cabin luggage only!

In the last of two weeks of school summer holidays we took a ten day summer break in Tenerife. There our discussions continued and we tested ourselves by each taking only 6 kilograms of hand luggage, including snorkels and goggles!

Late September 2014 during one of our regular visits to our son's home we announced our intentions. There'd probably been suspicions, but now it was on the table for full discussion, approval or disapproval. The only criticism given was that maybe we'd left it late for the necessary planning. After explaining we'd been doing that almost constantly since July, there was just encouragement and offers of help. I hadn't expected any less.

To obtain time off from her job, Chris needed a letter requesting a sabbatical. It was drafted and duly delivered. I'd already convinced her that if declined I would pressure her to walk away and pick up her career somewhere else on our return. I felt this wouldn't become necessary knowing that she was a dedicated long term member of staff. Knowledge and experiences she would gain on our expedition would only improve her value and teaching abilities. I was correct, she received the school's approval but with a proviso. The sabbatical period had to be two full terms. She would prove her loyalty by providing cover for staff shortage even during the weeks before we set off.

The not so secret was fully out. No backing down now! During the next few months life would be little more than consolidating plans. Flights soon to be booked, copious details written and saved in notebooks. I produced a calendar based spreadsheet, multiple copies for making permutations. We explored the possibility of booking some sections of the trip with travel companies. Visited one well known agent in Portsmouth but just plagiarised their South America itinerary. Chile, Peru, Bolivia, Brazil and all of the important destinations on the 'Gringo trail.' With a few adjustments we could do the same trip for half the cost.

India is a big subcontinent, my knowledge limited to schoolboy geography, history and stamp collecting. I was certain that I wouldn't be able to select any destinations except maybe the Taj Mahal and a beach resort. I contacted a tour provider based in Delhi. By email, the firm had sent a detailed itinerary which included destinations we'd not even heard of. We eagerly checked these on the internet. Accommodation mostly four and five star hotels so it didn't look much like back packing! Comparing this by price and quality with similar offered in England it seemed a no brain decision. The trip would be on a plate, turn up and do it, just what was needed for the first country. After reading the company revues I selected one or two of the higher profile contributors, searched them out on the web and emailed them. I received a reply from a Canadian Doctor stating that the firm could not be faulted. After that my mind was made up.

By now, Susie in Australia wasn't just informed but fully involved. Needing only our arrival and departure dates to work with, she would take care of much that would happen there, also volunteering to organise the Fiji Islands visit. While travelling together she'd help tighten my loose plans for South America.

October 2014. Started booking flights online. Skyscanner being the most useful website. It may seem strange, the first made being a July 2015 homebound from mainland Brazil. I'd made a decision that the last place visited would be the paradise island of Fernando de Noronha, 350 kilometres northeast of Brazil. I'd been there with Charles in July 2014 and Chris deserved to see it. Our flight to London had to be perfectly timed and linked with our return from the island. The February 2015 flight to Delhi was easier as India Airways flew there daily and could wait until the dates of our organised tour with Top Travel & Tours were confirmed.

By end of November 2014, the calendar spreadsheet contained the date and time of almost every entry and exit flight, continent to continent, country to country, including connections. New Zealand had been added, because it was more cost effective to fly from there across the great expanse of the Pacific Ocean to South America. Every pre-booked accommodation place and date were noted, along with possible and flexible stay durations for those not fixed. Many of these would be finalised whilst on the move. For that, Booking.com would become a great asset. Margin notes had possibilities for bus and coach companies, with times and fares. Much of our time was being used double and treble checking. As part of our preparations all of the definite details and dates were written into the pages of the note books that would become our diaries!

We also had to turn our minds to some other important details.

If visas are needed, information is on the internet and for most countries can be applied for online. They are needed for India and proved very difficult, complicated and expensive to obtain. I exhausted my patience trying to complete downloaded forms, eventually employing a professional service that is closely affiliated with the country's embassy. Less said is knowledge shared.

Travelling around the world we'd encounter many weathers, considerations for luggage and clothing became inseparable.

Even cabin size backpacks could end up in an aircraft's hold, if space didn't allow or they were considered overweight or size. This meant visiting the website of every airline booked to establish their restrictions.

Fortunately all companies allow a small personal hand bag and top coats. The latter we'd use to full advantage, pockets loaded with underpants, socks, toilet tissue and all manner of soft items. We could have just taken a coat from our wardrobes but needed multi-purpose and didn't want to spend a lot of money so bought two used items through ebay. Lightweight, waterproof, breathable with hoods and lots of zipped or popper buttoned pockets. So that they could be rolled with light weight hooded fleeces inside them, then secured and carried easily. I purchased four adjustable straps with plastic fasteners.

While internet shopping another item came to my attention. An ingenious fold away holdall, zipped flat it fitted into one of my coat pockets, unfolded it became a generous sized kit bag with shoulder strap. When we exited an aeroplane it was produced, while walking we became masters of being able to unfold it and pack it with the coats before arriving at immigration and baggage check areas.

We'd tested a clothing recycling process in Tenerife. Shirts, underwear and socks are easily rinsed and dried. Theoretically what lasted ten days, could do the same for one hundred and fifty.

Trousers, dual purpose, the zip off leg type with lots of pockets are essential, especially for those items that needed to be kept close, passports, money etcetera.

During the final weeks before our big adventure we laid out clothing and other items on a spare bed. Three piles, definitely, possibly and only if there is room! We did many packing and unpacking practices weighing the final results. The day bags would hold important electrical devices, cables and personal items. Chris decanted essential liquids into containers that complied with security limits.

We settled on the following luggage:

2 x Soft shell back packs, CabinMax™, 550 x 250 x 400mm.

2 x Hand/Day bags, Outdoor gear™, 300 x 250 x 100mm with shoulder strap.

1 x Foldaway Holdall, Aerolite™, 210 x 170 x 50mm packed, expands to 550 x 250 x 400mm.

Conscious that most garments could be replaced if necessary. Worn, carried or packed were for me:

Coat: Tenson™ waterproof hooded mid-thigh length, 1 x hooded fleece, 2 x short sleeved cotton shirts, 2 x Nosilife™ long sleeved safari shirts, 2 x cotton t shirts, 2 x cotton sports vests, 1 x lightweight safari trousers, 1 x walking trousers with zip off legs, 1 x denim shorts, 1 x swim shorts, 1 x canvas belt with metal buckle, 5 x briefs, 4 pairs cotton ankle socks, 3 pairs trainer shoe socks, 1 pair Karrimor™ lace up walking shoes, 1 pair velcro fastening sports sandals.

For Chris:

Coat: Tenson™ waterproof hooded mid-thigh length, hooded fleece, 2 x short sleeve cotton blouses/cover ups, 1 x sleeveless blouse, 2 x long sleeve cotton shirts, 4 x t shirts, 3 x vest tops, 2 pairs zip off leg trousers, 1 x black linen shorts, 6 pairs pants, 3 x bras, 5 pairs socks, 1 pair pyjamas, 1 bikini, 1 x swimsuit, 2 sarongs, 1 pashmina, 1 pair Karrimor™ lace walking shoes, 1 pair black Havaianas™ (flip flops), 1 pair Velcro fastening walking sandals, 1 pack of 6 disposable paper pants (in case of Delhi belly).

Final preparations

Although fully alarmed, leaving the house vacant for five months had to be considered. I explored the possibility of buying a 'temporary unoccupied' insurance, but we're fortunate in having a good relationship with close neighbours. When asked, they agreed to keep an eye on it for us, visiting the interior regularly and undertaking garden maintenance if time allowed. Shutting down services and isolating appliances was no problem. I prepared by fitting timed switches for lighting, ensuring alarm sensors had new batteries and leaving spares of these and lamp bulbs in easy access.

A friend, also a mechanic, agreed to take our car into his care, use it sometimes and undertake some minor works while we were away. It wouldn't need to be sold or put it into long term storage. Another piece of the puzzle solved.

Chris's fitness wasn't an issue but mine was suspect with torn shoulder tendons and knees that would no longer suffer running. Age and industrial chemicals has caused the skin on my lower arms and hands to be thin, fragile and susceptible to tearing or bruising. I need to be careful moving through confined spaces and to avoid obstacles that may cause such damage.

We'd taken to walking a good distance most days and steadily upped the lengths of those strolls until capable of ten to fifteen kilometres without being unduly tired. As an aside, we're not big in stature, five foot six and five foot five respectively so not a lot of leg room needed on aeroplanes!

As an asthmatic and prone to chest infections my doctor and dentist were thoughtful enough to prescribe courses of antibiotics 'just in case.' Later these proved invaluable but at the time were added to our small first aid kit, plasters, pain killers, Imodium, etcetera. Appointments were made for dental check-ups and at our local GP surgery we arranged for the important vaccinations, some compulsory, others optional, some paid for. Certain countries won't allow entry without a Yellow Fever immunisation certificate. I was also entitled to a free flu jab. One or another of these injections laid me low for a day, so ill that I thought I wouldn't make it through the night let alone the trip!

After travel insurance was arranged, telephone calls were made to our respective banks informing them of the countries and dates that credit/debit cards maybe used. Online, money was loaded to our ICE cards, failsafe currency in US dollar and Euro notes was obtained at the Post Office. Complete with visas our passports had been returned from the Indian Embassy and the final payment had been made for the North and South India tours.

A one way taxi trip to Heathrow Airport booked and the clock was ticking!

The Diary. Touring Northern India

Friday 13th February. Day 1. Portsmouth to Delhi, India. Via London Heathrow. Air India AI176 Dep. 1.00pm. Arr. 2.50am 14th Feb 2015. 10,690km.

Up early, finished locking down the house after a breakfast comprising of carbohydrates, toxins and stimulants. Translating as Marmite on toast, tea, coffee and three cigarettes! Chris later noted in her diary, 'I felt so excited I was almost physically sick.'

The taxi picked us up at 8.00am, neighbours Dave and Jill waved us goodbye. Good ride to Heathrow, the driver, a Scot was good company and we discussed football and politics. Being nervous I probably waffled!

In the airport I bought some Indian rupee notes at a dubious exchange rate. The currency isn't internationally traded and certainly not available at a British bank or post office.

Afterwards, we had coffee, cost £4 and one of Chris's homemade pasties, free. Cleared check in. Quite a fuss at security and I had to lose some liquids. Lots of WhatsApp messages arrived on Chris's phone. I wrote a diary entry at about 11.10am. While waiting for the gate to open Chris had her first airport number two toilet visit ever. Definitely pre-match nerves! Having boarded I checked email on my phone, message received confirming our pick-up at Delhi Airport. A box ticked, late but ticked!

The seats weren't too uncomfortable and I took a nap for an hour before dinner was served at about 3.30pm. I had western style roast lamb after it was recommended by a steward. After another nap at about 6.30pm UK time, more food arrived, supper by way of malai kebab and other items.

We're excited and looking forward to landing in Delhi at 9.30pm UK time, it will be 2.50am in India.

Saturday 14th February. Day 2. Delhi Airport.

Landed about 3.00am, depart the plane, go through the usual airport security sequences and move through to the packed immigration zone. Cleared only after a very hot and sticky two hours. It became apparent that the delay was caused by the incorrect entry forms supplied by Air India and other airlines. New ones were supplied and had to be filled at the desk. We were stunned because they required exactly the same information as those discarded. Maybe it was the colour of the paper? Welcome to Indian administration!

Joined other arrivals walking through shopping areas to the exit zone and we're recognised by the waiting rep and driver, introductions followed. We all leave the lights of the building to a waiting car, this at about 5.00am India time. They are pleasant chaps, one of them slips skinny garlands of flowers over our heads, the driver even manages to find some matches in his car and I get to smoke a cigarette.

Outside it is almost pitch black. I'm obviously still nervous, how Chris felt I didn't know, she always maintained an air of calm. It turned out that her trepidations were the same as mine. We have limited ideas of what to expect, it's all so very now and real actually being in this sprawling city, with a population of thirty million and voted this year by the World Health Organisation as the worst place on the planet to live!

The car loaded with our baggage we're off, being driven to the first hotel of which we only know the written address. One heck of a ride through some very heavy traffic out of the airport zone, the car's headlights piercing the blue smog. Onward through busy dark streets, eventually arriving at the Clarks Heights Hotel 1/1 West Patel, Nagar, opp. Metro Pilar No.209. N Delhi. A poorly lit building with a small parking lot at the front positioned on a main road junction with a metro viaduct on pillars as the main view. We exit the car and enter the bleak even more dimly lit reception that reminded me of a back street car dealer's sales office. A semi-circular counter covered in clutter, papers, books, leaflets, cables etcetera. I am very tired and sign the forms proffered. I really just want to sleep. That wasn't going to happen soon.

The rep drew us to some grubby lounge seats. He was about to explain the itinerary and as we were to find out, the 'voucher' system. This we came to understand was very important and as the India trip expanded Chris and I often referred to each other as 'voucher people.'

A large envelope was produced, it contained a copy of the whole travel itinerary, contact numbers, a second small envelope, a feedback form and two small booklets of vouchers. For these a verbal explanation about the tear out pages was given, how they should be presented when arriving at each new hotel or accommodation for room and breakfast. The first was eagerly taken by this hotel's receptionist. Another booklet contained similar and were to be given to allocated tour guides. The other envelope contained rail travel tickets. Small hours moonlight is still with us, we thank the rep, he departs and we're eventually taken to our room. It's clean, ensuite, has a good bed and a curtain of sorts over the single window. We dropped our bags, lay down and slept.

After a couple of hours Delhi started to wake up. The sound of traffic, voices and vehicle horns soon became a cacophony of noise. Something we were to going to have to live with for most of the tour. About 8.00am we went down to the restaurant-cum-breakfast room situated just behind reception. The tables are laid with crockery and cutlery. In the centre an island with foodstuffs presented buffet style.

I suspect that this hotel hasn't had many visitors from England. As white Europeans and Chris being blonde haired we attracted some strange looks from other guests and the newly arrived morning staff.

We settled at a table tucked into a corner. I couldn't help noticing that next to me was a small shelf with a

1980's era green slim phone. It and the cables had obviously never seen a cleaning cloth in their lifetime. The ground floor of the hotel is very affected by the dust and fumes raised by the almost constant nearby heavy road traffic.

A kind little waiter came to serve us. I ordered toast supplemented with papaya and coffee, Chris had the same plus cornflakes and warm milk, a first for her, she actually noted in her diary, 'yuk!'

Afterwards at about 9.15am. Chris joined me when I went outside for a cigarette stood in the car park. The hotel vista only had a vague similarity to the pictures seen on the internet. We watched and listened to the pandemonium of the street and junction for a while. Back at the room and our first experience of an Asian style bathroom. There's a porcelain toilet bowl and paper. A tiled and curtained shower area with fixed spray head above a tap, also provided is a large plastic bucket and a pouring jug. After ablutions we went back to bed, more sleep definitely needed.

Our tour proper starts tomorrow, the extra night here necessary because I'd booked a cheap unsociably timed flight. The saving on airfares easily outweighing the additional cost. On waking, sat on the bed and carefully checked through the itinerary. We hadn't really been giving full attention when it was presented at just before dawn.

The welcoming garlands of flowers had wilted and were binned. At about 3.30pm we went down and arranged a snack, chicken sandwiches and coffee. By that time had found out that the free internet was non-existent. We were both still very nervy about the days to come, certainly weren't in a tourist district at this time and I was neither confident enough to take a walk any distance from the hotel or desirous to do so. I'd wandered up to and just around the corner once on the unmade pavements and seen enough to satisfy a curious mind.

We relaxed in the room, talking and speculating, later going to the restaurant for dinner. While waiting for service we did some observing, not just of the grimy surfaces on show but people. By the clothing worn the other guests were all of Asian or similar origin and notably there weren't any females, guests or staff.

Two turban headed teenage Sikh males came out of the elevator into the lobby, Chris made a quiet comment to me only, probably prompted by nervousness, said in the UK it wouldn't be perceived as politically correct but we giggled like naughty school children.

Still on duty, the kind little waiter came to attend us. Selecting from the menu we ordered two large bottles of Kingfisher beer for starters. They took an age to arrive. I assumed that a woman drinking beer, a white one at that, would have probably required an inquisition at management level.

After taking advice from our friendly waiter a main meal was selected. Chicken murga, which was eventually served on the bone in a watery brown sauce with a side dish of boiled stodgy white rice. I noted in my diary that waiting one Greek minute had been outdone by the Indian waiting indefinitely. People came and went. We had another two bottles of Kingfisher beer.

Chris went to the room. I smoked outside the hotel as the night closed in. The road was still very noisy and stayed as such until about 2.00am. We went to bed at 9.40pm, it was a very edgy night for both of us but we were still in high spirits with excited expectation of the unknown.

Sunday 15th February. Day 3. Tour of Old and New Delhi. Overnight Rail Journey to Jaisalmer. JSM Express, Class 2 AC sleeper. Dep.5.35pm. 790km.

Diary reminder: 'pick up food and water for the train journey.'

Up at 6.40am, after breakfast finished packing ready for checkout. It's going to be a busy day. The itinerary is a tour of Old and New Delhi then we're booked on an overnight train for an eighteen hour rail journey to Jaisalmer.

My first big shock arrives when my ICE travel card is not working and have to pay the hotel account by credit card. Waiting in reception as this happened is our first guide. He introduced himself as Gupta and asked for the voucher. We said our goodbye to the hotel staff and the waiting car was loaded with our bags.

Although looking forward to the tour destinations I couldn't shift the travel card problem from my mind. Fortunately Gupta had a good understanding of spoken English and once I'd explained my need for cash in rupees he directed the driver to several banks with ATM's where I tried the ICE card without success. Eventually in desperation I used my credit card to obtain some money at an HSBC machine. I was very worried but with a heavy heart carried on.

During the morning in New Delhi visited an area containing the Presidential Palace, Parliament Buildings, The India Arch, Humayun's Tomb, Qutub Minar Minaret Tower, its related ruins and the first of what would be several in India, a Ghandi Museum.

Gupta ordered the driver to take us through the Delhi Sunday market. Here was a mind blowing plethora of sights with thousands upon thousands of people going about their business or milling in narrow side streets. I can state categorically that I became frightened for our welfare. Maybe unnecessarily but as the driver slowly squeezed the shiny white car through the throng, people were rubbed and nudged. We would have been obviously apparent as tourists and most likely to be the only Europeans in this area.

When we could 'actually' see things other than people through the car windows, at the stalls animals were hung and being butchered, large fish similarly treated on trestle tables, a small mountain of used clothing and piles of shoes was being picked over by the ragged and the poor. In places it was like a scrap yard, used goods being traded and all manner of small industrial manufacture and repairs active.

While we were taking all of this in Gupta continued his commentary explaining that the historic massive market was Muslim and Hindu sectored. I didn't think that the poverty stricken folks that we saw actually cared. It was a first for us and will be an enduring memory of massed humanity in a scene seemingly from a medieval period.

The driver moved the car through to a slightly less populated area of the market as Gupta declared that the next place on the tour was the local active Jama Masjid Mosque and we'd be stopping, parking and visiting. I wasn't keen, in fact still very nervy. The thought of being western tourists out and about on parade here didn't appeal to me for one second. Chris and I had already made a whispered agreement, so I firmly stated that we had seen enough, would like to move out and on, to take lunch if necessary.

An adjusted quote from Chris's diary, 'The Sunday market is a dreadful place, thousands of people everywhere. Lots of poverty in Delhi, homeless living on the streets, kids begging at cars and always filthy dirty.' I think that one particular event had struck a chord. Our car was held at a road junction where Gypsies actually lived. They exist as communities on traffic islands and below motorway bridges. Women will press a child or baby to the vehicles window and beg, indicating a need for food by pointing clustered fingers at their mouths. The vision of true poverty for this non class of human being was inescapable.

My thoughts about the market visit. 'Muslim and Hindu but a divided area. Chris and I had spoken about our concerns while in the car, the milling crowd, the vehicle nudging people. It's surprising how vulnerable one feels even in a vehicle when surrounded and only bodies from the waist up can be seen, no faces but you know that you are being looked at. At the time we hypothesised, having not long left our own Country which was still ringing with media reports of hostage taking in Pakistan, Syria, Libya and elsewhere, along with barbaric executions by terrorists. What chance would I or we have if it got ugly? What if the vehicle broke down? As it did later that day. Our total World travel possessions were on us or in the car. What could or might happen if the driver had hurt someone? Would the milling throng turn into a mob? Who would bear the brunt of their anger? Sure as heck it wouldn't be the native language speaking driver or guide. We as European tourists would probably be assessed as guilty in a micro second.'

Maybe these spoken thoughts were completely unnecessary, just prompted by our nervousness of the unknown but they were there in those moments. As it turned out we never again found ourselves in such a situation whilst in India, and moved as pedestrians through many other crowded places including markets, but our raw emotions were never raised to the heights touched that day.

This, the first tour day we were totally reliant upon Gupta the guide for all aspects, but our learning curve was in overdrive. Senses being almost overwhelmed by what we'd seen, heard and smelled and if this is called culture shock we both had the symptoms.

Having left the run down surrounds of the market we arrived in what seemed a nicer quieter area of Delhi. The car parked and Gupta indicated a place we'd take lunch. In a side street, a first floor restaurant above a small terrace of shops.

My mind was still in some turmoil from what we'd just seen, I had concerns about the failure of my travel card and couldn't get a connection or anything sent from my mobile phone. Going to lunch had been an excuse to be somewhere else and I would have been happy getting a snack from a road side stall, but as I came to realise as tour days continued official guides were not only to complete the visits in the itinerary, they often had their own agenda. The restaurant was very plush, we selected a table and sat, one look at the menu prices and a glance at the obviously well off tourist clientele made me feel uncomfortable and out of place. Chris sensed my resentment at being here.

Interrupting my quiet 'I'm not happy' conversation with my wife, Gupta sat opposite and kept suggesting items from the menu, full scale meals in fact. I said that I wasn't hungry, but really I wasn't interested. I asked him to pick something for himself, he declined, just asked for water. This was my chance and I selected one portion of cheapest starter on the menu for me and Chris to share. By the picture some sort of hot spicy finger shaped batter over meat. The waiter looked furious.

I think I'd already sussed the game. Guide brings tourists and that equals commission. Over time I learned India works that way in nearly all aspects and at every level. Chris was obviously feeling uncomfortable with my irritability but with wisdom she knew the situation and how to react, or even better not to! We bit the ends off of a couple of the sticks and left the rest on the plate. While Gupta was nowhere to be seen I called for the bill. English Bob was in control at least for now, 900 Rupees, yes £9 for a starter. It was never going to happen again!

Left the restaurant, down the stairs, out to the street into the glare of early afternoon sunshine. Our car was parked with other white tourist vehicles, a couple of luxury coaches were further up the street. The next destination was the Red Fort. All safely in the car and it doesn't start. I thought to myself there is a God and it isn't Vishnu!

Later in my diary, I wrote, 'we had two cars, one broke.' It seems that many Indians especially drivers fancy themselves as mechanics. Chris and I took to the shade of a nearby tree and watched. The car is surrounded, bonnet popped and propped the driver tries the ignition again, trrrrclck. Any man jack or his wife would know it was a flat battery.

By now Gupta was filling his face with food obtained from a local shop. One of the drivers owned a large spanner. Thirty minutes went by as each man took a turn to hit the battery. I was highly amused and could barely contain myself. My mood had been lightened. I smoked a few cigarettes and we decided that this was an opportune time for our first shopping trial.

With warnings about eating railway food strong in our minds we'd already planned to buy some snack foods for the overnight train journey. In the place that Gupta had shopped we purchased a mixture of things that looked nice, pastries, samosas and crisps.

Gupta must have realised that the spanner and a sequence of blows wasn't going to get us anywhere and was using his phone. I'd second guessed correctly, a short while after, a fresh white car and new driver arrived. Our bags are transferred to the replacement, I double checked, all present and correct.

We were off, distance and time not recalled and we're dropped off at the entrance to the massive Red Fort, the car and driver left. At this time of the afternoon queues to enter snaked for yards. Historic monuments are very popular and well attended by Indian tourists. As Westerners we're treated as privileged but pay a much higher entry price. More on that later. I give cash to Gupta, he buys tickets and we get in avoiding the queues. It worked for me. Do I sound selfish?

Nevertheless we don't avoid security and our day bags are inspected by the guards. Nearby is an armoured pill box with a metal meshed viewing aperture. Inside is a uniformed soldier, his automatic weapon clearly visible.

During the tour of the Fort Gupta is very informative, he has been most of the day and gives historically insights as we walk.

As we leave there are still long entry queues. Gupta led us to the waiting car. At about 4.30pm arrived at the Delhi railway station, a sprawling complex of old buildings and canopies. My diary note, 'a really surreal place as seen on TV.' Exit the car and put our back packs on, thank the driver and give him and Gupta a cash tip then walked the short distance to the entrance.

Crowds of people are coming, going and just standing, it's noisy, cluttered with all sorts of objects, sack trolleys and many two wheeled vendor carts. This is Sunday, I think to myself what it must be like on a weekday? I wave away the attentions of a porter wanting to take our holdall and we're swallowed into the melee. This is very much an unknown for us, nerves are jangling. Obviously having done this before Gupta had already taken a look at our ticket, knew where to take us and indicated to follow him. Up, over and down an iron walkway bridge we find ourselves on one of the many platforms. It's very hot, I'm feeling quite dishevelled and grubby. Chris and I stand close together. This was probably the first time we actually looked like proper travellers, with backpacks on, day bags shoulder slung and me with the holdall containing coats, food and water.

We must have been quite an unusual sight, men women and children don't just glance at us they stare. From every angle we're being looked at! We made small talk. The things we saw were amazing. In addition to people in all types of dress there are hessian sack piles, the contents unknown, boxes are on and off trolleys. Stacked nearby are some large and worn polystyrene cartons, by the leakage and smell we guessed fish! This was just one section of *'one'* platform. Nothing seemed to stay still except for the packages being used as seats. Just across the rail tracks are blue train carriages that look of some age, rusty and in pretty poor condition. Apertures where windows would be expected have bars, doors wide open and people hang from both. Other folks just walk over the rail tracks from one platform to another.

Daylight faded, an orange electric light semi gloom took its place under the canopies. Gupta seemed on edge and left us a couple of times, presumably checking for train delays. One contracted duty of the travel company was to ensure our safe departure from one place and to be met by a representative at the next. India is a very big country and we're to travel some great distances.

The Jaisalmer Express was due to depart at 5.35pm, it was after that already. Gupta is back on scene, un-talkative and moody. Maybe he hadn't been happy with his tip? His spoken English had become harder and harder to understand as the day wore on anyway. Out of nowhere close to us appeared a smartly dressed young man. Apparently our exit strategy rep, about introduce himself when Gupta interrupted, spoke sharply, then left. He obviously didn't like overtime!

We didn't catch the young man's name but he proffered and Chris took a small gift. A hoop handled, highly decorated straw posy basket, containing fruit, cakes and small cartons of orange juice. A nice touch by the tour company. He suggested we should move along the crowded platform to a place he estimated that our carriage would stop. Trains are very long in this country and he was completely wrong. When it pulled in a short time later, we, heavily laden, had to battle our way through the moving crowd and static baggage, back to virtually where we'd started. While doing so getting several bruises on my arms.

Carriage found, on we went, so did other passengers carrying light and heavy luggage bumping and boring through the narrow corridor. It was frenetic. Our curtained section and allocated seats-cum-bunks found, the rep showed us how to convert the hinged backs of the lower bench into a bed platform. All of the compartment's cotton sheets, rough wool blankets and small pillows are stored on the permanently fixed top bunks. After assuring him that we'd be fine, he left.

Almost the same instant we were joined by our compartment companions. A young French couple in about their mid-twenties. They'd been allocated the top bunks. After introductions we talked, they'd arrived earlier and had come direct to the station from Delhi Airport. By now the train had started to move slowly out of the station. Through the curtained and heavily scratched windows there was just enough light to see masses of accumulated rubbish and shockingly the tarpaulin, cardboard and corrugated iron roofed shanty town existing near the rail tracks.

The beds had to be made and as Europeans etiquette was easily established. The young lady spoke excellent English so fortunately I didn't have to make use of my 1960's secondary modern school French. Anyway, when would I have been able to introduce 'La plume de ma Tante est sur la table' into a conversation?

In fitting the linen and blankets to the top bunks someone has to stand on the edge of the lower ones. Other people in the compartment need to sit feet up on these and lean back out of the way. Once the top beds are made, up go the passengers along with their essentials, water and food etcetera. Net baskets are fixed to the carriage walls to stow those bits and pieces. Heavier baggage left on the floor is chained or strapped through the handles and padlocked to the nearest frame bar for security. Afterwards Chris and I did similar for the lower bunks, at this level we had access to a hinged drop down table fitted below the window to place foodstuffs and other items. I disconnected the strap from our holdall and used it to secure the backpacks. The bag with coats inside is to be used as my pillow. Now dark outside the train had been rattling and rolling along for some time. It was very hot inside although there was supposed to be air conditioning.

Each compartment has a ceiling mounted light and a wire caged electric fan, ours whirred loudly, noisy as a helicopter. The bunks have an individual wall mounted light and some worn power points. I noted that most of the fixings had been moved many times, previous screw holes were everywhere. Chris and I talked about the days' events as the train and time moved on. The noise of the carriage on rails now being complimented by human sounds, snoring, coughing and the awful Indian custom of nasal growl and throat clearing.

The AC Class 2 sleeper carriage layout: Opposite and fifty centimetres from the sideways four berth frame work other upper and lower side bunks are fixed lengthways, also curtained. Plastic windowed doors made of sharp edge aluminium frame are at either end of the corridor and open to a section of carriage with the main entrance doors either side. These open inward and are constructed of heavy iron plate and have waist height apertures fitted with vertical bars similar in fashion to an old prison door. The locking ironmongery is more blacksmith than engineering production.

Inter carriage connecting doors are central, a short corridor to them is formed by the toilet cubicles either side. These with a floor space area of about one hundred and twenty centimetres square. The doors open outwards, sheet metal fabrication, hinges and locking fitments of mostly of rough artisan manufacture. Latches are flat metal, with nuts and bolts drilled and fixed through to use as finger lifts.

Inside, it would be kind to describe the facilities as grim. One is Asian style, for squatting and has a press moulded plastic floor with specific non slip feet shapes indented. Almost central is a hole about five inches diameter, any deposits here find their way directly out of the carriage to wherever it maybe at that time! In the corner about thirty centimetres from the floor is a wall mounted tiny brass handled water tap. Close by, retained by a chain, a small metal pouring jug jinks around on the floor in sympathy with the motion of the train. Its use is obvious, toilet tissue is rarely used by Asians.

The western style WC differs in that a pan and seat are fitted. Both cubicles have an aperture in the external carriage wall fitted with a fine metal mesh screen. Electric lights and wire basket covered fans are permanently 'on.'

Outside on one wall there is a basin. I couldn't establish the material because of the long term staining, above it is a small tap dispensing cold water. After several rail journeys I noted that these little sinks are used for many purposes, among them cleaning teeth, feet and hand washing.

We'd decided to rest fully clothed apart from shoes. By about 7.30pm, our French companions seemed comfortable on their bunks with earphones and listening to music. The compartment curtains were drawn the noisy overhead fan no longer whirred. We'd agreed to turn it and the main light off but unfortunately it was even hotter in the carriage now. Chris had stretched out as best she could. With nicotine substitutes no longer effective I was gasping for a cigarette and decided to sneak to the WC, partake and flout the railway no smoking policy. The worst that could happen a 200 rupee fine, two quid! To me definitely worth the gamble.

I left the compartment area and damn it, the guard was stood outside. The train was moving fast, the two heavy main carriage doors open, swinging to and fro. Making eye contact with the bare footed man I showed him my cigarette and pointed to the doorway, his nonchalant wave of the hand and the look of 'carry on mate' was enough for me. I sparked up, inhaled deeply and positioned myself at one of the swinging doors, put my foot hard to the bottom wedging it, locked my arm through the bars and stared out at the blackness seeing only glimpses of shadowy vegetation caught in the lights of the train. Goodness me the best smoke I'd ever had. I lit another!

8.30pm, back in the compartment I made myself as comfy as possible and wrote my diary. Had a sip or two of water then dozed fitfully being disturbed on several occasions. Because the train had stopped, by the noise made by new passengers and the exceptionally annoying chant of 'Chai and coffee' from the seller with his urns as he moved between carriages.

Monday 16th February. Day 4. Seven hours later, still on the train.

1.00am, having slept on and off I woke fully. Hot sweaty and hungry. I disturbed Chris with my rummaging and the crackle of cellophane packet wrapper removal. We whispered trying not to wake the sleeping French couple. We snacked on samosas, cake, crisps, drank water and shared one of the cartons of orange juice. She'd inserted the straw because I'm a liability confronted by such tasks. Needing a leak, I put shoes on, with a cigarette and lighter in hand crept quietly to the WC area. Both main carriage doors were now closed, it was cooler, a breeze blowing through the barred apertures. The sight before me came to epitomise the strength and resilience of the common Indian people. A bare plywood board hinged and suspended by chains from the carriage wall, on it lay the guard, curled in foetal position, barefoot and asleep.

In the Western WC I had a pee and smoked my cigarette. Back on my bunk I slept until 6.00am as daylight started to peep through the curtains. Many others in the carriage also started their morning routines, talking, eating and making those other sounds!

Desert and what looked like some cultivated areas could soon be seen through the windows. At about 7.30am Chris and I had breakfast, sharing similar to last night's feast, except banana, she didn't as they upset her stomach. From then on the train seemed to stop everywhere with people getting on and off. 10.45am arrived at another station, (who knew where?) we left going backwards so must have travelled for a distance on a spur line.

12.15pm, arrived at Jaisalmer. By then our kit was ready to grab, said a hasty goodbye and best wishes to our French companions then exited the carriage onto a station platform bathed in glaring sunshine. Dishevelled and grubby after near eighteen hours rail travel we were met by a very smartly dressed travel rep who proffered his business card and introduced himself as Babu. We talked while walking out of the station, heading for a parked shiny black Mercedes saloon car. Our luggage put in the boot and we're driven through the outskirts of town. A first experience of the many part and unmade roads in India, loose debris, large rocks, stones and areas with holes as big as craters. From the car windows could see the ubiquitous piles of rubbish, people, road side workshops, scrawny dogs, horse and donkey drawn carts, lots of scraggy looking cows. These privileged ugly animals go, stand or lay anywhere they want. On or off of the road.

Ten minutes later we're at the Dhola Maru, Jethwai Road, a large building looking recently constructed with extensive grounds and circular drive at the front aspect. The tiled floor reception area is bright expansive and clean. Babu is well spoken, just as well, because the male receptionists had no English language at all. To him I explained that I was short of cash rupees and would need to visit an ATM. Without prompting he counted out 4,000 about £40 and I took this as a loan. Passport copying done, voucher given and we're shown to our room. Spacious, with a big bed, chairs and table, an old TV and some large cushions scattered on the floor in the bay window. It has its fair share of dust here and there.

At reception earlier I established that the hotel for some reason didn't have a working restaurant. This would be important later in the day. Collection at 2.15pm for the tour of Jaisalmer but there was enough time to use the bathroom, cold water feed only we still showered. In between times grazing on the last of the snack foods. I also wandered the hotel and its grounds, they didn't quite match the internet description. An outside sports area and a dry unused swimming pool, all very barren, the whole place felt slightly abandoned.

Guide Mahendre is waiting at reception. Outside he introduces us to our driver Sarup, stood by a white tour car. A short stocky fellow with a belly overhang contained in his stretched buttoned white shirt. What we didn't know

33

was that he'd be with us until we left North India and that we'd come to trust and like him very much.

Some of the afternoon visits to historic sites. The Golden Fort which from its heights the views of the city are fantastic. Looked at Havelies, highly decorated homes designed and constructed to allow light and flowing ventilation. Into the Bazaar and market area and on the outskirts to a manmade lake, a folly built to honour a princess. Chris wrote in her diary, 'Jaisalmer is a very pretty place in parts, the buildings are made with a yellowish stone, giving it the name Golden City.'

About mid-afternoon we were driven on a very dusty tarmac road through the desert to a place approximately forty kilometres from the Pakistan border, this was for a pre-booked camel ride. Enroute seeing only the occasional tour car or lorry. Mahendre took the time to impress that we should not be tempted to purchase anything from the vendors there. Paradoxically he had been an excellent and very informative guide during the day, except for dragging us into a Haveli shop of his choosing, where we were given the full sales treatment to buy carved ornaments. Suffice to say we left without a purchase.

The camel ride would end up as one of our most amusing events in India. We arrived, proper desert with sand dunes, sky still bright blue, the Sun dipping in the distance. This is a tourist outpost, large tents set out with military precision the signage indicating accommodation for the ultimate overnight desert experience. There are souvenir and other sellers. Cotton sheets on their stalls fluttered in the light breeze. Plenty of cars are parked on and just off of the road, ours joined them.

Mahendre led and introduced us to a man dressed in full Arabian style flowing robes. He held one end of a long leash, the other end being attached to a camel. I'd seen them in zoos! Fortunately they'd been behind a fence and me the other side. I understood that if upset they could not only kick out but deliver a horrendous spit of throat growled phlegm. Not that dissimilar to many Indians then?

This was our ride and driver and I was hilariously horrified. Chris was sniggering and my laughter must have been off putting. The camel driver tapped the animal on its front legs with a stick, it knelt forward on its knees, the rear legs folded and its body came in contact with the ground. The long neck seemed to coil like a snake with an enormous ugly head. Its tongue lolled across a couple of brown teeth. Saliva hung like strings from its mouth. Not to mention the noises and lips working independently side to side. It was definitely in kissing range!

The camel was fitted with a two seat arrangement made of wood and blankets all strapped over the one hump. Taking the front Chris was first to clamber on, with a struggle I got onto the rear section but was pained and complained loudly. My nether region bits were crushed as my legs splayed across the enormous beast. Chris noted in her diary, 'Bob constantly moaned about the condition of his man parts.' The driver tapped the animal again and it went automatically into standing up sequence. Holding tight here is a must, its back legs first and this throws a rider forwards, next, up come the front legs, this tips a passenger backwards. While all of this happens the animal makes awful throat noises and gaseous issues from the rear. It must be the strain!

Led by the driver we're soon being walked and for me every camel footfall was excruciating. Chris seemed to think it hilarious. Lots of other tourists were having rides, like us as two up, others three, some in carts being drawn up and across the dunes. These folks seemed mostly Indian or Asian extraction, there was a lot of laughter and plenty of beer and spirits drinking, swigging from both bottles and cans. Shamefully once a container had been emptied it was simply discarded. This must happen regularly, in the clefts of sand at the bottom of many dunes lay clusters of empties and other debris. It was quite sad to see a laughing rider throw an empty bottle and watch it roll to join the other litter.

A young lad about twelve years old moved into a position to walk alongside us, he was also dressed in robes and carrying a large bag which we soon discovered contained liquid refreshments. Closing on us he called in one sentence, "You want coke beer Fanta where you from?" I was keen for a drink but say, "No." As part of what I knew would be negotiation. I lit a cigarette and said, "England."

His response being along the lines of, "You Manchester David Beckham." Relenting I asked, "How much is beer?"

"500 rupees", his instant reply.

Knowing 200 rupees was expensive I retorted, "No thanks."

Cheeky chap still up close came back with, "How much you pay?"

In one throw I returned, "Is it cold, 100 rupees? This lad was a master of his trade and shook his head. Then came the Del Boy moment.

"Do you know how much it costs to get beer in the desert?"

I offer 200 hundred, a headshake indicates no and he's got me.

"OK 300 hundred," I reply and he agrees. I was still laughing out loud as I stretched down with the notes while he reached up to take them and hand me the can. It was a welcome drink and the first beer I'd ever shared with my wife in a desert. The young man continued to pester and ask awkward questions with us replying as best we could.

The driver stopped the animal and made a couple of hand gestures that indicated that he was willing to take photographs, we were grateful. That done, a short while later we'd retraced our tracks and were back roadside. Tapped with a stick the camel did its collapsing sequence, we dismounted, me with much relief. A cash tip to the driver was definitely expected, his harsh stare as I gave him 100 rupees prompted another 100 note. These chaps often hide their mastery of English language and I joked with a question not expecting a reply. "I suppose that's your Merc over there?" He smirked and pointed his stick at a virtually new black 4x4SUV parked close by. I'd got my answer.

Guide, driver and car were waiting obviously keen to get back to Jaisalmer before sundown. I was still holding the empty can and glancing around to spot a bin. Mahendre pointed to a stall across the road, I crossed and quickly deposited it near the already accumulated rubbish. On the drive back into town he couldn't resist asking how much the drink cost. Informed, he made his reply slightly snide, actually meaning 'told you so.' He would never understand that for the entertainment we'd just had I would have paid treble!

The drive back was uneventful. On the way I reminded that an ATM was necessary, there was one on the edge of town. Sarup parked and I got cash, enough for use and extra to repay Babu's loan. Knowing the hotel restaurant wasn't working my thoughts were now about what and where to eat. Chris and I had already decided that we were going to stay in town for the early evening, find something there and make our own way back to the accommodation. Confident that we knew enough of the layout, had spotted some stalls and a beer shop and seen more European tourists here than in Delhi. Informed of our intention Mahendre was horrified, it was his and Sarup's duty to see us safely back to the hotel and that would be the end of their remit. I pressed home the point that if the tour company had booked a hotel with food facilities we'd have happily gone back. Apart from that Chris and I were desperate to test ourselves. He relented, we agreed tomorrow morning's collection time, I gave him a cash tip then he and Sarup drove away.

Another situation was resolved today, having found that Sarup would be a constant for a few days I requested that Mahendre explain that I would organise his tip at the end of his duties.

There was still early evening light. Having already wandered the streets and lanes close to the Golden Fort Chris and I were cautiously confident. On entering the town proper for the second time we agreed that if separated or lost our 'rally point' will be the hotel and she should go by taxi. Having rally points would continue throughout our world travels.

The sun went down, it became dark very quickly. First target was food. Near us were a selection of vendors with carts and mobile heated glass cabinets. We bought some hot spicy samosas and other pastries, then ate and talked on the move. Repetition of the many stalls and shops became confusing and at one time we lost our way but fortunately regained our bearings quickly.

Night time activities in the town were far busier than the day. An extreme annoyance was the appearance of what seemed to be hundreds of motor cycles and scooters, riders weaved in and out of pedestrians in the narrow lanes. Soon the town was choking in a blue exhaust fog. This prompted us to exit. We'd earlier noted a beer and spirits shop, easily remembered, as the large sign read 'CHILD BEER', an obvious misspelling but funny nevertheless. Strangely for all of our time spent in North and South India, we were never ever again to find any shop similar to an English off license. Bought a four pack of lager then selected from one of many a tuk tuk, the famous three wheeled taxi with a two stroke engine. The barefooted driver understood the hotel address and quoted a 90 rupee fare. Smugly satisfied with our achievements we got in and had a very hard ride in the smog as he attempted to avoid holes, boulders and other traffic to the hotel.

About 8.30pm our noisy transport pulled up outside of the Dhola Maru. Driver given 200 rupees including tip. Double bubble, I spoiled him, a big smile said that he was very happy. Only one person at reception, acknowledged him and went to our room and readied for bed. There being absolutely no Wifi I made a telephone call to the ICE travel card company and sent some texts to daughter-in-law Kerri. Wrote our diaries, played some music through the ipod speakers, talked and drank beer while lolling around on the fat cushions in the bay window. Leaning out of an open one, I smoked a couple of cigarettes. It had been a very good day.

Tuesday 17th February. Day 5. Jaisalmer to Jodhpur, 278km. 7 hours by car. Via a Temple visit at Ossian.

Both slept well, the room air conditioning had kept us very comfortable. Got up early and part packed our bags. Today we'd have a few suspicions verified. I went outside for an early morning cigarette before breakfast. We knew where to get that. No other guests had been spotted or encountered during our exploration of the many roomed hotel. So if there were any surely they would be here. Entered the very big downstairs dining room, plenty of tables and chairs but not another soul. One table had been part set so we sat at it. A chap we'd not met came over and it became obvious that he was to be our breakfast waiter and cook. There was no menu card and after a brief discussion a meal of toast, omelette and coffee was ordered. Chris and I chatted, about what the day would bring and this strange place. As the foodstuffs were being prepared we heard the clanking of pots and pans along with the sniffing, growling and coughing, and hoped not to hear the expectorating!

The breakfast meal arrived in good time. As we ate, the man hovered waiting for compliments which were given. Afterwards, cleared our room then went to reception to sign out. A representative for Babu and the Rajastan Tour Company was waiting, not only to collect the cash loan, which I gladly handed to him but to ask if we'd been satisfied with the care and attention given. We had, and were pleased to impart that. I asked about the lack of clientele at the hotel and he explained that the region, very popular with Indian tourists, had recently been struck by an influenza outbreak. Wealthy and middle class Indians are very canny, with such a large country to visit they'd just decided not to come here. Was that good to know this early in our trip?

9.30am, car loaded. Before leaving had goodbye handshakes and a group photograph taken, staff and us. Departed Jaisalmer and were soon to enjoy the company and subtle wit of our driver Sarup Singh and find for ourselves exactly how chaotic and dangerous the Indian road network can be.

Left the outskirts of the city and attempted some small talk with Sarup. Seemingly it was going to be hard work. His driving concentration levels were obviously paramount to him. As drivers ourselves we quickly became confident in his abilities. As such I even took naps during the long distances travelled. Today was our first proper road trip, afterwards Chris noted, 'The drive from Jaisalmer was an eye opener, went through arid land that stretched for miles. Passing through lots of small villages and saw very isolated dwellings made of stone, some of mud, others of both. Irrigated fields mixed with barren dry country.'

Aside from the scenery, these are my recollections about driving and road craft in India. Apparently there are no rules or highway-code that we enjoy in Europe. The only safe living being on any road is a cow, they are sacred which simply speaks volumes about this country. Vehicles of all shape size and condition share the highways, motor cycles, scooters, mopeds, cars, trucks, tractors, trailers. Carts are drawn by camel, bullock, horse, donkey etcetera. Some are people propelled, cycled, pulled and pushed. Goods transport vehicles of every type are always overloaded by weight, width and height in whatever is carried, straw, tyres, boxes, bricks, even rubble. Motor cycles can and do carry whole families, two adults, two children and a baby over the petrol tank is normal and crash helmets are a rarity. It can be expected to meet one or all of these vehicles at any time in any direction, sometimes towards you, animal powered especially.

Overtaking is also undertaking, with speed of about 50 kilometres per hour, a favourite manoeuvre is positioning the car bonnet just below a lorry tailgate then edging out to get past as the truck driver slows to change gear. Scary but usually successful, unless another driver has started to over or undertake your vehicle. As westerners experiencing these awful road travel conditions we expected to see some road rage. Strangely the social pecking order of India seems to exclude this. Only once seeing any driver berate another road user. This in fact was Sarup who had words, not an argument, with a cart driver, who was badly positioned in the centre of a road and blocking our route.

Today he was driver and guide and we were happy with this. I think that after he saw our determination and independence yesterday we'd gained a little of his respect. He never had any other agenda than getting us to a destination safely. Obviously if there was an itinerary visit to make he made it. He didn't want to take us shopping for

41

tatty souvenirs or meet a cousin who owned a manufacturing workshop.

With very limited English language but as best possible making pertinent comments about things, events, road incidents, places and sights. During a journey, for bathroom or refreshment breaks he'd ask at what time we wanted them and how long they should last. He certainly didn't want to socialise. If we ate or drank anywhere, would never join us at a table but mix with the staff out of our sight. We'd meet at the car afterwards where he was waiting or us for him. If he had a fault it's the one running very deep in male Indian culture in that women are lesser mortals. He showed this quite unknowingly in that a car door was always opened for me but never for Chris. All comments were addressed to me as Mr Robert. As an opened minded Englishman who treats women as equals I found this annoying. To assuage my feelings I played a little game, not just with him. I'd wait for a car door to be opened then call Chris to take a seat then I'd go to the other side and let myself in.

Reached the town of Ossian at about midday. We're here to see an important ancient Hindu Temple. Our car was parked under trees with other tourist vehicles. The highest parts of the temple could be seen from where we stood. Nearby are some artisan built shacks and vendors of refreshments. I asked Sarup if he was making the visit with us. It was quickly clear by his hand gestures and facial expressions that the answer was no! So we agreed a time to meet back at the car. We hadn't had lunch so I quickly scoffed a banana before walking into the small town. As we did, were confronted by a beggar, a stooping old woman. Unfortunately we'd get used to the one extended hand and the other motioning to the mouth indicating a need for food. Right or wrong we always ignored the pleas.

Entrance to the temple is by payment, then our shoes have to come off. That done we went upwards using the sheltered stepped walkway. It's a busy place with a two way pedestrian system in operation. In addition to tourists, Indian and foreign, uniformed school children their interest in the historical aspects seemingly limited were clambering barriers, laughing and running amok. At the top we walked through a wire caged one way system past the altar, checked out the view over the town, took a few pictures, made our way down and retrieved our shoes. Before putting them on using wet wipes to clean our feet. A sequence that as the tour and visits continued would become a laborious and eventually very annoying task.

Back at the car before the appointed time we could see Sarup sitting at a stall taking tea with other drivers. As white Europeans we always attracted attention and soon had an audience of teenage school children. Always wanting to practice their spoken English they asked questions at an alarming rate, we always tried to oblige with polite answers. As this was happening another tourist driver beckoned Sarup from the tea stall. We said goodbye to the interested small crowd.

The journey continued, entering the busy city of Jodhpur, joining the rush hour traffic until arriving at the Hotel Park Plaza, Airport Road, Nr Panch Batti Circle. At the opulent reception, using the voucher I checked in for two nights, then agreed tomorrow mornings collection time with Sarup and he left. While we and our three bags were waiting for a room to be assigned we took note of our new palatial surroundings. What a hotel! 5 star at minimum, how must we have looked to the immaculately dressed reception staff? Stood in our multi-pocketed safari trousers and crumpled top shirts. More like refugees than the tourist and business clients normally welcomed. Chris had obviously been reading the tour notes, her diary quote, 'Lovely hotel, 4/5 star, I think it's possibly the best we'll get. Jodhpur, aka Sunshine city, aka the Blue City.' On reflection she had excellent perception.

It was here while sat in the hotel garden that we first noted the abundance of Sea Eagles, big birds with large wingspan that dominate the skies in India.

With free and very good Wifi the hotel is modern in design and very plush. The room and its facilities are excellent, much more upmarket than expected and a very pleasant surprise. We showered and put on fresh underclothes. Unfortunately I had to use the late afternoon and early evening attempting to solve the cash card problem and unblock my email account. Day light had faded, I left Chris in the room, went downstairs and outside for a cigarette. I stood watching the night time traffic roll past heading for the town centre just down the road. As the city before and I expect the next, exhaust fumes coloured the air blue.

Had dinner in the restaurant, a very nice meal while we chatted, afterwards enjoyed a couple of beers in the publicly accessible bar. Late to bed at 11.20pm, another super day with some good experiences.

Wednesday 18th February. Day 6. Jodhpur, sightseeing.

Both woke early, I didn't wait long before heading downstairs and out for a smoke. I'd noticed that the hotel is next door to a school, it looked like an infant facility probably a nursery. The morning sun was already warm, children were being delivered by parents, the sight of youngsters wearing woolly hats, top coats and even ear muffs I found quite amusing.

9.30am, after a very good breakfast met at reception by Sarup and today's guide introducing himself as Parbat Singh. From the hotel it's straight to the Mehrangarh Fort which contains the Palace Museum. For the scene as we walked the approach I quote from Chris's journal 'what an amazing place, high up on a hill overlooking Jodhpur, carved out of stone, truly magnificent.'

Parbat explained that he is an ex-Army Officer, had a later career in law and is now enjoying a new lease as an authorised guide. He obtained all entry permissions and tickets, I reimbursed him. He is very informative and gives a fine commentary about the local history. Stayed two hours in this magnificent building viewing its exhibits. We started to properly understand India's long history, its art, religion and divisions, warring and rich moguls, family ancestry of kings and rulers in ancient times, those that co-ruled during the British Colonial years and the ancestors that have power and enormous wealth to this day.

After many text messages a representative of the ICE travel card company informed that our cards should be unblocked and usable here in India. I successfully made a test purchase buying an illustrated booklet published by the museums trust, (this I intended to send home with other papers, thereby not increasing hand luggage weight during our onward travels).

On leaving the Fort, just outside I bought some cigarettes at a street stall. In the car we made a short journey to a memorial site, the Jaswant Tada nicknamed the Mini Taj Mahal. Afterwards, Parbat directed Sarup to a place we'd take lunch. In a busy street a café called 'On the Rocks.' Behind main road buildings, the eating area is nicely sited in landscaped planted gardens with shade giving trees. It was well patronised. I correctly guessed Parbat's army connections as the reason we were here, the waiting staff being dressed in pseudo military uniforms.

I invited him to join us to eat, he declined but did sit for a time and we talked. When not with us I presumed he was snacking for free and socialising with old comrades. While waiting for sandwiches I wrote my diary and we indulged in a refreshing beer. Much safer than water always the excuse for a daytime beverage.

Afterwards, a short ride to the oldest part of the city containing the Sardar market and Clock Tower. Car parked nearby. Walking with Parbat leading, the famous tower could be seen a short distance away through a magnificent archway as if framed. From here we entered and explored the very busy and colourful market, crammed with people going about their daily business, shopping and selling. Along with linen, silk and silver jewellery workshops, there were road side shoe repairers, knife sharpeners and other artisan trades. It was fascinating seeing these entrepreneurs sat cross legged beavering away at their work. In this a picture would say a thousand words but the smells and sounds are never portrayed. We meandered through narrow alleys that had buildings leaning toward the walkways. Goods were strewn everywhere, on the ground, tarpaulins, blankets, in baskets and racks. Overhead an amazing cable network hung precariously seemingly always looking about to fall. Sagging, trailing, connected, not connected and looked like spaghetti at junction boxes. Thick and thin, maybe electricity or communication. Who knew? Moving through the throng of people we attracted a lot of curious glances, even staring but not once feared for our safety.

Mid-afternoon Parbat led us to a wholesaler's premises that offered supposed handmade fine cloth. Knowing instantly that this was the alternative agenda we wouldn't be buying, whatever or however offered. Nevertheless we went in. A ramshackle old building of three floors on different levels linked by steep steps, some masonry, others wood. As we moved through and up every space was packed with cloth of all colours, bundles, piles and bolts. There must have been air conditioning as it was cool. In a top floor room a young chap invited us sit on some upholstered bench seats in front of large open floor area of polished wood, everywhere else is more piles of cloth. The man introduced himself as one of the business partners. I immediately explained that because of weight and lack of luggage space we were unable to buy or gather souvenirs, but we were still given the full sales pitch. He was well practised, I wondered how many tourists had been led here and left with items having succumbed to his slick selling patter? I whispered these thoughts to Chris and she agreed. We politely acted interested and listened intently while he and an associate deftly folded, unfolded and then let beautiful pashminas, throws and silk sheets flutter to the floor. While saying, "These we export to so and so, you will only find these at such and such." And name dropping famous retailers from around the world. Hopefully our blank expressions gave him a clue that there was no business to be done with us!

Sat in that room, my mind was made up that situations like this would never happen again. The event over, accepted a business card, wished the owner every success for the future and left the building. Parbat was waiting, no commission for him this time! Back on the street the late afternoon traffic was heavier, motor cycles and scooters. The air become increasingly polluted, it could be tasted. Chris remarked that she felt a cold coming on. I hoped it was just a symptom of the exhaust fumes.

It was time to return to the hotel. In the car Parbat was thanked and tipped then dropped off at a place of his choosing. Now routine, I agreed tomorrow mornings collection time with Sarup. The evening was ours to enjoy but unfortunately I was to be met with more I.T problems.

In our room I attempted wireless transfer of pictures from the camera to the ipad. Frustratingly this method is excessively time consuming because the connection frequently drops out. The annoying consequences being having to start the loading sequence afresh. Yet again I have to unblock my email account. Such a f*****g drag!

Wrote my diary at 7.45pm then we prepared ourselves to go for dinner. I shaved my head for the first time since arriving in India. By now, if they were available, we were selecting hotel supplied items to supplement our travel packs. Soaps, shampoos, toilet tissue, sachets of tea and coffee. We'd never know if they would be provided at the next accommodation.

In the restaurant a buffet was available but we selected from a fine a la carte menu. Dinner was enjoyed with few beers while watching an outdoor private party taking place at poolside. Attended by some obviously wealthy Indian families the hotel staff served them drink from a table top bar and barbequed food cooked on outdoor ranges. After eating we moved to the plush indoor cocktail bar, had a beer and talked.

11.00pm, back at the room intending to get an early night in anticipation of the early start tomorrow. I shouldn't have but attempted to upload some photographs again and failed. I was annoyed with myself, had spoiled the moment and was no longer totally relaxed. I'd been greedy and tried to get more from the day than was possible so wandered down through reception and had a last cigarette outside. Went back straight to bed at 11.20pm.

Thursday 19th February. Day 7. Jodhpur to Udaiphur via Ranakpur Jain Temple. 6 hours 255km.

Up at 7.00am, Chris said she had a runny nose, a worry as any illness would be difficult to contend with. Cleared the room, prepped our baggage, checked out after breakfast and soon on the road with Sarup at the wheel. He made a refuelling stop on the outskirts of Jodhpur. At the petrol station Chris and I never left the vehicle but were closely and inquisitively observed by customers and staff alike. We were starting to get used to this behaviour. I noted in my diary 'petrol cost 51.73 rupees per litre, about 52 British pence.' The journey continued, initially the landscape was quite flat, dry and dull to look at. Even at a good distance from the city it was mostly industrial buildings with some cultivated areas and a few farmsteads. At about 10.00am in the Pali district Sarup stopped for a refreshment break. He'd chosen a place that would be of interest and we could get coffee at the same time.

Here we briefly met two English women. Several times we'd noted their tourist car travelling the same road as us and had seen them plainly. Now, they'd stopped here at almost the same time. Strange, but India can make a European person feel very isolated so it was pleasant just to exchange greetings. Chris had more of the conversation relating it to me later. In their sixties one of them had come to India seventeen times and was acting as a guide and companion to the other on her first visit.

The place is a roadside shrine at which over the past few years a small business community has flourished. Not only are light snacks and souvenirs sold, also available are flowers and candles. Both are given as religious offerings. Sarup explained as best he could but I researched the story at the earliest opportunity on the internet. The shrine comprises a Royal Enfield Bullet motorcycle in aged and damaged condition contained in a slowly deteriorating metal framed glass case. This on a stone plinth next to a small tree. Of course, any visitor here with hope of a safe journey on this road is expected to make a charitable contribution to obtain a blessing. This is India's way! There were plenty of people doing so.

The popular story. 'Rider and motor cycle were involved in a fatal crash having collided with a tree, bike retrieved and impounded at the nearest police station. By the morning of the next day the motor cycle had made its way back to the crash site. Retrieved and impounded again, tank drained and wheels chained again made its way back to the crash site. The mysterious actions repeatedly continued. The story spread and the miracle motorcycle was born.'

What else could be expected with a Hindu population believing that some of its Gods can be reborn as part elephant or even as a river? As English folk with Christian ethics what should we do? Surely best to err on the safe side? Yes, made an offering and got the first red dots on our foreheads. Shouldn't have worried though, Chris's diary note, made at the end of the day, 'Sarup is a great driver, the Stig of India.'

Onward to Ranakpur the scenery improved, green and lush. Upward through quite a mountainous area on tree lined winding narrow roads, Sarup's skills were evident as we met oncoming vehicles, especially big ones such as coaches and lorries. Chris noted, 'drove through some amazing countryside, so much to see! Women and girls washing clothes in rivers, bullocks turning a water wheel for irrigation whilst the young lad attending is using his

49

mobile phone, very bizarre, 21st century meets 1st century.'

11.30am, arrived Ranakpur. Drove through open gates and parked in the landscaped managed grounds of the active Jain Temple. This religious sect has difficult to comprehend complexities. The simplified principles of the followers are that they do not harm any creature from insect to human and live without a desire for any material possessions or physical pleasures. This visit became quite a disappointment, especially when the religious context of the sect are taken into consideration. Again Sarup let us off the leash to do our own thing and we agreed a one hour visit.

In the busy car park we took time and care to read the large entry information and restriction signs. 'NO Cameras, NO Food,' on the list. Leaving our day bags in the vehicle Chris and I joined other tourist's queueing for access. First booth for tickets, 500 rupees per person obtained. Next booth to get headsets for the recorded commentary. Not something we'd normally do but these are compulsory to enter the temple. We overhear western words from other tourists. 'Why? What? Never.' Without any previous notice the teller was requesting passports as deposits for the equipment. There was no way we'd give ours up and anyway they were in the car. The clock was ticking and we could also see the rigmarole on the steps of the temple as uniformed armed guards bodily searched those who had made it that far. Get a refund? No chance, the ticket queue was snaking several yards so we quickly agreed that the visit would be a walk round. The ancient building is quite a wonder. We met an Australian couple who had decided similar, exchanged pleasantries, used their camera to take a picture of them, they used my phone camera to reciprocate. Several signs in the complex read, 'Do not give money to the sweepers.' We presumed complying with this request would assist in keeping the Jain followers from temptation or breaking their faith. Not so, they hovered everywhere, hands out, especially at the

50

toilet block expecting the ubiquitous tip as payment for use of the facilities.

Afterwards, Sarup drove until about 12.45pm then stopped at a roadside restaurant called 'Harmony.' A charming little place with a stepped and covered terrace. We took lunch here. Other customers seated were American and we engaged in idle chat. The serving area was set out buffet style. Earthenware pots holding several different preparations, meats, vegetables, some simmering on hotplates. Hand written wood signs in English were placed to aid customer choice. Chris and I would normally have just eaten a sandwich and some fruit at this time of day but the offerings looked and smelled delightful, so we each made different selections and shared them from two plates. Coffee followed. Before leaving, took some photographs near the restaurant's roadside sign, from here are good views into a valley below. Sarup continued the drive, this time travelling down the mountain roads then into Udaipur, the Lake City.

Late afternoon, arrived at the Hotel Rajdarshan 18 Pannadhia Marg. A magnificent place with landscaped tropical gardens. Checked in for one night and shown to our room, beautifully furnished, an excellent bathroom and as a bonus a balcony with Lake Swaroop Sagar below and views of the bridge that spans it. Wifi is free, best accessed in the lobby and bar areas, both luxurious places to be so who would possibly complain? Certainly not me. We readied for dinner as night came. Views across the lake at this time are fantastic. The city lights reflect and shimmer on the water. Although having an early start tomorrow tonight was to be enjoyed. The superb restaurant offered buffet and a la carte menu and certainly wasn't over populated. Other clients were families, tourists and business people, all Indian. We not only enjoyed a fine meal with beverages but the most genuine attention at service level received so far in this country.

After dinner we retired to the bar, in here just us and a barman. Kingfisher beers were enjoyed while chatting and keeping half an eye on a television showing World Cup cricket. Made good use of the Wifi, Chris used her cellphone, me the ipad. We updated family and friends with photographs and anecdotal stories by Facebook and Whatsapp. I also noted a gap in tomorrow's itinerary, a long time between the end of the day's touring and the train departing. This would need discussion with the appointed guide. We'd also written our diaries, my note, 'hotel, so far, the best menu, best meal, best served!'

We'd really enjoyed the evening, it was getting late, I had been outside smoking several times, the barman had noticed and when I returned for the last time he politely requested a cigarette. I proffered the opened packet and he deftly removed a clutch of four in number, thanking me while slipping them into his top pocket!

Back at the room we prepared our baggage for the early start, readied for bed, then I had a late smoke while stood on the balcony taking a last look at the night time view.

Friday 20th February. Day 8. Udaipur tour as itinerary. Overnight train to Jaipur: UDZ KURT EXPRESS Dep. 10.20pm. 419km

Diary reminder note, 'Get food for overnight train.'

After breakfast met guide Mahendra Singh and immediately brought to his attention my concerns about the spare time that is apparent today. He would make some telephone calls. Check out completed and I must admit that I'd have been very happy to stay, relax, and enjoy more of the hotel facilities for a couple of days. That was not to be, car loaded we were soon on our way to the first place on the tour of Udaipur, the Palace. A large opulent building with one side built on the edge of Lake Pichola.

Mahendra gave an interesting and informed commentary during the visit. Chris and I learned more about the enormous wealth of certain individuals in this country. A reoccurring theme as different Indian states were visited. This particular palace is owned by *this* State's Royal Family and has been for many centuries, even during the British Colonial period. Although no longer reigning, the family still keeps large areas of the place off limits to the public. Their enormous wealth is supplemented by hiring out the building for events such as weddings. In fact preparations for one were taking place today. A spacious courtyard being fitted out similar to a music festival, a stage, temporary tiered seating etcetera. These ceremonies can cost the Indian equivalent of millions of British pounds and on the event day the palace will be closed to all but invited guests and staff. There are a lot of very rich folks in India and the money obviously never flows down the food chain, the excruciating poverty for millions of the population is on show daily.

Next, to a highly carved stone Hindu Temple, shoes on and off again for this one. A lengthy wait listening to chanting by the followers while Mahendra queued to make his offering, receive a blessing and forehead red dot. From here to The Princess Gardens, after which we had a basic lunch of coffee and chips at a small café. Then on to an embarkation pier joining many other tourists for a flat bottomed boat ride on the lake. A sign said 'life jackets are compulsory.' When issued we put them on and took our seats. Plenty of oriental tourists on this trip with cameras neck and shoulder hung like paparazzi. It's a slow ride, enabling passengers to enjoy the views and take photographs. The boat moored at an Island, everyone disembarked to see what was described as a visitor centre but also doubled as a hotel and an events facility. A nicely laid out garden had quite an amusing sign posted in a scraggy flower border, it read 'please do not pluck roses.' Refreshments and bathrooms being available I took the opportunity to add a quality toilet roll to my stock. Boats were frequent so we took the next available back to the start point. Odd, but life jackets were 'optional' for the return journey. That made me smile. At 2.30pm the organised visits of our tour over Mahendre was given his voucher and cash tip.

My diary note, 'the locals are continually edging for tips, at WC's, shoe lockers, waiters, etcetera. The guide today was an odd chap, having good English, seemed moody but efficient. Our driver as always, safe and proficient.'

Met Sarup at the car. A plan for the rest of the day had to be formulated, effectively we were homeless. A local tour office being available, it had been arranged that we'd use it as temporary storage for our luggage. Within walking distance is Leela Park. This locality has many upmarket hotels so in effect, a safe area. Chris and I decided we'd be comfortable being left to our own devices. A pick-up point and time of 9.00pm was agreed for our ride to the railway station and the bags would already be in the car. That could be a concern but Indian organisation had been impeccable so far and we didn't see it as problem, it didn't turn into one.

At about 3.00pm we took coffee in the grounds of a nice hotel, the Garden Palace. We had about six hours to use, so afterwards established our bearings and walked to the park. It was hot and humid, plenty of vegetation, some areas managed others not. The grounds are extensive with many paths and some buildings. Wandering we found a library. People strolled, monkeys occasionally appeared. There were a few joggers. We talked while walking, then tarried sat on a bench, fortunately we carried insect repellent and put some on, knowing that as dusk arrived so would mosquitos. Eventually made our way out and back to the hotel, took a table, ordered more coffee and decided that we'd have dinner here, albeit later. Filled time by writing our diaries. My mind wandered to thoughts of the pool at the Hotel Rajdarshan, we hadn't had time to use it. I was hot and sticky now, a cooling dip would be heaven.

After dinner and at the appointed hour a white tour car pulled into the hotel grounds. The driver identified himself, but being security conscious I asked him to say my name. He scrabbled around inside the car for a piece of paper, 'Mr. Robert' his eventual reply. I requested to inspect the luggage, the car boot was opened and our bags were there. I double checked mine, I'd left the ipad in it, something I couldn't afford to go missing.

Put on our backpacks at the station. For our second overnight rail journey I was determined to establish the platform and identify the carriage. The place is old, dirty and smelly, the stink of urine prevalent. Not as busy as Delhi but still cluttered with baggage, goods and carts. Plenty of people, the usual strange looks and staring. It is impossible not to be noticed as foreigner in these places and quite unnerving when someone fixes their eyes on you. A train arrived, all of the numbers painted on it tallied with our tickets. It was early. I confirmed our carriage, close to the door it had a passenger list pasted and our names were on it. We got in found our compartment and were about to settle when a rail employee in no uncertain terms made us get off. The carriages weren't prepared and ready to accept passengers. Cleaning and laying out bedding was still in progress, the air conditioning wasn't operational and so on. This is India I mused, while finding somewhere to stand on an increasingly populated platform. We were eventually joined by a tour rep, another new face, I can honestly say I don't remember him to this day. He was here to see us safely onto the train. There's no doubting the care and attention of the tour company.

About 10.00pm after what seemed an eternity, passengers started boarding. The three of us got on. I quickly convinced the young rep that we were fine and he could leave. The carriage was still very hot. In our compartment we'd been allocated the lower beds, one of the upper to an Indian. He was quickly organised, bag and shoes below Chris's bunk. His bedding fitted and in sleeping position within minutes. I expect he'd done this many times before.

Chris and I started to sort out our sleeping areas much as we did on the Delhi to Jaisalmer trip. The train was still at the platform when there was an interruption.

A woman had arrived in the carriage, speaking in English and addressing both of us in a very flustered manner. Late middle aged and noticeably dressed old style hippie traveller. Heavy denim shirt, ankle length skirt, scarf around her neck and shoulders with greying hair pulled tightly into a pony tail. Quite a shock for us, we'd been in the country for several days, only had one fleeting conversation with British people and that was yesterday at the road side shrine. Not many of us about in a population of billions! She had an air of experience but was definitely expressing concerns, there were no introductions or pleasantries. It was all spilling out in a fractured manner, she was looking for a berth and could see the spare above mine was unoccupied. It was at the time but with even limited experience I knew that it would be taken eventually. Probably by someone down the line getting on at some unknown station in the small hours. She had a First Class sleeper ticket but to her horror the other three passengers in the four berth compartment were men. These compartments are a grade up from the curtained second, they are cabin style with doors. In India of late there'd been reports of attacks on Western women, very rarely, but I understood her concerns and suggested she looked for the guard or an inspector. She left the carriage, excitement over. The train was on the move.

We settled on our berths. Now past 11.30pm, resting, OK not for long, the curtain is pulled back. A man is visible, cap and uniform with lots of badges asking for passports, I thought instantly, "what on a f*****g train!" Ours were in my day bag and didn't take long to produce. I handed them over. A cursory glance at mine and it's returned but Chris's is fully scrutinised then given back to *me*. Nothing else was said. A strange interlude, I never did get to understand why.

Saturday 21st February. Day 9. Tour of Jaipur.

Night had turned to day, it's about 5.00am and so far a horrid journey, noisy and hot. Yet again we're dishevelled, feeling grubby, tired and neither of us is in good spirits. I could be described as 'hanging.' The knowledge that there were two more overnight train journeys didn't bear thinking about. We'd just eaten breakfast, biscuits, cake and banana as the train rolled slowly towards Jaipur station for the 6.00am arrival. Later I noted in my diary, 'It was an awful 7hrs, probably only two hours sleep and that was one before and one after midnight'.

We're met on the platform by a tour rep and a young lad assistant. They were thoughtful enough to help with our bags as they led us to the car park. Here with the car was Sarup, looking bright as a button. I expected him but thought at least there would be a different vehicle. He must have left for this city the minute we parted company in Udaipur. How I wished he'd brought us, I'm sure we'd have had a better journey. The young lad rode off on a moped. Sarup drove me, Chris and the rep to the Hotel Glitz Sitarampin, Nr Police Station, Amer Road, Shankar Nagar. While we checked in, the rep waited and a guide had turned up. By now I was on automatic pilot!

It's about 7.00am and obviously apparent that the guide, who introduced himself as Sandeep, (I have not included his second name and much more about him later), expected us ready to start the tour of Jaipur as soon as possible. There'd been no indication of this in the itinerary and we certainly weren't in a good condition, at least needing to freshen up and eat. I had a brief discussion and agreed reduced time at the listed visits. Used the lift and went to our room, had showers and washed some clothes while doing so. Dressed and went down for some proper breakfast served buffet style in the ground floor restaurant.

By 9.30am we were all in the car and on our way to the Amber Fort Palace a marvellous structure that gives stunning views across the city. Stayed for about an hour, at one time watching tourists on highly decorated elephants, enjoying rides from the lower ramparts up and through one of the magnificent tall arched entrances specifically designed for the purpose. In ancient times the animal was not just used for ritual but military purposes during many interstate wars. Unfortunately because of our late arrival, massive queues and other commitments we'd have to forego our booked turn.

The fort is a very popular destination and populated by many souvenir sellers and touts. They are an extremely annoying, uncontrolled and unwanted interruption. Persistent in presenting their goods, physically taking the ground in front of a person while walking and constantly offering barter terms. This was the first time we'd encountered such behaviour. The only method of dealing with this is to attempt ignorance or walk into them. Any form of acknowledgement is deemed an entry into negotiation.

From the fort we were driven into the city, on the way making a brief roadside stop to take photographs of a building's façade, all that remains of The Palace of Winds. Other interesting visits were to the Pink City, Maharajah's City Palace and the Jantar Mantar Observatory.

Back at the hotel by 1.00pm. A very busy place. Income from guests plainly supplemented by custom in the restaurant, which by the condition of furnishings is well used, many of the chairs had damage, finials missing and backs split. The heavier under cloths laid on tables had frayed and torn edges, curtains hanging at the windows were holed, ragged and sun bleached. In many places water and other stains seemed to hold the material together. Nevertheless a popular all day food stop for companies or maybe just the guides and drivers. Coaches, mini-buses and tour cars come and go frequently. We noted Oriental, Indian and Western clientele, groups, couples and single. For some, food would have been inclusive, alcoholic beverages and branded soft drinks never are, they are charged as extras.

We ordered a light lunch, a pay as you go situation for us. There is great competition between waiters to place the account wallet on the table before a meal is finished, even more to collect it. This proved to be an observation of Indian greed and selfishness. If containing a cash tip, the waiter's deft ability to slyly remove and get it to pocket in one movement would have impressed a magician. No sharing rewards here!

In a corner of the busy car park is a shed type building, the drivers congregated here, laughter could be heard often. I imagined generated as they exchanged anecdotal stories about the strange needs and habits of their clients. I'd taken a walk around the block that contained the hotel and grounds. There was very little for a tourist to see or do, a few scruffy shops, locals going about daily life. The demarcation of unmade road from unkempt pedestrian walkway only delineated by accumulated rubbish, rocks and other debris.

Of the morning's events, my diary note, 'it had been a whirlwind of sights and sensations.'

Chris and I slept for three hours waking about 4.00pm. Had obviously needed the rest, maybe because of our age but more likely the heat and rail journey. Our room was more basic accommodation than luxury, it did however provide all of the essentials. These included a kettle and some crockery but no condiments. We'd been collecting sachets of sauce, tea, coffee etcetera. I made hot drinks using our supplies. I'd stopped taking milk in any beverage some time ago. Any valuable spare time was often used for personal grooming and minor laundering. While getting on with these chores we'd discuss the events of recent hours or previous days, today was no different. One topic being how expensive this country is for Western tourists, given that an Indian could gain access to an attraction for 20 rupees but we'd need to pay 500, about £5.GBP per person.

Another subject was today's guide.

I can safely say that by the end our visits in Jaipur Chris disliked the fellow intently. I add that he was almost as much of a distraction to the enjoyment of the ancient wonders as the touts. In my diary I always made a brief note about the qualities of a guide. Today it had been one word, a vile swear word not to be recorded on these pages.

This morning we'd been presented with this slim smartly dressed young man wearing designer shoes, highly pressed trousers and a bright orange shirt. He'd introduced himself and given us his business card, a glossy little item. From the time we got in the car we were being delivered his take on things, politics, media and obviously, tourism. Then it was how we should conduct ourselves, not to do this, not to buy that. But there were three particular issues that he expounded, each in their own right would bring us to have great contempt for him. For Chris, one especially.

While travelling by car to the Amber Palace, he told us that he's a Jain by religion, we'd already learned of the piety and renouncing of possessions by followers. So we found this odd, paradoxical, especially as he further explained his family and business connections in the jewellery trade while flaunting what he described as a very expensive and flawless sapphire mounted in a gold ring, worn with others on immaculately manicured fingers.

Walking as a group of three, up by way of a winding path into the fort we're assailed with his opinion of the media. Reports of gang rape and crimes such as attacks on tourists are being manufactured to sell newspapers. I suggested that if even only one of the accounts recently reported were true it should be enough to concede that by any civilised standard a heinous crime. According to him they don't happen. By now I was seething, Chris maintained a dignified silence but I knew what the look on her face meant.

The subject of poverty in India broached he wasted no time or words as his opinion spilled. There is none! Chris having seen with her own eyes plenty of examples of abject destitution then posed a question, asking about cardboard shanty towns, the people who live at roadside or under bridges. Easily explained away, they want to live in this manner, most have been given apartments and an allowance of 500 rupees per month, more than enough to buy rice and other foodstuffs. They rent out the apartments to supplement their chosen lifestyle! Our anger at his arrogance was contained, but only just.

Nevertheless the day had been far from a bad one, we'd accomplished many things, touristic and domestic. It would soon be time for dinner but I had an appointment before that. A meeting with the guide Sandeep to complete an interim feedback form and for him to collect his tip. About 5.00pm a phone call to the room beckoned me to reception. He was waiting. The form was duly completed, not able to use old English swear words I put the word good for most of the items listed, except where a section enquired about the driver. It's always nice to write 'excellent.'

7.30pm, dinner, a buffet on offer but we preferred to select from the menu. I ordered a couple of beers to wind down with while making a meal selection. They were quickly delivered, the waiter hovered pen and pad in hand. No we hadn't selected, so easier to put up five fingers and tap a wristwatch than to explain, away he went. We scanned the menu. One item intrigued us, chicken and yellow sauce. Far less than five minutes had elapsed the waiter was back. Time to enquire.

I ask, "What is the yellow sauce?"

"Yellow sauce," his reply.

Ok a rethink, "What is in the yellow sauce?"

"Yellow sauce," again the reply. One more try, I can see Chris in the corner of my eye, cheeks up eyes welling and about to burst into laughter.

"What ingredients are in the yellow sauce?" I should have known better, by now Chris had her hands covering her mouth and nose suppressing laughter.

The waiter's answer, "Yellow sauce!"

As Chris stifled her giggles I gave up and ordered two chicken and yellow sauce. It turned out to be a nice meal, as usual meat on the bone, with a mild sauce of which we'd never establish ingredients but it was yellow!

While enjoying dinner we and other clients were to be entertained. We'd seen drums sited on the floor where the buffet tables had been placed at lunch time. I'd hoped to have been long gone before any such thing happened. A group of 'strangely' dressed men seated themselves crossed legged at the instruments, women dressed in tunics and trousers were soon dancing to the sound of the drums, a folk show. I can't say I was impressed, especially when diners were encouraged to join in. A dancer came to our table as we were talking and was politely waved away. I knew how it would all end. Passing the hat, and it did.

Sunday 22nd February. Day 10. Jaipur to Agra via Fatehpur Sikri. 5 Hour drive. 240km.

Woken at 6.00am by the sound of bells and drums from outside. What they indicated, who knew? They could have been of some religious significance. Before breakfast at 7.30am Chris informed me of a slight bottom accident, a wet one. Probably the yellow sauce! As a bonus her suspected cold hadn't become serious. She noted later, 'Woke up with a slightly dodgy tummy this morning, thankfully it's been OK so far, nose starting to feel better, not so snotty.'

By 9.00am we'd checked out, Sarup and car were ready for us. It's to be another long driving day. The sun was up and beaming through the windows, although air conditioned it was still hot. About 11.00am we stopped for a leg stretch and for me to smoke.

Near midday arrived at Fatephur Sikri the abandoned City of one Religion. Built using red sandstone, inhabited for fourteen years only then deserted because of the scarcity of fresh water. Today the place was mobbed with people, tourists, touts and souvenir sellers. Sarup temporarily parked, left us in the car and went to fetch an official guide. Its tour company policy for us to have one when visiting these ancient monuments. He returned with a big fellow who introduced himself as we drove to a permanent parking space. I don't recall his name and didn't bother to note it.

Here we again experience the Indian method of money extraction. Tourists and guides have to use a bus from the parking area to the city entrance, a short distance that could have been comfortably walked. Return tickets obtained we all boarded an old single deck bus, which was soon crammed with passengers, seated and standing. The drop off point was reached in minutes.

City entrance tickets were purchased, no extra cost for cameras as is the case at many ancient monuments. In we went, there was much to see and admire. I took many photographs. The guide gave his commentary, an obviously well practised story. These chaps all seem to have their own take on the religious history of India, all conflicting! Maybe I'll have to read a book sometime.

The walk through visit ended in the grounds of an active Mosque. Not such an abandoned place then? Waiting for the next available return bus an awkward situation arose, in that a young tout became very persistent. Chris and I employed the usual methods of dismissal, ignoring, hands up or waving away but this fellow would not desist, he was in our faces and the guide didn't intervene. For the first time in India my anger rose and fists clenched. As always Chris noticed and became the needed calming influence physically getting between me and the pest. He went, I turned my ire onto the guide and made my feelings known in no uncertain terms, not swearing, but he certainly got the point.

The return bus used, it arrived at the edge of the car park. We were walking and talking now, Chris wasn't convinced that I had calmed. I was, but had revenge in my heart and it was easy to exact.

The biggest insult that can be given to an official guide is not refusing to give a cash tip but giving a very small one. He knew that my comment was politeness only as I thanked him for his services and gave him a one hundred rupee note, an amount that would have satisfied a toilet attendant.

On we travelled toward Agra only making a brief stop for lunch. The drive was very interesting with further examples of Sarup's skill. Chris later noted in her diary, 'again saw some amazing sights during the drive from Jaipur, women carrying small babies on motor bikes, horses, camels, pigs, monkeys, lorries etcetera, all on the roads.' Today we learned that if an animal became a static obstruction across the road he would hardly decelerate and always pass it while aiming the car at the beast's rear end. Bringing chortles all round he explained "They never reverse." Another amusing incident brought more laughter. A horse had straddled what was an excuse for a central reservation, other obstructions opposite narrowed the gap which the car had to pass through. I didn't realise that these animals expressed horror or surprise by facial expression. This one did as the car door mirror almost brushed its nose. A 'be there' moment but we enjoyed it.

Arrived in Agra at about 4.00pm. Sarup stopped the car at the gated compound of the Clarks Shiraz Hotel, 54 Taj Road, Agra Cantonment, Tajgant. Guards made him open the boot and bonnet and the underside of the vehicle was checked using a mirror. This is a very plush place sited close to a Military Establishment. All luggage is taken to a secure room and passed through an airport type scanner before entry. Contents of handbags are inspected, phones, electronic and personal items placed on trays for examination. This hotel was certainly on a high security footing. Clients not only included obviously wealthy tourists, we heard German, French and English spoken, saw Japanese and Koreans. It seems that politicians and higher rank military personnel are also guests. Security is bolstered by uniformed soldiers. I noted in my diary, 'at night, at least one automatic weapon is on show.'

We checked in for two nights, the reception staff eyed us strangely, not the usual type of clientele. Most others booking in had multiples of baggage, aluminium and hard shell cases almost spilling from trolleys. No porter required, we shouldered our kit, were shown to our room and left our bags there, having decided to explore the expansive grounds before darkness fell.

The complex comprises linked buildings of several storeys with a selection of restaurants and bars, one on a patio roof top doubled as the breakfast room. From here are superb views across the city. At a distance the Taj Mahal is visible, sometimes clearly otherwise shrouded in mist or smog. Monkeys and noisy peacocks are on the roof and in the gardens. We wandered past the outdoor swimming pool, a few people were laying on beds catching the last rays of the setting sun. There'd obviously been a recent party, the remains of a decorated platform were on a lawn bordered by tall spindly trees, branches hung with strings of tiny lights and long ribbons. We bought coffee at the all hour's café and sat under part of the covered walkway that bounds the building's perimeter, talked and exchanged opinions about many things including our new found surroundings. Afterwards, back through the marble walled and floored reception and went to our room. Wrote my diary at 5.30pm.

Showered and dressed, then checked the menu prices on boards outside the main restaurants. Not surprisingly they read like telephone numbers, international and area codes included! We had beers at the ground floor bar then went to the café and ordered burgers and chips, washed them down with a couple more of the very expensive beverages. It can be noted that we spent our money very wisely! Chris wrote, 'beer at the bar then dinner, mushroom burger, made a nice change from curry although it was still spicy.' Went to bed at a sensible 10.30pm. Big day tomorrow, the Taj Mahal visit.

Monday 23rd February. Day 11. Taj Mahal & Agra Fort.

Up at 6.15am, had breakfast at the rooftop facility and took photographs of the views. Back at the room I made a diary note, 'my phone is not connecting with any server, put data on last night to send a text to Kerri, eventually picked up India Airtel at 8.00am.' When internet access was unavailable or as here is ridiculously priced at 750 rupees per hour, we made a point of getting one message back home to daughter-in-law Kerri, to advise of our position and condition, she would share this to family and friends.

9.00am, Sarup arrived to collect us without a guide and was on his phone sorting this out. One was picked up enroute, introducing himself as Arif Khan. As we made the journey to the Taj Mahal he explained the ticket prices and very strict entry rules that apply for carried items. Briefly, nothing is allowed that could be used to damage the monument. The list of permitted items is far shorter than those banned and anything that security guards deem illicit will be confiscated with no argument and no storage or return facility. Later we see this process enacted. Chris and I rearranged the contents of our day bags, permissible items are, water, prescription medicines, cameras, cell phones. We carried one bag the other remained in the car.

Walking the short distance to the entrance is not an option, we're led cross the road to ride in a highly decorated horse drawn cart. The guide and I in the rear seat, Chris in the front next to the driver. Offered, she takes the reins, clip clop clip two hundred yards later 400 rupees spent and he'll wait for us!

Close to the entrance touts are persistent but ignorable. Tickets bought at 750 rupees each for westerners, Indians 20 rupees! I knew the cow was sacred here but was starting to feel like a milked one. Security is military, real soldiers, one visitor entrance for males another for females. For both, first the frisk and pat down, next the bag search. Chris didn't carry one, mine was Ok, but a very unhappy American and his family weren't so fortunate. Pens, pencils, gum, sweets, fruit juices joined the pile of confiscated goods on show. I certainly couldn't complain about the advice given by our guide.

Chris noted later, 'surreal moment of the day.' While being searched by a female soldier wearing full uniform and surgical gloves, was asked. "Where did you get your top? It's beautiful." Chris explained it was from England but didn't expand that the short sleeved, white buttoned blouse with an embroidered front panel was an ebay purchase and obtained expressly as a cover up for use in religiously sensitive areas of India. Fashionably sensible my missus!

The Taj Mahal, 17th Century, a mausoleum for a Muslim wife and Queen, built at great expense, is justifiably listed as one of the seven man made wonders of the world. It, the landscaped grounds and complimentary buildings have the most amazing architectural geometric symmetry. Much has been written and is freely available so I need not expand. We were here!

Entry and exit to the building is up wooden steps where a two way system operates. The queue is long but moving. No shoes on and off here, the pile of footwear and resultant confusion at retrieval unimaginable. Shoe nets are provided, a quick and simple solution.

Views across the Yamuna River enhanced our appreciation of this visit. My camera was used to good effect, our guide even taking photographs of us as a couple, touristy shots through pierced and carved fretwork marble panels. In the grounds he encouraged us to pose in similar fashion to those that became so famous taken of Princess Diana. We did, tacky being the describing word. No serenity for us, the place was closed to the public for her and Charles's visit, we had the world and his wife up around us.

I know my wife well and couldn't help wonder what she was thinking but I didn't want to spoil the moment. Diana died the day after Chris's mother. Only one of these deaths had made the news the other was kept close to home.

The visit over and thoroughly enjoyed we all made our way to the grounds exit. True to the promise, cart and driver were there. Who was responsible for this clockwork timing? I'd never establish this, maybe the guide, everyone had mobile phones, it was a certainty that he wouldn't have sat waiting just for our return and had probably been up and down the road many times in the interim.

An almost identical return journey to the car except that Chris and the guide were in the rear seat, with me in the front alongside the driver. Yes I'm offered the reins, no thanks, clip clop clip two hundred yards up the road the cart stops. Arif is out and has the camera, click, click, a few more tacky but enjoyable memories.

Indians are opportunists, there must have been two lads per wheel holding spokes keeping the cart still as Chris and I dismounted, more tips, 400 rupees. Maybe I should stop talking and moo!

68

Later I made a note in my diary, 'Legalised begging and touts are f****** pests, quite fed up with the constant expected "tipping," they are at all places, take a p**s, they want money for opening a door, a piece of tissue, even today after paying 400R for the cart ride boys expected money for holding it still for our dismount, will be glad to get South, just for a change!!' Bad English but written while in a mood of annoyance and frustration.

At about midday arrived at a marble merchants much against my desire and this place probably the guide's commission agenda. I didn't make a fuss but was more determined that these types of visits weren't to happen. Fortunately it was nice and cool inside the building so avoiding the purchase of a miniature Taj Mahal was at least to be done in comfort. We were treated to a demonstration of the marble inlayer's art, lectured about the qualities of Indian marble versus European varieties etcetera but our interest was low.

Afterwards we're driven to a car park just off of a very busy two way four lane road, noted only because crossing it to get to our luncheon destination was quite perilous. The café is called the Taj Mahal, pretty low grade, apparently Muslim owned and run establishment, so there was no beer. I presumed the guide chose it for the western style toilet facilities available. Chris and shared a couple of ropey sandwiches and a coke. It was the first time we'd got up close and personal to people eating without cutlery, using the fingers of their right hand only. Hygiene purposes, supposedly?

After using the toilet Chris found that her Saint Christopher medallion had come adrift from the neck chain and had lodged in her blouse. Very fortunate, I'd given it to her as a gift many years ago. We'd have to wait until much later in our travels to get a repair made.

About 1.00pm arrived at the enormous structure of Agra Fort. This place has fantastic history that compliments its imposing presence. Built as a fortress and a palace, used by many rulers and administrations from the

15th to 20th century including the British. We certainly enjoyed our time here and had a good conversation with Arif about many topics, not just his knowledge of history. He even touched upon the discontent he has for American and German tourists. If I remember correctly saying they are arrogant and needy. Strange because that's how I had come to perceive quite a few Indians.

Back at the hotel by 2.45pm, made and drank coffee in our room and were thankful for the air conditioning. It had been and still was a scorcher of a day.

After showering had a couple beers in the bar. We had a lot to talk about and did. The conversation continued through dinner at 8.00pm in the café. Tomorrow we'd be leaving north India's Golden Triangle and flying south to Chennai. In our room we had coffee and started preparing our baggage for the airport. Were in bed by 11.00pm.

Our diary notes for the day are very different, I wrote about the hotel. 'Again all male staff for housekeeping and cleaning, a token female presence at the front entrance for security, one or two at reception. These people are Arab in any other way in treatment of women. The hotel is immaculate, front line staff almost fawning but this is a false front it has the atmosphere of a hospital, dull.'

Chris was in reflective mood, her notes were, 'so far my thoughts on India are mixed. There is great wealth for a few and grinding poverty for the masses. Many beautiful places but also massive slum/poor areas with dirt and filth everywhere. India, it seems is the same in many ways back in history with the Moguls and Maharajas. It will be interesting to see southern India in comparison to the north.'

Tuesday 24th February. Day 12. Delhi to Chennai. 2,200km. Air India A142 Flight. Dept. 5.15pm. Arr. 8.00pm

Plenty of time spare to double check our packing and clear the room after breakfast. At the desk I checkout. Sarup wearing a rare smile is ready for us. The car loaded, we're about to get in and suddenly a female reception staff member is beckoning. I have to go back and pay for a room mini bar beer. Couldn't remember having one but went back and literally threw some cash at the problem. We were off, not quite the words I used in my diary.

Out of the city of Agra and on the way to Delhi using the almost new Yamuna Highway that links the two Cities. A concrete and tarmac road with similarities in design to a European motorway. Proper signage, lane markings, speed limits and overtaking restrictions. Here the resemblance ends, the engineers and planners hadn't taken into consideration the Indian people. Either side of the new road are the tracks and lanes that service farmlands and other agricultural concerns. So the beasts of burden, carts and labourers bring goods and people to convenient locations such as small bridgeworks or anywhere with access to the highway then motorised trucks stop to collect the goods and people from these unauthorised 'way stations.'

Approaching the outskirts of Delhi we passed the Buddh International Grand Prix Motor racing stadium and track. From there onward saw a lot of construction work, skyscrapers in varying state of completion. There were signs, very sensory, stirring and suggestive. They reminded me of a futuristic film extolling the virtues of a new order but these were here and now, encouraging and enticing the nouveau riche of India that these places and the way of life they offered is the way ahead. If they have the necessary multiple millions of rupees to spare!

At Delhi airport. Said goodbye to Sarup, a gratuity of 7,500 rupees being given with handshakes and thanks, he had truly been a good driver.

It seemed India always has twists, we have paper tickets for the internal flight but as foreigners must use the international departure facilities. Other than that, the usual airport sequence is followed. Through security with hand luggage only. Damn it, they found my tiny scissors and that was them gone! We snacked on burgers, bought some sweets and cigarettes. Through to departures and were soon on the aeroplane.

Touring Southern India

Take off was fifty minutes late, we were given dinner in flight, landed in Chennai at 8.50pm, through customs and immigration and met just outside the retail shopping area by a rep called Joshua and a driver. Driven to the hotel, arriving 10.00pm at The Pride, 216 E.V.R. Periyar Salai, Poonamallee High Road, Kilpauk, Chennai. Checked in, Wifi by the hour or day yet again. Showered and washed some clothes. Couldn't see much of interest outside but smoked a last cigarette. Before going to bed at 11.45pm noted that the door lock was inoperative.

Wednesday 25th February. Day 13. Touring Chennai.

Up at 7.45am. We're on the 8th floor so used the elevator down to breakfast. While having a smoke outside I took another look at the locality, very city centre and not much for a tourist. Found a small shop locally, bought a lighter, water and some crisps. Wait on the guide scheduled for 10.30am. No decision has been made regarding visits. He arrives and introduces himself as T.D.Venkatesan. Not only do we agree a shorter mileage day, I also request that a place is found where I can buy a couple of beers. This being done soon after leaving the hotel forecourt. The event is a standalone story.

The car was stopped in a side road, Chris and driver staying, the guide led me into an alley with washing hung on strings between the rundown buildings. One had a barred aperture and a few men were hanging around. The guide relayed my request for beer to a chap behind the bars. I was shown varying containers, even offered a case of cans. A couple of bottles of Kingfisher was all I wanted. They eventually proffered these at 100 rupees each but I had difficulty in explaining that they were for later, the vendor being keen to uncrown them and expecting me to drink them immediately. Confusion was cleared up and the bottles obtained for 120 rupees each. Back in the car, T.D as he preferred to be called, explained that Chennai among other big cities has a problem in the male population. With wages of 500 rupees a week and that amount only available for a few, drinking can wipe that out and leave families starving, so the supply of alcohol of any type to the public has been pushed underground. Back in the car I put our 'contraband' into one of the day bags and slid it under the front passenger seat.

Continued to Kanchipuram 140 kilometres from Chennai. Traffic in town was busy as expected with heavier industrial vehicles on the outskirts. We're told that some of this road is new but its condition seemed fifty years old. Anyway we arrived and visited a Hindu temple, in fact two! Shoes off and on for the first but fed up with doing this, at the second decided that I would only look at the outside. Afterwards went for a lunch of sandwiches and beer at a classy hotel in town.

Later in the afternoon on the way back into Chennai the car is parked outside a silk workshop and it looks to be another guide organised shopping stop. Earlier, using my best spoken English language I'd warned TD politely, firmly and in no uncertain terms that souvenir shopping was not wanted and wouldn't be tolerated, so I was very annoyed to have been plainly ignored. These fellows seem to resort to a pigeon English when confronted. Adamant that Chris and I would never again be trapped as tourists in a sales mission organised by a guide, point blank I asked. "Why are we here?"
"We go in." His reply. The new driver sat in stunned silence as I requested of Mr Venkatasen if he actually understood what I had said this morning and was saying now. The situation became a silent 'what do we do now?' Then he said those actual words and my reply was easy. "Go to the hotel."

From the outskirts we entered the city, ten million people and traffic to match. There are lorries everywhere and it seems that in addition to the no rules driving it's a must to use tyres until they shred. On one occasion we were behind a petrol tanker, in poor condition and without mud flaps. Shockingly, the metal core of one rear tyre could be seen easily.

4.45pm, in the hotel room before going for dinner I loaded some photographs from camera to the ipad while we shared the Kingfisher beers and listened to music. Later at the hotel restaurant I had Byriani, Chris ate vegetable curry, meals enjoyed with a very nice eight percent strength lager. I took the 'British Empire' label from the bottle as a keepsake. At about 9.00pm I paid for an hour's worth of internet, posted some pictures and sent messages. In my diary I wrote 'possibly Microsoft email problem again.' A reoccurring situation every time I move districts. In bed by 11.00pm.

Thursday 26th February. Day 14. Tour as Itinerary. Overnight train Chennai to Madurai. Pothigai Express. Dep. 8.55pm. 470km

Up at 7.30am. Had breakfast, packed and checked out, all by 10.00am. Same guide and driver today. I requested that TD took me to a Post Office before our first scheduled visit. I had small package of brochures, tickets and a couple of illustrated books I wanted to send back home. Not that heavy but eventually items that would encroach on hand luggage weight allowance. We're in Chennai, Madras as it was called in British Colonial times. Now properly grown up and in areas a modern city with an international port. So I fully expected to find myself using the facilities of a twenty first century Post Office. How wrong could I be?

The car stopped and parked in a busy road. TD led me into a large Victorian Gothic building, didn't think I'd enter a time warp. My package was ready to go, I'd used a large envelope which had originally contained just one book, on it I'd written the recipients address, I expected it to be weighed, to pay the transit fee and a receipt be given.

Nope! Entering a room my head spun. Had I really gone back in time? Presented with what looked like a scruffy second hand shop, furnished with tables, chairs, cupboards, filing cabinets, all well used and from several periods but mainly Edwardian England. There were open ink pads, hand stamps laying nearby or hanging from their metal trees. Piles of packets boxes and parcels on show, some wrapped in card, others by sack cloth or brown paper. Sticky tape was a rarity, most were secured with string or skinny rough hemp fibre string.

Method was being used here, I just hadn't seen it! A sequence, one person took your item and examined it, the next weighed it, another wrapped it then someone else addressed the packet. Only after all of that shipping costs are calculated and paid. Surely the cost could be given once it was scaled? TD looked as confused by my hesitancy as I was with what I was seeing and trying to understand. As soon as I'd realised the futility I snatched my package from the table, turned away, left the room and made my way back to the car. TD followed. I explained to Chris what had just happened, she was amazed. I hoped TD had grasped my disappointment and surprise while listening. Sending the packet would wait until much later.

Close by we visited the British Colonial period coastal Fort Saint George. The older buildings are not well maintained and the whole military compound has been amalgamated in to the city. The museum exhibits are mostly military and very interesting. Collectors in England would pay a fortune to own them but their display and presentation is tired. Probably made fifty years ago most of the hand written description cards are now faded and stained. Dead insects, accumulated dirt and dust lie at the bottom of cabinets. Plainly a lack of care.

In the vast compound we visited the Church of St. Mary. Built in 1690, constructed to serve as fortified redoubt in times of trouble. Areas of the interior were under repair. Unbelievably, again it's shoes off to enter. This was the first Christian place of worship we'd found or been to since arriving in India, so we sat and reflected. It would have been rude not to. Outside, engraved flagstones mark the burial places of some of the earliest British pioneers and family members. Walked around for a while passing Clive of India's House and other colonial era buildings.

From the fort, drove and parked on the coast road for a short stroll on the promenade. This area was devastated during the recent Tsunami. Some has been rebuilt, the fish market being first to recover. Had lunch in a multi ethnic café, the food was quite pleasant. Afterwards to Saint Thomas Cathedral and then a longer visit at a zoo and reptile park. Took some good pictures of the exhibits, especially the chicks in a glass fronted vivarium, there as live food for the snakes!

As an additional and very special part of the tour itinerary, I'd requested that we were taken to the British Commonwealth Graves Commission Memorial, to pay our respects for lives lost in World Wars One and Two.

For me being the first member of my Cooke family to have ever visited, I knew it would be a very emotional time. Here is where my Great Uncle's name is remembered in perpetuity with others. Dudley Clarence COOKE, S/34038 Rifleman, the Kings Royal Rifles. He died in service of the British Empire on 9th November 1918, killed by disease, influenza, which would become the pandemic that killed millions.

Sited at the edge of the city the commission's grounds are immaculate, a condition they are kept all around the globe. After parking I asked our guide to give me and Chris some privacy. The names of the WW1 dead are carved into a stone plinth, WW2 graves have individual headstones. The gravity of these places is emotionally stirring in any circumstances but I would be a fool and liar not to admit that by the time Dudley's name was found I was looking at it through misty wet eyes.

Chris was also affected, standing close to me as I sent my thoughts into the ether and not forgetting the other souls remembered here by saying the words, "At the going down of the sun, we will remember them."

I went and stood at the foot of the white stone cross centred in the close cut lawns. I knelt, had a private word and took time to reflect.

A while later, having regaining at least some composure I took some photographs.

At the time we'd been the only visitors. Before leaving, our guide organised the gardeners into a line. I was offered and signed the visitor book, duly shook hands and thanked them for their care of the grounds. A small gratuity was given to each.

Back into Chennai. As a group we had coffee in a very busy snack bar. The first time we'd enjoyed the company of driver and guide, a very rare event indeed. Maybe after the CWGC visit they'd realised that we weren't detached from humanity. With time spare before Chris and I were due at the railway station we relaxed sat and chatted sharing views on several topics.

Later, taken to Chennai's 'Egmore Station.' Car unloaded, bags back and shoulders slung. I gave cash tips to guide and driver. It was early evening, still light and we knew there'd be quite a wait for the train. This time we were on our own, no escort! The tour company had either realised we were competent or forgotten us. It was busy but didn't seem as frantic as the previous stations. We certainly weren't looking forward to the overnight journey, knew what could be expected, we were confident but not overly, after all this is India! Chris and I purchased a selection of snack and drinks from the array on offer at the many vending booths. Happy and with that done made our way into the station, past a lonely soldier who on occasion did some cursory bag checks. The information hall was crowded, plenty of folks moving through. We viewed the signage, comparing train numbers, times and platforms against those on our tickets, two pairs of eyes, double checked and one agreement.

Didn't even have to cross the rails, we were in the correct place, so found a low concrete stepped wall and sat down, the weight of our backpacks relieved by the rear of the structure. Chris and I talked and people watched. We were watched! I occasionally wandered to the ticket hall to check the information displays.

Waiting time soon past, night had fallen and the train arrived at the platform. It must have started its journey somewhere else and was ready to receive passengers. Carriage identified, we got on and found our berths. Chris had a passageway side lower bunk, mine was a low one in the curtained four person compartment opposite. We departed a little late at 9.05pm, settled into our respective berths and grazed on snack foods.

Friday 27th February. Day 15. Madurai.

The noise and bustle of the carriage woke me fully at about 5.30am. I'd managed several hours of fitful sleep but again we were tired, hot and grubby. The train rolled slowly into Madurai station nearly an hour late at about 6.30am. We were met by a rep and driver then taken directly to the Hotel Germanus, Sammattipuram Main Road, Kalavasal. It looked very nice and had the facility of free internet wifi. After checking in, left our bags at the room and went for breakfast at about 7.15am. That left us three hours spare before the city tour started. During that time I found that I was still having problems with Microsoft email.

Having been travelling for two weeks and although we'd kept a lot of our underclothes cleaned and rinsed using hotel bathrooms, Chris selected some top wear clothing needing proper laundering and decided to use the hotel facilities.

While waiting to be collected we witnessed a people protest, a large number, mainly women marching, then stopping at a road junction close to the hotel. They held up traffic until Police arrived and dispersed them. We found out later that the local government had promised the issue of free food grinders and fans. Neither had materialised.

At 10.00am new driver Pandiya Kumar and today's guide Luke met us at reception. After a quick chat explaining our tiredness it's decided that our city visit will take in only the most important sites.

First stop the Nayak Palace, a superb 17th century building of Italian architectural design. A very busy tourist attraction and of interest to local school groups. Our visit here is best described from the notes in Chris's diary, 'Uniformed Pupils on a school visit seemed more interested in me and Bob. The younger girls 'mobbed' me, wanted to talk, touch my hand and have photos taken with me, the same with the senior pupils and the teachers. It was an awesome experience, one I'll never forget.' She also drew a little smiley face!

True warmth and affection, the first time we'd enjoyed this, maybe Southern India would be less harsh, not as formal as the North. While Chris engaged in conversation, Luke and I stood back and watched. I took photographs, it was wonderful to see her fully engaged, the centre of attention and almost in her element.

Later that morning, Luke took us through some of the city streets. A good intelligent guide and nice fellow, we talked as we walked. I mentioned that his name was Biblical. He explained that he was baptised as a Catholic but had his own opinions about religion. We shared some similarities, in that gathering to worship or joining with others to say prayers wasn't a prerequisite to being or having a Christian attitude. If needing a word with who was ever running things in the spirit world he'd have a private one. I understood this.

I believe he actually grasped that we were genuinely interested in not just India's history but its current state, world position and especially its people. He told me that bribing the Police in this city is called 'giving a smile.'

He led us to the market area. We walked down Onion Street. Yes, that was its name. The vegetable in all types, sizes, colours, boxed, crated, racked, spilling on sheets and tarpaulins, a stunning sight with an all pervasive odour.

Through side roads or better described as alleys and into the Banana market. The fruit in all shapes and sizes, yellow, red, orange, green in bunches, hanging in giant clusters from trestles and frameworks, shaded by woven branch and leaf covers. Men were shouldering loads that I would find impossible to lift. We squeezed through the narrow gaps left between the stalls and came away with new knowledge. There are over two hundred different types of banana. A snippet for the trivia library.

After the city walk we visited to two Hindu Temples, Meenakshi and Tirupara Rock, deciding not to enter either but wandering the grounds admiring the structures and carvings. Later, I noted in my diary, 'the shoes on off bit had done my head in!' Luke seemed a little put out that we hadn't wanted to go into these buildings but I took time to gently explain that we'd seen so many. I don't think he would have understood that we were just 'templed' out!

Back at the hotel by 2.00pm and we had lunch. Here in the restaurant a hilarious exchange of words came about. Something like this as a waiter offered beverages. "Coffee?"

Our reply, "Yes, black please."

Waiter while pointing at us, asking "milk?"

Us again, "No, black please!"

The remainder of the afternoon was ours. I uploaded photographs to the ipad and spent some time online. Made a diary entry at about 4.30pm. Then it was panic!

An email from Air Asia notifying a flight time change for the 2nd leg, Kuala Lumpar to Perth, Australia. The date had been changed completely and it would throw our travel plans in to disarray.

Calm down first! Then using Skyscanner find a new flight for the correct date and book it, afterwards cancel the Air Asia flight by email and telephone. All done. Sounded easy but I wasn't happy. Obtaining flights this late costs far more money than booking early. The airline was now on my hate list.

The cancellation email clearly offered three options. Take the first leg and the rearranged later date flight, a credit note for all or part of the two leg flight or a full refund. I had taken the third but found out much later when back in England that their refund process was so complex that many people just gave up trying.

The new flight was with Malaysia Airways. Recent incidents such as them completely losing an aeroplane were at the back of my mind but as travel manager I had to quickly re-join the broken link in our plans!

Our fresh laundry had been delivered to the room, Chris checked that it was all present and correct. We freshened up and at 8.30pm enjoyed a dinner selected from the buffet, it was quite good. We had a lot to talk about and did.

Afterwards Chris went up to the room. I popped outside for a cigarette and could hear a loud voice of what seemed to be a preacher. Across the wide road there was a building with a wall mounted neon cross. Below it, doors were wide open, the interior brightly lit with a blue fluorescent glow. It was definitely some form of religious meeting hall. I could see people moving as silhouettes against the bright background. There was almost certainly preaching going on, sometimes multiple voices gave a joined reply to a single call or what sounded like a question. Catholicism with a touch of American Gospel? It was certainly different. I couldn't imagine a place like this surviving in the North of India.

Saturday 28th February. Day 16. Madurai to Kanyakumari. 5 hour drive 250 km.

Up at 6.30am. Last night I'd downloaded a new application for Outlook it seemed successful. I was hopeful that this would be the end of the constant blocking by Microsoft and the unblocking sequence that had become so frequent and frustrating. I checked for emails before breakfast and messaged Kerri with details of the changed flight. Completed packing, then checked out. Driver and air conditioned car ready at 9.00am, we set off for the long drive to Kanyakumari in the southernmost district known as the 'Cape of India.'

Pandiya started to prove himself as a worthy contender for Stig of South India. Traffic conditions had the usual hazards and animal presence but the drive was thankfully uneventful. He seemed a little more sociable than Sarup, spoke and understood more of the English language, even initiating conversations. At one time pointing out the Tamil Nadu identity letters on vehicle number plates. I dozed on and off, so was either confident in him or just plain tired. The landscape scenery was lush, lots of greenery, more space between buildings and farmsteads. Only one stop made at a road side booth for coffee and for me to smoke.

We arrived in Kanyakumari at 1.00pm and parked in the forecourt of the Hotel Singaar International, 5/22 Main Road. There was work being carried out at the front elevation, an interesting bamboo and wood scaffold was erected to one side. The main entrance wasn't affected. Chris and I entered the glass fronted, lavishly marble fitted, beautifully furnished reception and checked in for the overnight stay. The usual rigmarole, passports copied, voucher handed in. As a welcome gesture we were even double dotted, red and yellow on our foreheads. Unfortunately, from then on the place started to disappoint.

Our room was on one of the many floors, we used the lift, so small and slow that for the duration of our short stay taking the stairs was quicker. The room seemed fine, furnishings were tired but there wasn't any kettle or condiments. There was a view, through the dirty windows we could just about see the ocean. There was early stage construction work at this flank of the building.

If the ground work practices that amused me while I watched are a temper of the quality used in this country, I'm not surprised these places fall over when shaken by Mother Nature. Men wearing steel toe capped flip flops, (I jest about the steel), were prepping the footings of an extension. An excavated trench being built into, large varying shaped boulders laid on hand trowelled beds of mortar. Add a couple vertical rebar rods, a shovel or two of tamped aggregate with a float finish. Job done or recipe for disaster? I did take some photographs.

With some time to spare I tried the free wifi. No connection found ever, anywhere! So we decide to freshen up before lunch. In the bathroom, toilet pan, fixed shower spray head over a tub, hand basin and taps to suit. No cold water, the hot was just that, scalding. Toilet used, cistern flushed and it doesn't refill, turn on a tap to fill the bath tub and it does now! It's the old hot water toilet flush trick. We could have requested a change of room but both agreed that as a 'one nighter,' why bother. Tomorrow we'll be somewhere different, probably better, it couldn't be worse! Actually we were so chilled and just didn't give a toss. This was all part of the experience.

I could have listed so many faults for this hotel but left it noted in my diary as 'by far the worst we'd stayed in.' I wrote a Tripadvisor review to post online as soon as possible, and as the tour company wouldn't know of the situation, I informed our rep just in case they wanted to divert clients.

Had a light lunch in the grimy restaurant, a highlight being the dead flies trapped between the glass table top and wood frame. Enough said.

Back at the room I had a nap. We were to be collected by Pandiya about 5.30pm for the sundown visit to the tip of India where three seas meet. The Indian Ocean, Arabian Sea and Bay of Bengal.

The drive to the point was about two kilometres and we joined a queue of cars trying to find a parking space. That done Chris and I walked the last few hundred metres to the foreshore. A gentle cooling breeze was coming off the sea, unfortunately it just served to bring the litter and debris to our attention. Trapped in the spindly branches of bracken undergrowth was paper, cans, bottles, cartons, card wrappings and lots of flimsy blue polythene bags.

Having run the gauntlet of souvenir sellers, food and drink vendors we arrived at the beach. Leaving aside the detractions, a beautiful place. Very large, climbable rocks with sandy paths between them. Children played and paddled. For all of my time here I was never sure if Indian folk actually swam in the sea. Fishermen work this area, were tending nets and making general repairs oblivious of the tourists. Small clinker built boats were beached on the sand. Nearby were some very old dug out log canoes that had certainly not been in water for many years.

There was hardly a space on the concrete sea wall and pathway. Tourists, many of which were Indian, sat, squatted, stood, with cameras at the ready, many on tripods. All hoping to get that elusive shot of the sun dropping into the ocean. Mother Nature is the production manager for post card quality pictures. Clouds were low in the sky, nothing better than the last rays of the sun piercing these.

My camera was also ready. We'd wandered through the rocks, found a space and now waited. The big yellow ball slowly dropped, even bigger clouds rolled in, the clock was ticking, but soon it was just clouds touching the sea. That postcard shot was going to have to wait.

We joined many others in a trail back to the car park and found Pandiya. He eventually got us out of the disorganised melee of parting vehicles. Back at the hotel we agreed tomorrow's collection time.

Having experienced the poor quality of the restaurant we decided to take a look locally for somewhere to get tonight's dinner. Walked up and down the main road, didn't find anywhere with a semblance to a café so had to admit defeat.

Back at the room, made the best of the bathroom facilities, with no cold water available filled buckets with hot, let it cool, then washed and rinsed camping style.

The grubby grimy restaurant had one more twist for me. I'd had a good day, regardless of how my diary read. We ordered a couple of beers and two different basic meals in the same instant. Chris had been served and finished eating while mine, although I had enquired of it several times, never appeared at all. I cancelled, frustrated and annoyed but not angry. This was always going to be one of 'those' places. Ate some crisps in the room and crashed into bed at 10.00pm.

Sunday 1st March. Day 17. Tour of Kanyakumari, on to Kovalam. Our 40th Wedding Anniversary.

Up at 7.00am. After a poor breakfast we brought our diary entries up to date. Checked out at 9.00am, collected by Pandiya and today's guide to begin a tour of Kanyakumari for a couple of hours. First to the harbour and our guide using his influence gets us aboard a ferry avoiding the long queues. It happened that the Ferry Captain was his brother, so we had the privilege of using the first class cabin just below and behind the bridge, in which someone had placed a couple of old settees covered with tatty blankets. Other passengers were seated in the deck mounted benches. Motored out to the Vivekaranda Rock, a small island about ten minutes from shore on which the main attraction is a Hindu temple. Declining the shoes on and off routine we wandered around up and down the many exterior stone steps, enjoyed the views and took some photographs.

While waiting for the return ferry Chris got film star treatment. Indian tourists, husbands and wives, families and groups queued for the opportunity of having a novelty photograph taken in the company of a white skinned, blonde haired woman. Crazy! With a shaved head I must have looked so much the English thug that they didn't bother with me. Eventually embarked the ferry, its departure delayed while the tourist paparazzi took the last shots!

I travelled back to the pontoon at Kanyakumari inside the bridge of the boat and took some nice photographs from this high position. The skipper was keen to obtain English coins, I had none but he was very happy with a British ball point pen as a gift.

After the boat ride we walked through the harbour's busy souvenir market. Most of the items on sale were sea and shore oriented, bracelets, necklaces and ornaments made from shells. I saw an ice cream vendor, so ignoring the possibility of food poisoning, bought and enjoyed a cornet. It was very hot here!

Next place of visit was a nearby Gandhi Memorial. There are many of these in this country. Again we didn't enter, shoes on and off the prime reason. Realising there'd be no tips the caretaker came outside. He also wanted to exchange a banknote received earlier into rupees, if it had been a dollar or a pound I probably would have done but an Iraqi one thousand dinar note held no interest for me.

Continued the drive to Kovalam. On the way a land scape with rice fields, banana and coconut tree plantations. Arrived at about 1.00pm. Checked in for two nights at the Hotel Uday Samudra, G.V Raja Road, Samudra Beach. It's some place! Has the biggest open plan reception area I've ever seen, with tropical plants, a fish pond and small waterfall, lots of plush leather and cloth upholstered settees and armchairs. It's explained that Wifi is best obtained in this area and that complimentary tea and coffee is available at any time whilst in the grounds. Our room in one of the many low rise blocks is luxurious in all aspects.

With no visits booked we had the rest of the day and the whole of tomorrow to enjoy the hotel facilities. After nineteen days of almost constant travelling I was overjoyed at the possibility of relaxation. What a place to have our anniversary dinner. Chris and I had lunch in the garden café, afterwards wandering the grounds for a while to acclimatise. There is a small selection of shops, several eating places and a swimming pool. Just outside the secure compound is a short stretch of narrow sandy beach, the sea wall supplemented by large rocks so I guessed that the sea could get rough here. At one end the promenade a restaurant had tables set on the walkway.

The Arabian Sea beckoned, it's hot and I'm determined to take a dip, doubting that I'll ever get the chance again in my lifetime. Back at the room, we changed into swimwear and with just towels, my cigarettes and lighter went back to the beach.

Not that we were difficult to notice! A local vendor hiring out beach chairs saw us. He was dressed in a flowing almost white robe and looked more like a slave trader, his mouth was missing many teeth and he had one white eye, resultant from some sort of fracas I presumed. He wanted conversation, we didn't, but he told us that the hotel pool wasn't clean. He wanted a cigarette. He could have that!

If only briefly, I got to swim in the Arabian Sea, there was quite a swell and strong undertow. Probably the reason we were the only people in the water. I was in first, Chris followed and within seconds we were smashed and swamped by a roller wave. She suffered most, shipping sand where it shouldn't get and got a few knee and elbow grazes. I would have rescued her but didn't need to, because the ocean spat her out on to the beach. I never even had time to think about the possible insurance claim!

That had been enough for Chris, we were still laughing while walking to the hotel pool. This had very warm water and no waves. Took sunbeds, I had a snooze, later we had coffee. Back to the room at about 5.30pm and showered. While drinking a beer from the mini-bar I uploaded photographs and prepped them ready to put on Facebook.

We had our 40th Wedding Anniversary dinner in the main restaurant, selecting from a very generous and varied buffet selection with beer served by efficient waiters. Chris had brought a celebration card given to her by a work colleague, she posed it with a flower from the table decoration, one of the staff noticed and kindly took photographs for us.

Afterwards we took seats in reception and made a pre-arranged Skype video call to Kerri and our grandchildren in England. Even though difficult to hear, it was good to chat and was almost totally successful except for the heavy mosquito infestation which was quite an annoyance.

In our room by 10.30pm and wrote our diaries, Chris noted, 'This is one Wedding Anniversary that I won't forget, it's been a great day.'

Monday 2nd March. Day 18. Kovalam, free day.

I woke at 7.00am but had a lay in. After breakfast I cash tipped the pool guy for unofficial reservations on sunbeds, that's how it works here. We got ready for a chilled, relaxing day by the pool. Had coffee delivered by a waiter who was interested in where we were from. We talked about the World Cup cricket, he knew the name of virtually every player. Took the occasional swim, chatted, sunbathed and both got pink skin even though using sun tan lotion.

There are other birds but it was wonderful to watch the dominant Sea Eagles swooping low and in between the trees.

There are more English people here than anywhere else we've been, so I did get to speak to a few. I exchanged India experiences with a Northern chap. Here on holiday and taking an advantage by purchasing cheap prescription spectacles available. He'd already paid a deposit but had concerns they'd not materialise because the optician hadn't been seen for some days. I related my 'guide' stories, how they proclaim to understand English but then ignore or misinterpret orders and requests. He'd experienced similar, telling that one day, much to his wife's disagreement, he'd set out to prove it by posing several queries and always getting 'yes' as a reply. So his final question was to ask if the guide wore women's clothing. The answer was obvious and we laughed.

Late afternoon, Chris stayed in the room while I visited an ATM just over the road from the front of the gated hotel compound. Close by, from a small booth I bought some cigarettes, sun tan lotion and a natural lemon based mosquito repellent spray. Last night we'd been bitten several times, likely while Skyping. Its mozzy central in reception during the evening, the pond and vegetation being a natural habitat for the horrid insect.

For dinner we'd decided earlier to use another of the resorts eateries, a small café cum restaurant bar near the beach. I was looking forward to a western style burger instead of spicy food, had a couple of lagers then ate. Afterwards took a night walk along the sea wall and around the complex then went back for a night cap beer in the same café. It was very late, just us and two barmen here. I paid cash and don't think it made it to the till. Back at the room we part packed for tomorrow's early start and set a phone alarm.

Tuesday 3rd March. Day 19. Kovalam to Alleppy. Houseboat on Lake Poonarmarla. 4 hr drive 180km

Up at 6.00am, finish packing. At reception ask staff to make up our account, then go to breakfast at 7.00am. The hotel restaurant is not quite organised at this time so we eat from whatever becomes available, toast, omelette etcetera, fortunately coffee arrived just in time. Back to the room and collect our bags. Pay and check out. 8.00am, Pandiya is waiting. I'll miss this place!

The road trip to Alleppy took over four and a half hours. Enroute the usual manic traffic and some bad roads but we see plenty of well managed agricultural land. The South of India produces enormous amounts of diverse crops. Drove through an area heavily planted with wind turbines. There seemed to be hundreds, all sizes, tall, not so tall, many different manufacturing names, some working, many not, two propeller blades, three propeller blades, one propeller blade, oops that one is definitely not generating. Pandiya pulled the car over at a little roadside refreshment cabin, here a proper Indian coffee cost a lowly 30 rupees. Chris and I were quite a novelty to the staff of two.

About 1.00pm arrived at a lakeside boatyard and pulled into a gravelled, scraggy, undergrowth strewn parking area. Out of the car we complete the signing in process, voucher taken, passports shown and my signature given.

Probably on a health and safety waiver form. We're shown the 'Houseboat.' There are quite few tied to each other alongside a pontoon. The access piers are pretty ropey with loose and some fragile timbers.

Before boarding we're invited to view a table laid with a small array of beers and spirits, then asked to select and purchase what we'd like to drink whilst on board. Decided on two large bottles of beer. One to share before dinner, the other after.

Some confusion came about. We were scheduled to depart from here and be collected at the Kumarakom disembarkation point. It seems that this wasn't to be the plan and Pandiya became involved in the discussion, taking our part, thankfully as it happened. Personally I wouldn't have known what alternative to have suggested, if any. It was decided that after the trip and overnight on the boat we'd be brought back here.

The boat looks quite old, about ten metres long, almost barge shaped with a metal hull. The plank wood deck shaded by a woven reed cover supported by a fretwork bamboo frame. Our air conditioned bedroom is ensuite and towels have been placed on the bed. Chris noted, 'Not exactly a palace but nice enough.'

Just us two passengers and a crew of three men. One is the cook, a charming, short, dumpy chap, bare footed, always smiling and wears a very well used blue and white pin striped butchers apron. He wouldn't seem out of place on a pirate ship!

At about 1.00pm the boat is untied and moves off. Within ten minutes of leaving it's secured to a mooring post and we're served a lunch of rice, pappadoms and very bony fish, which I presumed was lake caught. A dessert followed with coffee to finish. We were impressed and certainly over fed.

After that we start our journey on the lake. There are lots of houseboats here, all shapes and sizes, some have many bedrooms and others look quite luxurious. We see a few with clients enjoying parties on deck, glasses chinking, being waved as salutes when passing us. Quite an industry it seems. We cruise, never knowing exactly where or what distance but I take lots of pictures. There's so much to see. Human life being eked out by the water's edge, small holdings, shanty huts, ducks in wire mesh water cages and pigs in pens. School children boarding boats to go home. Women washing clothes in the lake using the old fashioned machine, a stone and soap. Told Chris I was going to get her one of these when we get home, what a saving it would be on electricity!

It was all so wonderful, we were enjoying this, felt special, almost like royalty and I could smoke at will! We could sit anywhere, on the deck benches or just lord it in the two old armchairs just behind the bow, from where the boat was steered. Pampering was carefully considered and well timed, during the afternoon we were served coffee, cake, and a whole coconut, its juice to be sucked through a straw.

6.00pm, the boat was moored in a line with others alongside a concrete river wall. This was to be our overnight berth. Chris and I disembarked and went for a walk along a path. We were very careful not to trip on root growth, there was plenty of it and I didn't fancy a lake bath. Took some pictures of the rice fields nearby. The back drop was moody, a grey sky and it rained a little. The crew of another boat were indulging in personal hygiene. No embarrassment here, dressed in their smalls they soaped up, hauled large tubs of water from the lake, lifted, poured and rinsed. It was good to feel that we weren't an imposition and that these lake dwellers could be themselves. After all, we were the aliens.

While walking we met a Canadian couple making a similar trip. We talked for a while and exchanged experiences. Always a pleasure to meet nice people, even if it's for just a moment in time.

Back to the boat, night had closed in, the sky cloudy and dark, water glimmering with reflections of the lights on the moored vessels. Our crew had prepped the open deck with hanging mosquito nets. Chris and I showered and applied plenty of insect repellent.

At 7.00pm, a time agreed earlier, we settled in chairs at the deck table, it already laid for dinner. The beers were delivered, crown caps off. Next came the meal served on several dishes. Our 'pirate' cook had been busy. Chicken dhal, okra, rice, potatoes and breads. Chris noted 'How he could make a meal like that in such a tiny galley is beyond me.'

After dinner we thanked the crew and informed them that we'd be readying for bed then went to our cabin and they took their turn at the table. Being a small boat we could hear them talking. I uploaded today's photographs by wireless transfer, sometimes it actually worked! Both asleep by 9.45pm.

In my notes 'clean and comfortable, the crew and cook very good. The dinner was as good as any restaurant could serve.' Chris wrote 'Brilliant day.' That summed it really.

Wednesday 4th March. Day 20. Kumarakom. Backwater Retreat, Aymanam, Nr Pulikuttissery Bridge. 7km from Kottayam, Railway station.

I woke at 4.30am for a bathroom visit and eventually got up properly at 6.30am. Almost silence. It was lovely not to hear vehicle horns, just the occasional throb of a boat engine, water lapping and birdsong. We were served coffee as breakfast was being prepared. While waiting, I stepped off of the vessel, its rigging dripped with dew. I looked closely at a bird perched on one of the boats timbers, it stared back. The early morning views across the lake and rice fields were stunning.

After a fine early morning meal the boat was untied and slowly cruised back to port. On the way we said a heartfelt thank you to each of the crewmen and parted with a 1200 rupee tip.

Disembarked about 9.00am. Pandiya was waiting to take us to Kumarakom. Not a long journey and punctuated by a stop at a bird sanctuary. He waited with the car while we paid the entrance fees then made a short tour of the small visitor centre. There was a path indicated, so took that and made a very sweaty, sticky, round trip walk through the tangled forest 'jungle.' No birds seen, even after climbing a rickety, rusty, metal viewing tower. However there were many butterflies, so not a complete disappointment.

Met Pandiya back at the visitor centre. Here was a small but unattended refreshments booth. I suggested coffee and asked him to join us. He agreed, found someone to serve and ordered the beverages.

Drove onward, deep into a forested area and left metalled roads, the saloon car now being punished on unmade tracks of dry mud and stones. About 11.30am arrived at tonight's hotel, the Backwater Retreat. I didn't have an address. It didn't look five star but it's a handsome old building, lots of timber and white cylindrical pillars used in the structure. It has character, wasn't completely level or vertical. Its shape has been gently adjusted by heat and humidity. A family run affair, we noted a father, mother and two sons.

Checking in is almost as old school as the building. This happens in the open air at a table placed in the front aspect near a wooden deck with balustrade. Very little English is spoken but there are plenty of forms to complete. No photocopier, so passport details are taken and hand written. That done and the voucher is accepted.

Asking and being told that beer wasn't available, the hotel manager suggested that I should send our driver to the nearest shop. Standing nearby, Pandiya understood and volunteered. I gave him 400 rupees to buy a couple of large bottles. I did briefly think about the rough ride he'd have but only for a millisecond. After all, we had the perennial excuse, beer is safer than water!

The property is divided. Guests are billeted on the first floor of the rear aspect, this area accessed by external stairs. All of the rooms here are served by a building length balcony with a veranda roof. This overlooks a canal and a tree lined hillside on the opposite bank. Quite a view, we enjoyed this very much.

We're given a choice of two rooms, both with walls of painted vertical wood panelling and chose the one with lighter, brighter colour. Very clean and comfortable but dated by old furnishings. The bathroom didn't have a shower. It would be buckets of water again!

There being no bar or restaurant, food during the stay would be prepared in the family's kitchen. There was however a limited menu card. We had to select tonight's dinner and serving hour at the same time as ordering lunch. All meals are served at tables on the veranda.

Outside our room Chris and I settled in a couple of plastic chairs and wrote our diaries. There is free wifi and a good connection. We ate sandwiches, talked and looked at the beautiful surroundings, watched the clumps of floating vegetation on the water as it flowed quickly past. Saw long tailed birds flitting between branches in the tall trees on the steep bank opposite. Voices could be heard but with the thick undergrowth we couldn't see where or who from. It was hot, we were sweating and imagined that this colonial scene hadn't changed for many years. All a very pleasant experience.

One of the staff came to inform me of Pandiya's return. I went down to meet him, the beer had already been put in the kitchen fridge. Two 600 millilitre bottles cost 90 rupees each, cheapest yet He gave me the cash change then asked if we'd like to go for a walk. I jumped at the opportunity, seeing real India on the ground was never to be declined, said I'd get Chris and be ready in five minutes.

Met him by the car, he'd just finished changing from smart driver clothes into jeans and t shirt. It was here that I found out that he spent nights in the vehicle, with rooms costing only a tenner a night, I offered to pay for one but he declined.

Mid-afternoon and it was hot and dry. Pandiya led the way, I think he'd been here before. We walked past a few randomly placed concrete and block built shacks, barely the size of a good shed in England, these were local family homes. At some, clothes were strung out drying. Against others were piles of sticks, straw and cut vegetation. Scrawny chickens occasionally came into view. Such obvious poverty but strangely we could always hear sounds from television sets. Strolling along well used paths, saw spices, seeds and vegetables, spread and drying on linen sheets. At the edge of the village he took us to an unfinished road bridge. Under construction and had been for many years, unused steel girders rusting with plants growing alongside as and where they lay. To access the finished section of roadway leading to another village, locals used an old metal stairway, its footplates perished, holed and dangerously loose.

Pandiya seemed to enjoy being guide and information manager. He pointed out a banana tree, its finger sized fruits just starting to form in a cluster around the dark maroon cone shaped flower. This he tells, is used in many natural medicines. We'd never seen one before.

Came upon a working wood mill, several buildings in a compound with timber of all types, shapes and sizes, piled, stacked or randomly scattered around the yard. I could hear a saw buzzing and see people in one of the flimsy sheds. One fellow held a tape measure, surely he had to be the boss. I picked my way carefully through the debris, approached him and pointed at my camera. Understanding my intention he nodded approval for me to take photographs.

This workshop was constructed of gapped wood boards and topped off with a badly propped sagging clay tiled roof for shade. It contained a horizontal plank saw. I couldn't tell whether it was powered by a generator or mains electricity but the rest of the operation was definitely manual. On the floor of the saw pit old rail tracks are guides for the rolling frame. The sawyer wearing only a loin cloth and flip flops had a rope around his waist and was pulling a log backwards. I was glad to be able to use my camera because this scene needed a thousand word description.

4. 3.2015 16:00

Evening was arriving so went back to the hotel. At 7.00pm
we were treated to a brief but powerful tropical rain storm
with a touch of thunder for added effect. Dinner at 8.00pm
was a nice vegetable curry with rice, enjoyed with a beer
before and after. We ordered tomorrow's breakfast timed
for 7.30am. In the room we were joined by a cute lizard
hanging on the curtains. Wrote our diaries and were in bed
by 9.30pm. Yet another wonderful day had.

Thursday 5th March. Day 21. Periyar. 4 hour drive. 260km.
Nature and Tiger reserve.

Up at 5.00am, bathroom visit, must have been the curry!
Dozed until about 6.00am. Breakfast was served spot on
time, basic but enough, toast, omelettes, pineapple and
coffee. Cleared the room, packed and checked out. Paid
the bill for dinner and lunch, 700 rupees including tip!
    Left at 8.00am. On the way there were several phone
calls to Pandiya's mobile. He informs us of a change of
destination hotel, there is construction work at the original.
I often have to speak to the tour company via a driver's
phone, they inquire if we are being treated well.

It's a good drive, with a coffee stop made just before a mountainous area. The highway is narrow, traffic as usual, lorries, buses, cars and motor cycles all jockeying for position. We saw many tea and rubber plantations on the terraced slopes. Stunning views were had from the corners and bends of the winding hill road.

Arrived in Periyar at midday. Pandiya located the Cardamom County Hotel. We checked in at 12.30pm. A local rep for the main tour company was waiting for us. He wanted reassurance that we'd been looked after and that the change of hotel had been OK. I thought I'd done that earlier by telephone. Anyway, Chris and I said that we were perfectly happy. He then started to explain about the afternoon trip to the nature reserve. A recently man made landscaped lake purely formed as tourist attraction. I'd checked it out online, it didn't really hold any interest for us but we agreed to go. Quite honestly I'd have been happier to lounge by the hotel pool.

Took a quick look at the room and bathroom. Very modern style, superbly presented in a chalet type bungalow set with others on terraces and quite high up. Left our bags then went for lunch in the hotel restaurant. Here were many obviously wealthy and older tourists, some with their personal assistants. There's a big difference between having an appointed 'day guide' and a 'paid for travel companion.' The latter and sometimes drivers eat and drink at the client's expense. It amused me as they ploughed through the menu, ordering item after item, while their patron just picked over a salad and drank water. Leeches was the word I used in my notes.

Pandiya was expecting us at the hotel carpark at 2.45pm for the Periyar Nature Reserve tour and boat trip. We met him then drove off. The description starts with my diary note. 'Total waste of f*****g time and money, saw more on the way here by car.' It finishes with my Tripadvisor review.

'Ok, so you pay 500 rupees each to ride a very slow boat around the landscaped nature reserve, see a couple of birds, a cow and maybe a deer. Everyone knows that that wild animals only visit water early morning and evening. The ones here were more likely tethered, but don't take my word for it. Because before you get to the boat, you'll be paying 450 rupees each just to get through the tiger reserve, yes I hear you ask, tigers? No there aren't any but to get to the boat you have to pay. Also a camera fee of 40 rupees, to photograph from the boat, what? Yes, if you can negotiate the compulsory life jacket. If anything, the view maybe worth ten quid, or 12 dollars but personally I'd have rather spent the 3 hours in a bar.'

I knew it would be a waste of time and was proved correct, but were fortunately back at the hotel by 5.30pm. On the main road a short distance away I found a little booth and bought some cigarettes. We showered, posh place or not, did some laundering at the same time, in the hope that the clothes would be dry in the morning. Went for dinner, had a couple of beers, shared a biryani and vegetarian curry. I was still a bit moody not just because of the wasted time and money.

After twenty one days in India another gripe had surfaced, 'Mr Robert,' as I am always politely addressed. 'He' was always presented with and paid the bill. Never a word to 'Mrs Robert,' as if Chris was an appendage. Tonight these folks were to find out that we are equal partners. The account for the meal duly arrived in a restaurant folder. I indicated that my wife would pay by sliding the bill in front of Chris as she readied her travel card.

"No, no, Mr Robert." Came the waiter's startled response.

"No, no, Mrs Robert." My reply as I stood up. "Mr Robert is going for a cigarette, so Mrs Robert will pay." The waiter stood stock still as I walked out, I could feel his eyes burning as I left. Chris joined me outside. I asked how it went and she smiled.

Took the steep winding stone path and steps back to the room. Chris made coffee, I sat outside and smoked another

102

cigarette. It had been quite a day, we were asleep by 10.00pm.

Friday 6th March. Day 22. To Cochin. 170 km 4 hour drive

Up at 6.50am. In the restaurant, had a buffet style breakfast and then packed. Most of the laundry was dry, anything damp was put in polythene bags.

In travelling 'light,' we'd both developed the 'just in case syndrome.' Careful consideration given before anything is discarded. Reusable items such as shopping bags, elastic bands etcetera, being kept, but now, items like pencils, note paper, even string or a shoelace are likely to be popped into a day bag. We'd also become practised at relieving bathrooms of essentials, especially toilet tissue. We're also maintaining a small stock of tea, coffee and other sachet condiments. There's plenty of plunder to be had here before leaving!

Checked out at 9.00am. No account to pay as breakfast had been inclusive and we'd paid for snacks and meals with cash or by card. Started the long drive to Cochin. Plenty of sights on the way including tea, coffee and rubber tree farms.

At about midday Pandiya stopped at a road side café for refreshments. He sat with us and was very chatty. We were sharing more and more information about ourselves.

The diner is very popular, plenty of tourists arriving by car, coach and minibus. A sloping field next door is the lower reach of a rubber plantation, regular demonstrations are given in how the tree trunks are milked of the latex sap.

As we continued toward Cochin the countryside provided plenty to see. I'd requested an ATM be found, these were our last days with Pandiya and I needed cash for his tip. Our destination, the large manmade Willingdon Island in Lake Kochi. A between the two World Wars British inception, which since India's independence has become a naval base and an international sea and airport.

Pandiya got the car on to the Island and struggled to locate the hotel, but we at least got to see many of the interesting colonial military buildings and warehouses. After a couple of consultations with pedestrians, at about 2.00pm, arrived and checked in at the Casino, C.V.Iyer Road, Willingdon Island, Kochi, Kerala.

Our room is exceptional, large, furnished for business with a desk, formal and arm chairs. Ordered a room service late lunch. While awaiting delivery we met with the local tour rep in reception, discussed and decided to cancel tonight's dance visit. We're not big fans of these contrived folk events. Enjoyed the club sandwiches then wandered the hotel and grounds, found the outdoor swimming pool and decided a dip would be good. Although the sky was overcast we swam and spent a while at poolside on sunbeds. Chris commented that the water was cold. At least she wasn't being beaten to a pulp by the Arabian Sea. 'Squinny' was the word I thought of!

During the afternoon the hotel reception staff were of exceptional help. Not only did they agree a later checkout without charge, I also needed paper copies of the airline tickets for the recently booked replacement flight to Australia. I forwarded the emailed documents, they printed them for me. I was very relieved and grateful.

Showered and dressed we went to the bar and had a couple of beers then into the restaurant for a buffet dinner. There was quite a choice, Chris liked many dishes but I didn't really enjoy any. At least an entertaining situation was taking place at a nearby table. An easy to overhear meeting, a wedding plan sale. Big business in this country, one side of the table father, mother and daughter, all smiles, presumed soon to be a bride. Opposite a heavy pressure salesman and his sidekick. It was all presentation, the virtues of this and that, the best place to obtain other things. When the different types and cost of gold wedding jewellery was broached, by his sweat, complexion and demeanour, I worried that the father maybe close to a heart attack!

Saturday 7th March. Day 23. Sightseeing in Cochin. Overnight train. Bangalore Express. Dep. 8.30pm. 550km.

8.00am breakfast, afterwards to the pool for a refreshing dip. A Korean businessman was teaching his eighteen year old son to swim. They took being in the water very seriously, goggles and caps essential. We had a brief chat with the father who spoke enough English for us to understand that he visited India regularly on buying trips.

Some depth signs were being fixed at the poolside edge. No health and safety here, a drill connected to an electricity cable that snaked perilously across the ground. We obviously didn't take to the water while this operation was in hand.

At the room, had showers and completed packing for the 1.00pm checkout. It was one of our largest accounts, 2,850 rupees about £28.00.

Pandiya collected us outside reception. Guide Philip Rojan was picked up on the way to the ancient Portuguese/Dutch Palace. We were given a very good history lesson here. Britain wasn't the only 17th and 18th century empire builder that had desires of trade with this country. The aggressive attitude of other European nations led some Indian state Maharajas to invite the Georgian British to be active in military defence. It seems that a very Romanesque method of influence was employed, India and Great Britain became closely intertwined, benefiting the rich and powerful in both countries. A phrase often heard, 'now many people have nothing, at least when the British were here, everyone had something.'

Drove a short distance to visit an Anglican church. Afterwards and close by viewed the Chinese fishing nets in the harbour. An ancient method of fishing by dipping a net attached to a timber frame in a crane like motion. Being done now almost purely for the benefit of tourists who are invited to take part, cash contributions are of course very welcome. Other modern methods are in use, the catch being sold on the shore line. With the heat and smells there are also a lot of flies here to keep a tourist company.

The official tour itinerary completed. As a group we had lunch in an Indian fast food outlet called 'ChicKing.' I kid you not! I happily paid for all refreshments. Following which we thanked, tipped and said goodbye to Philip. He'd been very informative.

Pandiya is to remain with us until we're delivered to the station for the overnight train journey. We obviously weren't looking forward to it but words like, last and thank goodness did spring to mind.

Being early afternoon and with a lot of spare time he drove us to the Cochin market area. Here for the better off consumer is a main road with similarities to places in England but more frenetic, having multi storey arcades, electrical superstores and fashion clothes shops. There are also pavement stalls selling cheap toys, costume jewellery etcetera.

He then led us a short distance to a road that runs parallel. Here are many different shops but much smaller with goods piled high and sometimes spilling out of doorways. These retailers cater for the less well off. The road itself had kerbside gullies, basically open drains bridged with paving slabs placed like stepping stones. With so many people moving through, great care was needed, not least to avoid tripping, worse was imaginable. We briefly wandered through the stalls of the vegetable market, much the same as we'd seen in other cities, hundreds of people, goods laid out on sheeting, trestles and barrows, a very busy place. On the way back to the car, Pandiya took the time to buy some items, including gifts for his wife and children. He was going home after his tour duties with us.

From here we drove to a shore area with views of Willington Island harbour. Part of the promenade has modern shops and food outlets. Suffice to say the wash of the sea brought a lot of debris, in places the smell was foul. Bought coffee in a fashionably new place with electronic, wireless, button push waiter requesters. The staff were young and they'd already developed the fast food chain attitude that we know and love!

Here we exchanged more stories and experiences, shared phone stored photographs of our families. Out of the blue Pandiya told us that he'd cancelled his trip home and taken the job of escorting a Scandinavian couple for a south India tour.

Walking through the shopping mall Chris and I bought some snacks and water for the rail journey. Time moved on, so did we. At about 6.00pm arrived at the Cochin railway station. Out of the car and we loaded our backs! A young tour rep was waiting for us. To Pandiya we said thank you and goodbye with a 9,000 rupee cash tip. He'd been a good fellow for us in all aspects and had definitely proved himself the 'Stig' of the south.

While we were stood waiting at the station the rep made excuses and disappeared. Chris and I found a clean wall to use as a sitting place among the goods on carts placed around the platforms. I left her for a few moment to view the signage and confirm the platform we were on was correct. Evening came and went, light faded and night took over.

The young rep returned, found and took us to the Class 2 waiting room, no charge to sit in here. It has metal chair benches and is full of people and luggage. It's also hot, noisy and stinks of urine among other things. The rep disappeared again. At 7.15pm Chris and I decided to move from this sweaty confine, walked along the platform and found some concrete bench seats formed as part of a wall.

The area was crowded and we discovered that the train was delayed by at least an hour and a half. No surprise there! Rumours from people waiting were of a breakdown, the next train due, therefore the one after, ours, couldn't get in. As probably the only fair skinned English folks here, even in the gloom and poor light we attracted attention. Most people just stared although it was a nice surprise when others acknowledged us. One local chap even decided to have a conversation, it was limited but a welcome interlude.

By 9.00pm we'd eaten our snacks. I topped up supplies with some bits and pieces from a platform vendor and bought coffees served in the popular small Styrofoam containers. Always made with sugar but at least milk could be declined. The area became infested with mosquitoes, Chris and I applied repellent.

Our temporary young tour rep returned, we obviously weren't difficult to find! He looked bored and tired. I said that we'd be able to find and negotiate access to our train carriage but he insisted on staying, sat on the bench and was soon asleep, phone next to him as he leant on Chris, his head slumped on her shoulder. We couldn't help smiling as he dribbled, a dark wet patch forming on his purple shirt.

The train eventually arrived about 10.15pm. Watching the ordinary 'sleeper second class' commuters rushing to get near a window or a top tier in the triple stacked bunks is a sight not easily forgotten.

Carriage found we checked that our names were on the freshly pasted paper next to the door, confirmed the berth numbers tallied with the tickets, boarded and said goodbye to the rep.

Our booking had us designated to side berths, Chris the upper, me, the one below. The corridor had passengers with luggage moving through but we almost routinely prepped our bedding. I stowed and secured the back packs below my bunk, the canvas holdall again became my extra pillow. Unfortunately the suspension straps for my platform bed were over stretched and it wasn't level. In fact it tipped towards the curtained corridor and I would spend most of my night attempting not to fall to the floor. It was also extremely hot and I wasn't looking forward to calls from the chai wallahs.

Sunday 8th March. Day 24. Bangalore. Tour of City.

Fully awake at 6.00am. The bustle, hustle and noise of people preparing for journey's end had been continuous since about 4.00am. I must have got a few hours of broken sleep. I'd had to get up and take a leak once or twice. I was now tired, dirty, hungry and tetchy. I cleared up and once Chris had got down from her bunk we reconstructed mine into the alternative two seats. While sitting I dozed on and off. When awake I took some pictures of the slums through the windows of the train as it continued to our destination, Bangalore.

We always tried to be prepared well in advance of the due stop, this morning it was to prove invaluable. This city has three stations, our scheduled exit being the second, the first is Bangalore Cantonment. The train slowed as it entered this station, as it came to a halt we suddenly heard my name being called, "Mr.Robert, Mr.Robert!" In the carriage we're confronted by two men, dressed in suits who identify themselves as tour reps from India Travel. Without a second wasted, in some urgency and with little explanation, apart from, "this is a better pick up place," we're asked to get off of the train. I grabbed my bag and the holdall, Chris picked up her backpack, we bundled ourselves to the carriage exit and followed these fellows onto the platform.

It's about 9.00am and this particular station is very busy. Neither of us have had a chance to put our backpacks on and I am not a happy boy! These chaps are now striding away from the platform across a walkway bridge. Amidst the milling pedestrian crowd, we in disarray are attempting to follow. Chris slightly in front of me and by now I'm seething. My brain kicked into 'English Bob' mode, I called her to stop and say, "This isn't on," as she turns. The reps have walked on ahead but glance over their shoulders to see where we are, I dropped my bags, hand clapped hard and shouted very loudly. "Stop! You come here." Along with most of the other folks on the bridge this definitely catches their attention. You should have seen the look on their and other faces, Colonial Bob had arrived in Bangalore!

They walked back meekly and picked up our bags, we followed them to a parked car.

In my mind I'd already cancelled any thought of doing today's city tour. By the time we arrived at the Hotel Solitare, 3 Kumara Krupa Road, Madhawanagar, the tour rep had been made fully aware. I think I told him without swearing. I knew it wasn't his fault that the train had been late leaving and arriving, nevertheless my anger was obvious.

9.30am, checked in for one night. Left our bags in the very smart modern room and then ate a late breakfast. Afterwards we showered. I went outside and smoked cigarettes, quite a few. Back in the room and we got some sleep. Later, me having calmed, Chris made us coffee, we wrote our diaries and listened to some music. At 3.00pm, both dressed then went and found the basement bar. Almost a night club, dimly lit in blue florescent and publicly accessible for those who could afford it. We

110

talked and watched television, Australia beating Sri Lanka in the World Cup Cricket. Also we drank a few beers. Actually four each and smoking was permitted here so the day had got better.

About 7.30pm had dinner at the 7th floor restaurant, partaking in a Chinese food selection and more beer, all very nice. By now the day had totally improved! Bed at 9.30pm.

Monday 9th March. Day 25. Bangalore to Mysore. 150 km. 3 hour drive.

Up early, had breakfast in the glass covered roof top restaurant. Took some photos of the staff and the unused empty indoor swimming pool that's up here. There's a good view across this modern city, the famous Bangalore horse racing track can be seen, steeds and riders on the gallops out for early morning exercise.

Packed, used the bathroom and cleared the room. Checked out at 9.00am. Our biggest bill yet, £48.00! Some food, mostly beer, needed, enjoyed, no regrets!

While waiting for our car and driver I took some pictures of the bald tyres on an Audi Quattro parked in the hotel forecourt.

A car arrived. The new driver is Chandru. We loaded baggage and we're on our way but stop within a few minutes to visit a Hindu temple. Construction completed in about the year 2000. An ugly place, we didn't go in, quite honestly we're now utterly 'templed out.' Not only that, there's a fee to enter and it would have been shoes on and off yet again. We walked around the perimeter and fifteen minutes later we're back at the car. The driver looked slightly surprised. So with little delay we're on our way again. After one more ten minute stop at a road side café for a coffee and me to smoke, continued into the City of Mysore.

1.00pm, the Hotel Fortune Park JP Palace, 3 Abba Road, Nazarbad opposite Government Guesthouse,

111

Mysuru. Checked in for two nights and are given a 2nd floor room. The place is very plush with free Wifi. Another five star hotel with gated vehicle entrance and added security. A sign at the main doors says 'No Firearms Permitted,' amusing or maybe not! There is a swimming pool set in a quadrangle overlooked by hotel upper rooms and corridors. The remainder of the day is ours, no guide or itinerary. Fantastic, sometimes it's good to be rid of the tour staff.

A big screen TV is in the hotel lobby so before and after lunch we watched England get a trouncing at cricket by the Bangladeshis. By 3.45pm we're in changed clothes and sat by the pool which was in shade but we did swim. Although cold water it was worthwhile exercise, especially having been in transit for quite a while.

At the room I dozed on and off, uploaded photographs and occasionally wandered down and outside for a cigarette or two. Eventually I shaved, we both showered and readied to take dinner in one of the three rooftop restaurants on the fourth floor. Ate and drank a few beers, Chris had lamb chops, proper baby sheep, tiny little ribs. Her diary note, 'like I've never tasted before.' We talked about the past few days. By now I'd really had enough of India and confessed that I was looking forward to leaving. I didn't know that this wasn't going to be as easy as it sounded. 10.30pm, back in the room, caught up with diary writing before sleeping.

Tuesday 10th March. Day 26. Tour of Mysore.

Up at 7.30am. After breakfast collected by driver and guide Ahmed. Drove for about an hour and a half, then stopped and viewed an abandoned 13th century Hindu temple, very picturesque and interesting. Then back into Mysore to the very opulent Maharajas Palace designed by a British architect and built in 1912. Did an extensive tour of the interior which annoyingly again required shoes off. Afterwards retrieved our footwear, agreed a meeting point and time with the guide to ensure us leaving together, then we're left to our own devices to wander the grounds.

Yet again Chris came to the attention of Indian visitors, a young family with children requested to be photographed with her. As usual she obliged. Some teenaged Indian fashionistas, 'Jack the lads,' also approached, one wearing a 'pork pie hat,' an English skin head era accessory. We're always wary of the unknown and these lads were a definite for the category. My assessment was that they probably weighed about ten stone, (65 kilos), between them but as usual there was no nastiness, just inquisitiveness. Being photographed with a white woman seemed to be quite a trophy, even for this age group. I jokingly asked for 200 rupees for the privilege, laughing out loud at their shocked faces. The leader of this five man crew was rightly proud of his Ganesh and own initials chest tattoo. When shown my Portsmouth and England arm inking for comparison, initially they thought the town crest of star and crescent was for Pakistan, then, a few of them believing it was drawn with felt tipped pens, had a good rub!

Met with Ahmed, then located the vehicle and driver in the car park. Close by there was another perfect example of India, piles of rubbish against the palace boundary walls.

Guide tipping done, back to the hotel. Had beers and club sandwiches for lunch. The small pool was busy, a couple of Indian families enjoying the facility. Males in swim wear, females clothed in t shirts and trousers. Some folks had taken lunch here so most of the loungers were in use, we waited a while and a couple became available, took those, had a swim and at about 2.30pm wrote our diaries. I had an afternoon nap. In the early evening we did some internet postings. Later we took our last dinner in India. Coffee in the room then bed about 10.30pm. Tomorrow it's goodbye!

113

Wednesday 11th March. Day 26. Mysore to Bengaluru Airport. To Perth, Australia via Kuala Lumpar, Malaysia. 7,200km.

It's a big travel day. A long journey starts this morning and my pre-match nerves are jangling. We're up early and go to breakfast. Afterwards carefully pack our bags. Hand luggage only means sifting through and discarding to a bin any liquids, powders or other items we've gathered that may cause a problem at the airport, because of weight or content. Sad moments, losing so much when you have so little!

The room cleared and checked. At reception pay the account, 6,000rupees. Over indulged here, £60 for two nights, lunches, dinners and most of all, beer. Lovely, by now I really don't care.

The day, night, day is planned thus. Today the 11th, arrive Bengaluru Airport. Just after midnight a departure flight to Kuala Lumpar, arriving 7.00am on the 12th. The connecting flight to Perth Australia leaves at 9.30am and arrives at 3.00pm. All times local, easy!

My immediate intention is to arrive at Bengaluru airport early, find the Air Asia desk and remonstrate about the cancelled flight, unanswered emails and no refund received. I have a little anger in my heart.

Just after 10.30am the driver collects us at hotel reception. A three hour ride gets us to Bengaluru and we're in the extensive grounds of the modern airport at about 2.00pm. Here we're met by a 'Top Travel Tours' representative. This company's care and attention cannot be faulted. Car unloaded, Chris and I put on our backpacks, day bags are shoulder slung, mine with today's paper work and ipad easily accessible. Chris took charge of the holdall containing our coats.

The first shock is now delivered by the rep. He tells us that people are not allowed into the airport earlier than three hours prior to a booked flight. This I supposed is understandable considering India's security concerns.

In fact, whilst glancing around at the airport terminal entrances, each door had two armed soldiers outside and two more inside. Worst still, we're then informed that no one is allowed into the terminal the day before a flight. Our new one with Malaysia Airways is after midnight, in effect, tomorrow!

I still wanted 'in,' so after some frantic but controlled discussion, the rep asked if we still had the Air Asia tickets. Of course we did. This flight was to leave at 11.20pm. The three of us presented ourselves at one of the security entrances, passports were shown to a soldier and the rep talked to him while showing the redundant tickets. We were in!

After a short search we spot the Air Asia desk, all three of us walked to it. It's attended by a young woman. I present myself and immediately recount the story of the cancelled flight, the unanswered emails and the lack of refund. The retort, I am told that our tickets have 'not' been cancelled! My anger is rising, Chris keeps me level headed but I demand an email confirming the cancellation that I made by telephone on the 27th February. The rep also speaks to the receptionist. I'm promised an email but doubt that it will happen and eventually proven correct, because this problem was not resolved until my return to England in July!

We turn away from the desk. I thank the rep for his and the company's good services which are now at an end and assure him that he can leave. After handshakes all round, he does.

About 3.00pm, in the airport terminal illegally. Chris and I are on our own and know we need to keep a low profile. It's going to be a long wait until twenty minutes after midnight. The lounge area has very limited seating and food outlets. At one I ordered coffee and filled bread rolls. We sit, discuss recent events and reflect our opinions and experiences in India. The clock ticked away. We rolled and strapped our coats, the collapsed holdall is in mine. We both cut our fingernails, just in case the clippers are discovered. Several hours, coffees and snacks later the Malaysia Airways gate opens. We present ourselves and the printed email ticket confirmations, passports are checked, the usual questions are asked about baggage, especially as we're travelling hand luggage only. Through security my back pack comes under scrutiny, it's searched and my tiny watchmaker screw driver is discovered. I explain that it is used to tighten my spectacle arms and it's let through. One small victory for common sense!

Not that long a wait before boarding. We're on the aeroplane, yes, using an airline that has just recently lost two craft. We find our seats, I load the overhead locker, sit down and buckle up. My high excitement, nerves and emotions are disappearing, relief washes over me because as far as I was concerned, in this aircraft I'm no longer in India!

So, how was India?

What did you think of it? I hear the questions. Believe me, I'm still asking myself. Had I been too critical of the people we interacted with? Did I find those serendipitous events and moments so sought after during the Hippy era? No. But presented with a country of this size with much to admire, plenty to deride, such a diverse and massive population, I did form many opinions. How could I not?

We were given history lessons at almost every place visited. The complexity of religious beliefs here are almost beyond comprehension, an indigenous Indian surely has no chance of understanding all of them, especially when his or her main aim in life is survival.

The class or caste system that has operated for thousands of years is still adhered to. It bears no similarity to the three of four blurred society levels that we as westerners understand. Theoretically, as citizens we can move and improve by work, education and other means, being born into poverty here is to die poor. There is also the gypsy population, an underclass, highly visible but paradoxically they supposedly don't exist. Nevertheless, here as in many countries the poor and lower classes underpin the rich and have done so for many years.

Education is either government organised, private or charitable, even then there is not much time for poor children to learn, because for many hours they are beavering away in fields or back street workshops. However, I do give a deserved compliment. People here are mostly industrious, entrepreneurial and opportunistic.

The cities resemble multiple land built gigantic ant nests. In most, construction started three thousand years ago, now they sprawl with ancient and modern buildings side by side. Much like its society, some folks exist as those did many years ago but now the rich drive new cars using the same roads as people using animal or hand pulled carts. Sharing just about finishes at that point.

I enjoyed hearing of the Colonial and Imperial eras, especially coming to understand that it was not so much a singular ruling. It was also pointed out that certain British administrators were responsible for saving and restoring many important ancient structures. Before this period, in the process of consolidating a captured area there would be destruction of buildings, antiquated or not, that didn't fit with the new ruling dynasty's ideology or religion. Right or wrong I have pride in what was achieved by the British during the time. Notably many newspapers are still printed in English and learning the language is a prerequisite for any Indian wishing to maintain or gain any position.

No visitor can come here and not notice the high revere that Mahatma Ghandi is held. Taking advantage of Britain's weakened state after World War two, he is credited with attaining India's independence and thereafter its partition. The countries that are now, India, Pakistan and Bangladesh were as one under British administration. I'm not sure that all he craved for his fellow man was actually achieved.

I take time here to impress that even having travelled much of this country, in no way would a single visit be enough to appreciate its full diversity. That said, a thousand books could be read and its history would never be fully understood either.

For all that the country offers, would I go back? I'm still undecided. Would I recommend it? Yes, because it is unique.

Adventures in Australia

Thursday 12th March. Day 28. Kuala Lumpar, Malaysia to Perth, Australia.

Once airborne a meal was served, afterwards I got some sleep. On arrival at Kuala Lumpar's futuristic airport at 7.30am local time, we put our watches forward by two and a half hours. First thing to do was find the transfer gate and confirm that our onward flight was on schedule. That done we found a nice café and bought some coffee, our US dollars being useful for that purpose. I used the time spare to bring my diary up to date. Within another hour we'd boarded the connecting flight to Perth and departed just after 9.30am. I slept for a while, always taking the opportunity for peaceful rest while on aeroplanes, something I had learned while in Brazil, if there's no planning or pressing matter to be discussed, why not? After all, you are in the hands of the pilot and crew, can't make phone calls or access the web, so shutting down for me was easy. Apart from that, travelling burns a lot of mental and physical energy, tiredness is inevitable.

Later, half watched a film and filled the immigration entry forms supplied by the airline. Put our shoes back on ready for the 3.10pm landing. Disembarked and we did the coats to bag loading trick, then went through two security checks, the second being 'Bio,' a new one for us. Australia not only has strict good's importation limits but a serious attitude in preventing the country from being contaminated by alien species, not just by us humans but plant and animal life. No problem for us, we'd dumped any uneaten fruit on the aeroplane and the 'only' fifty cigarettes import rule I'd found out in KL.

After clearing immigration I picked up some Australian dollars at an ATM in the front lounge of the airport. Outside I smoked a couple cigarettes. The sun was blazing and temperature very high. We weren't in any panic but didn't see any reason to hang about and got a price from a taxi driver for the drive into Scarborough. First reality check, $80Aud about £60Gbp. We'd chosen to stay in this town for several reasons, it's a coastal resort with the famous 'Brighton Beach' and in easy reach of Fremantle and Perth City Centre. We'd visit both.

The ride was heavenly, air conditioned large car, driver an ex-patriot Pakistani who spoke superb English and we chatted. The roads wide, organised, clear and clean. No carts, cows, camels and not a horn sounding! After sitting in a couple of rush hour traffic jams we arrived at the Indian Ocean Hotel, 27 Hastings Street, 6019. Bed and breakfast booked months ago. Passports were copied as usual and the cost of the stay payable in advance but we're allowed to run both a bar and restaurant credit tab. The web revues of this place had been mixed, suggestions that live music could disrupt sleeping. We never found that a problem. Allocated a room on the third floor with a double and single bed, fridge, kettle and crockery, an ensuite toilet, shower and a small balcony overlooking the car park. Wifi is free and excellent. The receptionist Hannah of East European origin spoke perfect English, she proved to be an absolute star. Helped me confirm that I had yet again unblocked my Microsoft email and when informed that our daughter Susie would be arriving to stay here, volunteered that she could share our room free of charge, including the breakfast facility. There is a God!

So, here we are, actually in Australia, we sorted our kit, had showers and at 7.30pm went down to the 'Bistro Bar.' I supposed now that we were in reverse culture shock, having been in India for almost a month and mostly only having ourselves to talk to, here we had English speaking company, bar staff and inquisitive customers enquiring of our wellbeing. Where are you from? What are we doing here? And general chit chat. Brilliant!

Ordered some lagers, not halves or the schooner, that strange interim measure found on this continent but proper pints in tall glasses and kept them coming. We ate thick steak sandwiches and played pool against some locals but never won a game. My diary note, 'bed about 10.30pm, p****d and very tired.' It had been a special day.

Friday 13th March. Day 29. Scarborough.

Chris and I discussed our new situation while drinking coffee and eating from a good buffet breakfast. After the hectic previous days we decided to try and have a relaxing one. Easier said than done, having been on the move for so long, this would be the first time we'd spend five nights in one place since home. Did some walking around this small town, took a look at the local beach and made our minds up to spend a few hours there later. Viewed what was on offer at the promenade restaurants and also found a 'Coles' supermarket. Went in, needing to get some snack and lunch foods to keep in the hotel room, bought ham, cheese, butter, a couple of pre-packed sandwiches and cans of beer for the beach.

After dropping off the shopping and changing into swimwear, we went back to the 'Brighton' section of Scarborough beach. The weather overcast but still warm, there was even a brief rain shower. The Indian Ocean was quite rough with some breaking waves, we eventually got in and did swim for a while. At least Chris wasn't beaten up like last time. Sat on our towels and talking she mentioned my primeval fear of sharks, I knew that would happen, all's fair in love and war. On the way back through the sea side carpark a chap, a churchman, was handing out uncut loaves of bread. We graciously accepted one.

At the hotel, planning to visit Fremantle tomorrow I used the ipad to study bus routes and timetables. Later we showered and changed for the evening 'Indi bar' session, which was quite good. Being Friday night it was well patronised, predominantly by youngsters. Pay to enter for the public, as hotel guests we got in free. A sign on the door said 'No entry wearing thongs or singlets,' to me and you that's 'flip flops or vests.' An Irish folk band were the live entertainment. We mingled with the friendly crowd, paradoxically many were wearing 'thongs and singlets.' Had several beers and quite a few conversations, during which as the time lapsed, found out that we'd missed the last ordering time for dinner, so later had to make do with 'room food.' Churchman? Bread? Must have been a sign!

Saturday 14th March. Day 30. Tonight, having travelled from Sydney, Susie would join us.

Up about 8.15am. Had breakfast then went to and from Fremantle by bus, two there, two back. A quiet place. Had a good look around the town and the docks then visited the Maritime museum, which is a quite impressive modern building and had some interesting exhibits. For lunch bought hot sausage rolls and coffee from a stall. I know how to treat a girl!

Back at Scarborough, just in case Susie hadn't eaten, picked up extra snack foods and a few beers for the room fridge. Did some internet research then showered. At 7.45pm, wrote my diary. According to messages received Susie should be with us at about 11.00pm. Excitedly anticipating the prodigal daughter, we went to the bar. Chris and I had dinner and limited our drinking to a pint each, being Saturday, not something that others were doing, many indulging to real excess. Doormen were having quite a difficult time and refusing entry to some very well lubricated folks. We saw the police arrive several times. Small clusters of youths indulging in their own drinking sessions were hanging about close to the car park and up and down Hastings Road. Being from Portsmouth I wasn't at all unnerved but did consider that my daughter would have to run the gauntlet of these groups. Being a black belt in Tae Kwando she wouldn't have a problem, but would be carrying her worldly goods in a back pack and other bags. I suspected these would slightly restrict a reaction, if one was needed!

More text messages confirmed that she'd landed, was taking a train and bus to meet us and her e.t.a. would be after 11.00pm. Chris and I decided to wait outside reception. Here we were entertained by a very drunk local resident. Telling us that he lived in one of the posh flats next door, being over friendly if anything, offered for us to meet his wife and drink with him. In England the instant classification would be 'pest.'

By about 11.30pm there had been a couple of car park scuffles, so knowing which bus stop Susie would get off at I decided to walk down Hastings Road. I saw a little flashlight torch flickering, it was her searching for building identification numbers. A quick hello had to be enough for now even though we hadn't physically seen each other for eight months.

I grabbed what bags I could carry, she had several. At the hotel she had hugs with her mother, the reunion is good, almost tearful. At the room we chatted, shared a glass or two of beer and ate some snacks. Catching up is hard to resist, it was past 2.00am by the time we all went to our beds.

Sunday 15th March. Day 31. Visit to Perth City Centre and Road Trip planning.

We had breakfast together, the talking never stopped. It didn't stop all day! Susie is our family's most experienced traveller. She'd already done a lot here in Australia, including camping road trips. I took that virtual step back, whatever she decided or suggested to do from here on would be better than good enough for me. I knew Chris would agree.

Day travel passes for bus and trains purchased, we went into Perth City. Susie helped me get a sim card for the ipad, it could be essential on a road trip. Walked up to Kings Park, great views from here. After a while we found an unoccupied bench and had the lunch which we'd made from breakfast foodstuffs from the hotel. OK it's not quite within the rules but there's little difference between someone who eats six slices of bread as toast at 8.00am and that of me who has two then and takes two for later.

At the West Perth War Memorial we paid our respects to the fallen and walked the beautifully landscaped grounds. It doesn't matter what country, city or town, these places always make Chris and I very emotional. Wandered through to the botanical gardens, up and over the suspended walkways. I took a lot of 360 degree pictures. Back in the city and visited The West Australian museum for a few hours, much to see and enjoy here. Outside we sat and ate the last of our snack foods. By now its late afternoon, Susie used her phone mapping app and found an Irish themed pub within walking distance. Here we enjoyed a few beers and steak sandwiches, all the while our conversation and planning continued. Left at 10.00pm, buses are limited, so travelled using two trains and a taxi back to the hotel. Coffee in the room, then bed. It had been a fantastic day. Almost as if the three of us had never been apart.

Monday 16th March. Day 32. Road Trip planning and beach visit.

Up at 8.30am. Breakfast, then back to the room for determined road trip planning until it's all sorted. Susie has penned out a loose route. From here, drive the West Coast route to Exmouth with camping and places of interest stops on the way up and back. Twelve days in total. She's been to some of them before. Excitement is mounting. I use the ipad, she uses her phone, we need to locate and hire a camper van, unfortunately it's a holiday weekend coming up and our choices are few, in fact they become limited to one company, 'Wicked Campers.' A firm started in New Zealand many years ago, catering for that 'cheap trip,' mainly for students and back packers on tight budgets. A four berth van is booked, to be collected tomorrow morning, the first day of 'our' road trip.

Mid-day. We walked to the local Coles supermarket, picked up bread rolls, cheese, ham and beers. Made up a picnic lunch in the room and head off to the beach. 2.00pm, towels laid out, hardly another person here, it's a lovely day the sun is shining, the sea inviting. Now I have two females ripping into me about my shark phobia. I can take it. As a land based creature it's just one of those things, a primeval fear. I have great respect for all sea dwellers, they're equipped for it and I'm not. Most of them, big, small or micro have stings, barbs, teeth and or both. The fact of the matter is that as a human on land I am the predator, in the sea I am the prey, part of the food chain. In my mind it's that simple.

Stayed on the beach until just after the beautiful sunset which we obviously photographed. Back at the hotel we showered and dressed. I loaded pictures from camera to ipad. Susie made a road trip playlist on Chris's ipod. At the very quiet Bistro bar ordered food, fish and chips times two and share three ways. At the room we all part pack in preparation for the big day tomorrow.

Tuesday 17th March. Day 33. Check out of Indian Ocean Hotel. Road Trip Day 1. To Jurien Bay 220km.

Up at 7.00am. Finish packing after breakfast, when during a discussion it's decided for the best that Susie and me go into Perth to collect the camper van. Much better than all three of us lugging our baggage, which can be left temporarily with Chris in the hotel lobby area. As it happened, the luggage stayed in the reception office and she was allowed to keep the room until our return. More brownie points for the place. Having paid the account and checked out, Susie and I travel by bus and train into Perth.

We find the hire place in Miller Street and then go through the rigmarole of getting the van. Plenty of wagons here, the yard reminded me pretty much of a car recycling centre. Bits of vehicles, wheels and tyres, a couple of workshops and a grubby old port-a-cabin office. Although the staff, an expat Mancunian and his daughter were friendly enough. There was plenty of paperwork, a form for this, a form for that. Only after a deposit is paid and a bond backed by a credit card lodged, we get to see the allocated van.

There it was in all its glory. An auto gearbox Toyota campervan. About eight years old, covered inside and out with designer graffiti and stupid hand written slogans for which the company has some infamy. Susie didn't care, I was only marginally taken aback. Although later during the trip I would scrape away some of the viler swear words. The basics rules for the hire, we were responsible for oil, fuel and water and the van is to be returned in a condition comparable to its leaving. More sexual innuendo written on the roof head lining or maybe clean graffiti?

Susie is no fool. Check out the vehicle and photograph every bit of damage, then make sure the 'condition report' tallies with the one you sign. That took some doing. I propped the bonnet and did an engine bay inspection, hadn't wasted part of my life in the English motor trade I

126

supposed. The tailgate is lifted and basic equipment noted, a one ring gas cooker, sink with pump tap, water containers, fold out stools and table, cutlery, crockery and a few pans. There's minimal bedding, a thin foam mattress and couple of pillows in suspicious condition. We were given a verbal run down on how to use the roof mounted top tent. This would eventually become affectionately known as the loft room.

From the office, collected a satnav, gas canister and the completed paperwork which included road side assistance telephone numbers. I took the wheel, drove out of the yard and we were on our way back to Scarborough. Susie did the guide bit until the satnav took over. The van didn't look much but it went well, we could only hope that fuel economy was good. My diary quote 'the van doesn't drive badly, but it's a pig to look at.'

Rolled the wagon into the hotel car park at about 2.00pm. It drew comments and glances from people, none of which were complimentary. We loaded our new home as best possible. Being past midday had some biscuits as a snack, then drove to Coles supermarket and liquor store for victuals. That done, on to a K mart to get some cheap pillow cases. What we didn't have now we'd source on our journey. Petrol tank filled on the way out of the city and a course set to Jurien Bay on the Indian Ocean Drive coast road.

Today Susie and I would split the driving duties, Chris would take turns later. It's highways to the outskirts of the city, here they change to simple tarmacked roads, on which is very little traffic, something we'd get used to. It wasn't long before the ipod was connected to the van radio, Prince, The Who and Prodigy among others entertaining us now and for coming days. Concentrating on the road meant not much sightseeing for the driver, although a few emus were spotted in the scrubland. To reach Sandy Cape Park, our chosen site for the first night in the semi-wilderness, we left metalled roads and went onto graded clay tracks for a bumpy final ride of about 6km.

5.00pm. Arrived at a very small campsite in a hollow behind some high sand banks. The only facilities, organic toilets. There were only a few other vehicles parked and a couple of tents of differing sizes pitched in among some scraggy, scrawny trees. It was dusk, the low sun behind thick cloud but there was still light. We jointly picked the first available space using these protocols, not too close to any other wagon or tent, no overhanging tree branches that would hinder erection of the 'loft tent.' Done, we all got out and first mistake noticed, the back of the wagon was facing the wind and that wouldn't do. Cooking on a one ring gas stove would be a trial even without the strong breeze.

Imagining the already settled campers smirking. On the same plot I manoeuvred the van into a more favourable position, front facing into the wind. Before setting up camp we applied insect repellent then took a short walk through the dunes. Had a look at the shore and Indian Ocean, look left, look right, not a soul in sight for miles.

We'd taken a couple beers with us to celebrate the success of 'road trip' day one. The sun was setting and we took photos.

Back at the wagon, in what light remained, work in setting up camp and organising the van began in earnest. Our first efforts were going to have to be our best! The last time Chris and I had been in a camper van was over thirty years ago, for a one week stay in Hampshire's New Forest.

The top tent is mounted on a frame, half the length and full width of the roof, it's contained in what can only be described as a giant soft black suit case. The soft outer cover has Velcro and other safety strapping at the sides and rear, these when released allow it to be flipped over the front windshield. A hinged laminated board with a telescopic ladder fixed on is then exposed. The rungs of the ladder are grasped, by stepping and pulling backwards it extends, with little effort the board flips up and over forming the second section of a floor. The nylon tent which is completely and permanently fixed to the floor sections becomes fully formed, popping up as the operations are performed. Ingenious! This would be Susie's berth, kit that she needed, bedding etcetera are bumped up into the tent later.

Unfortunately none of us are seven feet six inches tall, so one person needs to access the van roof and assist in the unstrapping and definitely needs to be there for the refolding. It became obvious to us that this had been done many times before, the route to the roof indicated by damage already incurred. The passenger door arm rest is crushed and the seat has a collapsed outer edge. The door window wind deflector also cracked and the factory fitted radio aerial broken. Later, we established that better traction is gained walking up the front windscreen bare footed, although slippery if wet and avoiding breaking the wipers is a challenge.

During the next eleven days, we three became masters of the sequence, each having a different job during the operation, whether construction or dismantling. Susie took responsibility for the high work, me with the ladder. As the trip continued we honed it to a fine art, five minutes for the put up, ten for the pack up.

To sort the van's internal sleeping arrangements the vehicle needs to be cleared of all larger bags. Small items can be put on the dashboard or in the front footwell, but here they are always in danger of damage.

The individual front seats are moved forward, so is the rear bench seat to the fullest extent, then the back is pushed down backwards flat on its hinges. Behind it is a loose lidded wood storage box with an aluminium retaining strip fixed on the front top edge. A loose plywood board is then laid on the collapsed rear seat arrangement. This board also has an edge fixed with section of angled aluminium which slots in to the one on the box. A very thin foam mattress is placed on top of the lot. Hey Presto! A two person sleeping berth where Chris and I would bed down. During the first night it not only proved very uncomfortable, the ply board also kept separating from the storage box. This would need some serious thought for improvements. By the second night, necessity being the mother of invention I'd resolved at least the ply board problem by placing our back packs on the seat to level it and preventing separation from the aluminium slot. The reality was that it being so rough and ready, it would never improve.

The kit bags would be placed onto the empty front seats or any spare footwell space for overnight.

While I took responsibility for the van interior Susie and Chris prepared our evening meal. How they managed to produce a fry up of sausages, beans, tomatoes, mushrooms and eggs on a tiny, portable, one ringed gas stove I will always wonder. By now it was night, the sky full of stars, an amazing and wonderful sight, it was as if you could stretch a hand up and touch them. They gave light but our head torches had been extracted from luggage and put on. The fold out stools had been found, we sat and ate and washed the food down with a couple of small cans of beer.

Insects are a problem. We learnt quickly not to open the van doors with interior lights ablaze. Once inside, moths and the like ping around in the darkness.

The day had been very hectic, a fantastic experience. We were all very tired and in our respective sleeping berths by about 9.00pm. Chris and I lay down on the board and thin mattress. I used the holdall as an extra pillow. Trying to sleep, I thought of the guard on the Delhi to Jaisalmer train and his ply wood bed!

Wednesday 18th March. Day 34. North to Waminda Wildlife Sanctuary via Geraldton. 200km. Road Trip Day 2.

For me and Chris it had been an awful night, broken sleep, hot and uncomfortable on the hard board bed which had continually slipped from its retainer. I had to take a leak about 3.00am. Eased myself out through the side door of the wagon and decorated a rear wheel while all sorts of crawlies walked over my bare feet. By 6.45am I was fully awake, out and about. Chris and Susie soon followed. They made a welcome breakfast of eggy toast with mushrooms, tea and coffee.

Bathroom time, another first, using the drop bog or as it's properly known a bio toilet. Contained in a lean to type shed it's basically a porcelain pan fixed over a very, very, deep bored hole. Lift the seat, check for spiders then use the facility as one would at home. There is no flush, so wash around the pan using the brush and blue organic liquid from the bucket found in the cubicle. Outside, rinse soaped hands under the tap supplied by tank fed water. These places are inspected and cleaned daily by park rangers.

None of us had washed properly, the remainder of boiled water is used for a face rinse. We brush our teeth and swill from a cup. Then, as the phrase goes, we break camp, load the van and leave about 9.00am just as rain starts to fall. When pulling away from the parking spot a double check is made ensuring nothing has been left behind, especially rubbish.

With stops it's going to be about a four hour journey. I take us out of camp heading back to the main road via the graded track. A 'Who' song Baba O'Reilly is soon playing through the radio speakers. We're still getting used to the van, splitting driving duties and will get fuel at the first opportunity.

On arrival in Geraldton, a small seaside town with colonial history, we find a parking place close to some public toilets. It's stopped raining but the skies are threatening more. With the van tailgate up the girls make sandwiches for lunch. Afterwards we moved and parked close to the town's Maritime museum and visited it.

Close by is the original jail house which although still retaining many features has been adapted as crafts and art shops. By now the rain is pouring down. Another move, to a supermarket to buy tonight's supper and other victuals. That done, drive on towards our night time stopover, the Waminda animal sanctuary. Here the owners allow camping for a voluntary cash contribution toward the upkeep of the place.

Susie had stayed here before but we let the satnav take the strain of finding it. Tarmacked roads all the way. Although raining again we're soon at the gates. The land looks unmanaged, size of the plot is hard to establish. The boundaries are only marked by tatty fencing, wire, wood and bushes. After entry through the air lock type double gates, we're on a pitted, wheel rutted mud and clay track. All around there are vehicles, coaches without wheels, static cabins and caravans on blocks, most have been converted into temporary accommodation. Abandoned tractors and other farm implements randomly lay where last placed, vegetation growing around through and over them.

The track is followed until we approach some buildings, one is a house with a picket fence and gate. The rest are workshops or sheds, brick block, metal clad and timber. There are animal pens and some wired cages visible.

Susie had mentioned that when she had previously been here there was a party atmosphere among the campers. There would no chance of that tonight, today we're definitely the only human visitors.

I waited with the van for instructions while Susie and Chris went to and from the house. We're directed to park up in a small clearing we'd passed on the trackway. With nimble manoeuvring the van is edged into a neat little area near some trees. Close by is a toilet cubicle, a static cabin and water stand pipe. Perfect.

3.00pm, the rain stopped but it's still overcast. The loft tent is up and the van rearranged ready for sleeping, except for mine and Chris's backpacks, which are to be used as levelling under the horrid bed board. The girls had set out all the equipment and victuals needed to prepare tonight's dinner. That done we had a cup of tea, so British. At 4.00pm we're to join in and help feeding the animals.

We followed French girl, a 'woofer' (World Wide Opportunities on Organic Farms) a foreigner in Australia who does work for food and accommodation. She carried large plastic buckets containing foodstuffs, among other things bread and cabbage. Sharing this out while moving through different enclosures, to a horse called Goldie, a mixed group of wallabies, kangaroos and emus. In mesh pens a piglet, ducks and chickens. Then into my absolute favourite. A large wired cage enclosure with all sorts of birds eagerly awaiting seeds and meal to be put into dishes dotted around. Some including budgerigars and parakeets perched on our hands and fed from the palms. Then 'Heath' arrived, a one legged large black parrot with a penchant for sunflower seeds. I'd kept birds in England so blew the smaller seeds from my hand, he was instantly on it, the sharp claws of his only foot punctured my skin but being close this marvellous bird was worth the discomfort.

As we wandered back to the van daylight was fading. The girls had dinner to prepare but discovered that we'd run out of gas! I thought that it would be sandwiches again. Susie went to the farm house, maybe they would have a canister or two? No such luck but ours did turn for the good. Ian the owner had returned, on hearing of our plight he gave Susie the keys to one of the static cabins. It was connected to a water and electricity supply and had a cylinder fed gas cooker. Outback chef's heaven!

The components of our meal were quickly transferred to the cabin kitchen. Half an hour later we're sat at a table enjoying burgers, rolls, salad and a few beverages. Well done girls! As we came to the end of our meal Ian joined us. Kind and thoughtful enough to have brought a few bottles of cold beer. Among stories exchanged the history of Heath. How this parrot had been advertised as an unwanted pet, how he'd travelled 800km then paid a lot of Aussie dollars to buy him. Now he'd see out his days in the company of other birds. Dedication indeed.

Didn't have the heart to tell Ian that we'd just eaten our first ever kangaroo burgers. After he left we played cards, finished our beers then made coffee. About 9.00pm we closed down the cabin. While we'd been eating, another vehicle had parked in the clearing. We went to our respective berths in or on the campervan. Road trip day two had been a cracker in all aspects.

Thursday 19th March. Day 35 to Kalbarri. 180k. Road trip Day 3

I was up and out of the van by 6.30am. I'd slept for longer spells between pee breaks, during which the opportunity to view the stars and the 'Milky Way' weren't wasted. From the wet patch on the ground below the loft tent I deduced that I wasn't the only one not making trips to the WC in the darkness!

The cabin facility was used to make coffee and brew tea. We joined the new guests to feed the animals. While in the pen with the sanctuary's emus and kangaroos. A veritable giant of the latter about two and a half metres tall, peered over the boundary fence. The French girl explained that visitors like him often took the opportunity to inspect for females of the species.

Ian then fed the dingoes raw meat, he and his big old dog the only beings permitted in that wired cage. Feeding duties all done, next was breakfast with him, his wife and guests in the farmhouse conservatory. All part of the experience. A table had been laid with toast, vegemite, jam and coffee. Nice except for the early morning uninvited flies. Everyone was introduced and had cuddles with a blind orphaned 'joey,' a young kangaroo. Its mother, as many are had been killed by a motor vehicle. It seems etiquette in Australia that if a driver hits one of these large animals the female's pouch is checked for living babies. Unfortunately on the outback roads evidence of road kills are frequent, stains or remains on tarmac and sun bleached or fly blown skeletons on verges.

We left our charitable cash contribution in a jar placed on the table. Said our goodbyes and thanks for the kindness received.

At the van took a couple of photographs for reminders, fully cleared up and broke camp. Drove down the lane and picked up the route to Kalbarri. Paved road and music all the way through the National Park on the way to this sea side town. On arriving we find it's as pretty as a picture postcard. Fuel and provision the wagon here, then drive back into the park mostly on graded clay roads, which are hard work but worth it once there. We walked in the blazing sunshine, looking at the rock formations and the gorge down to the river offered especially stunning views.

Afterwards drove back into town, find the camp Susie had researched on her iphone. Kalbarri Tudor Caravan Park, a glam site with swimming pool, flushing toilets and hot showers. We needed those having not washed properly for three days! At reception we're given a choice of plots. Picked one and found it. While manoeuvring I reversed into a f***** tree! A bit of a dampener really, here we are about to enjoy the marvellous facilities and I've jammed the van tailgate, all of our provisions stored behind it and no other access.

My problem and soon to be my solution. I scouted around, found a discarded angled iron fence post and a brick. Read as 'pry bar and hammer,' it's the builder in me and now I had tools! Sweating on success, I prised open the tailgate, fortunately not causing too much damage elsewhere. Relieved I took the opportunity to lubricate all locking mechanisms with washing up liquid and check that full operation was fully restored. By now black humour had surfaced and the girls are ripping into me. How many times was I to hear about fast growing trees or them jumping out of nowhere. However, we were all smiles now!

We changed clothes and had a swim, then showered and prepped the van for overnighting. Susie and Chris made a chili con carne in the camp kitchen. While there we charged our phones and I transferred some photos to the ipad. Had dinner sat at one of the nearby bench tabled eating areas, drank a few beers, talked over the day and played cards. Retired to the van at about 9.45pm.

Friday 20th March. To Carnarvon. 500km. Road trip Day 4.

After another broken night. Too much beer had me out of the van a couple of times, during which I noticed that small kangaroos forage the site in the darkness. Up at 6.40am, I made tea and coffee ready for Chris and Susie. They made breakfast of scrambled egg and toast in the camp kitchen.

By 8.45am, cleared, all packed up and on our way North to Carnarvon with Chris at the wheel for the first stint of what was going to be a very long drive. Tunes playing and all was good until about 11.00am when the van wiped out a medium sized lizard. To say it lowered our moods would be an understatement. It sent us all down, so far that even music wouldn't lift us, there was no choice but to carry on. Eventually stopped for fuel, afterwards, Susie took the wheel.

While in the back seat of the van Chris made up bread rolls with fillings, we ate those, all done on the move. So non-stop except for toilet breaks. We pulled into Carnarvon at about 2.30pm. We'd talked of trying to get further north but decided that enough distance had been covered. Susie checked out a couple of local campsites on her iphone and selected one.

In Perth we'd heard that Mother Nature and her agent cyclone 'Olwin' had made a mess here. Saw plenty of evidence, road signs and panelled fences blown down, some collapsed buildings, corrugated metal roofs detached from houses. Before going shopping we parked up near the shore. The estuary and sea a horrid red brown colour, silt and mud had been washed down the 'Gascoyne,' the longest river in Western Australia. However the area was still open for business. On the beach children were playing, dogs being walked. I bought some choc ices from a static van and we sat on the foreshore rocks for a while.

In town much the same circumstances. Storm damage. A couple of shops had temporarily relocated into vacant units. Supplies obtained and we drove onto the campsite Capricorn Park. Recently acquired by new owners, they and staff were very welcoming. A parking lot allocated, van set up, we took a swim in the small pool then showered. With a good kitchen available Susie and Chris prepared dinner of lamb chops and potatoes. Internet access being free we did some research about flights for me and Chris to Alice Springs and for Susie to Sydney.

Saturday 21st March. Day 37. To Exmouth, Ningaloo Coast. 500km. Road trip Day 5.

Up at 6.30am. In the camp kitchen the girls made poached eggs with cheese on toast for breakfast, very nice or 'yum' as Chris noted in her diary. I thought we'd get away from here early but it was 9.00am by the time we'd broke camp and got on the road. It was to be another long ride with limited stops on the way. Driving sequence sorted, me out of camp, Chris, Susie, then me again to take us into the destination. This arrangement worked well, it left Susie available to navigate the last few kilometres.

Came off of the main road just north of Carnarvon and made a detour to Quebba Point. Here for the blow holes, spectacular spouts of sea spray shooting skyward forced through the rocks by massive, powerful waves. The coast line is perilous, jagged, sharp and crevices with trip points and gouges. I noted in my diary 'scary, instant death.' On our way again. The landscape either side of the road is mainly scrub, little or no cultivation and feral cattle roam at will.

Drove on through an extensive area with hundreds of termite mounds from two to ten feet tall. An amazing sight. At one point on the open road, some way off on the opposite side to us, was a stationary van. On drawing closer we found out why. A big lizard about one and a half metres long, its tongue flicking in and out tasting the air had left the scrub hedging and was moving stealthily towards a roadkill, a large bovine dead at the edge of the tarmac. By now our van was stopped, I was out taking pictures. Unfortunately, at a distance coming towards us a road train appeared, I knew these monster trucks with trailers didn't stop easily so beat a hasty retreat to the wagon. The show was over.

Made two refuelling stops before reaching Exmouth. Here we did a supply shop that should last for two days. Susie had selected a campsite she had been to before, 17 kilometres from town, Lighthouse Park, named after the building high on the point. She hadn't reckoned with the area having no wifi and a plague of flies. The first wasn't really an issue, but oh my, the second was. The van was parked and the loft tent set up in minutes, we were experts by now.

There's a road to the Vlamingh Head lighthouse but that's for softies! Carrying a few cans of beer we climbed the rock strewn hill. I came across a small python during the walk up. The views out over Ningaloo Reef are astounding. We sat and enjoyed the sunset moment, the beers a bonus. Daylight was fading fast, we'd left the climb down late, a dodgy thing to do but did get back to the campsite with limbs undamaged!

All of us used the camp bathrooms to shower. Flies were everywhere, the problem seeming worse early evening and mornings just as the sun warmed. Susie and Chris made a meal in the kitchen, they reported that it had been hard work with many folks using so few facilities. Because of the flies, it had been decided to eat inside the campervan. This would be a first. While the girls were busy I rearranged the interior. There is a facility to rotate the front seats, difficult but manageable, the rear bench seat in its upright position then pushed back. A purpose made metal post slots into a fixed cupping on the floor with a table top placed over a similar fitting in its underside. Easy.

We ate a vegetable curry, had a few beers and talked. While the girls did the washing up, I set the van interior for sleeping. Retired at 9.00pm in anticipation of an early morning start.

Sunday 22nd March. Day 38. Cape Range National Park to Turquoise Bay. 40k. Road trip Day 6.

All up and about by 6.30am. Susie and I readied the van for the road as Chris made coffee and toast. Today's destination Turquoise Bay in the Cape Range National Park, right on the coast. Camping here is back to basics, so our drinking water was topped up and we fuelled the wagon before leaving. This site has its own fuel pumps, a little more expensive than road stations but we had to be properly prepared. Out and on our way by 8.20am.

Arrived at the park and went into the modern visitor centre. Fees paid and we're given a short talk on the 'Do's and Don'ts,' then watched a brief video. An information map indicated areas of shore line and tidal flow, all very important, basically there's a safe swimming and novice snorkelling area, if you go out of bounds on your head be it. I'd certainly be adhering to the rules and hoped that any sharks would do also. We hired a couple of sets of goggles and snorkels, paid the deposit, left and drove following signs to one of the daytime only parking areas.

By 10.00am. We'd changed into swim wear, made a picnic lunch, taken other beach essentials and were on the sand. So were quite a few other folks. The sun is hot and the sky bright blue. Here is a simply stunning long curved inlet bay, I walked the full distance. One end is a rocky shoreline, the other is a sandy promontory where powerful seas mix with the quiet waters of the safe beach. Warning of the dangers that can be met a sign is placed here, making good use of the shadow cast was a good size lizard. In the distance almost on the horizon big waves were crashing over the hidden reef.

Snorkels and facemasks on, Susie and Chris wasted no time getting into the sea. Standing at the water's edge I received reports about coral and fish. I had my turn later. Afterwards we all took the opportunity to relax, stretching out on towels and sunbathing. At 2.00pm we decided to leave, needing to drive further along the coast, still within the reserve but to find an overnight camping place. The tourist map showed several. One was found in about thirty minutes, the only facilities being the ubiquitous bio toilets. I parked in one of only a few vehicle bays marked out by simple low log posts topped with horizontal poles.

We're no more than 30 metres from the sea. There are some timber decking paths and steps that can be used to get through the scrub vegetation, then over high dunes to a crumbling sand slope that drops down to a few metres of dry beach and the water's edge. A wind blew, strong enough to cause some concern about using the loft tent. Still being daylight we decided to wait a while and see how things developed before putting it up. I took a nap while the girls played cards, sheltered from the breeze by the side of the van.

Well before night fall it was decided that Chris and Susie should berth in the loft tent. A bit of extra body and baggage weight wouldn't go amiss so the wagon was prepared. Daylight started to fade and the wind calmed.

It had been a good few years since I'd been sea fishing and seeing rods stood against their vehicle I struck up a conversation with two chaps parked nearby. An English father and son, the dad visiting his long time Australian based offspring for an angling holiday. They were preparing kit for a night time expedition and would be walking further along the beach to fish. Later that night they invited me to cast a line into the Indian Ocean, Susie had a go too. No bites, it was a one off and unlikely to happen again.

The girls cooked burgers, we had those and a couple of beers in the glow of our head torches. The sky was cloudy and very dark, no star show this evening. All in our sleeping quarters by 8.30pm. Tired and very happy.

Monday 23rd March. Day 39 to Coral Bay via Exmouth. 150k. Road trip day 7.

Up and about by 6.30am and noticed that our fishing friends had already departed the camp. I'd slept like a baby and only decorated a van wheel once during the night. At that time the night sky was clear, so got my view of the stars after all. Fantastic. I boiled water for beverages, Chris made French toast. After breakfast I packed up most of the kit then we all went for an early swim. Snorkel and goggles on, Chris again reported seeing coral, fish and a ray, I was unlucky, didn't see anything. By 9.15am all ready to go. On the way out of the park dropped the hired items at the visitor centre, cash deposits were returned.

Not a long drive to Coral Bay, we were relaxed enough and played music. On the way at road side spotted a good size salamander so stopped and took photographs. Went back into Exmouth to re-stock food and beer. Never missing an opportunity, also topped the van up with fuel.

Arrived at the 'Peoples Campsite' about 2.00pm. Susie negotiated, she was a little annoyed with the attitude of the receptionist and the price of $60, a deposit also had to be paid for an auto gate entry card. Hey ho, we needed to be here. The site was rammed, full of caravans, tents and people. Flipping Australians enjoying a holiday!

Drove slowly through the camp, children were playing and folks were wandering about. Found our allocated plot right at the back of the site. A fair walk to the shower blocks and kitchen. Didn't do much else except lock the parked van, then carrying our beach gear, left the camp on foot. This place and surrounding village size community is totally tourist oriented. The beach is flat sand, much of it was still wet, so obviously tidal. Plenty of people here too, a couple of coaches had just disgorged their occupants, at least one organised school trip and a group of oriental visitors. We walked to where boats were moored at the water's edge, there is a quite a steep coastal shelf.

On the way down we'd seen shops that hired out snorkelling gear, the girls definitely wanted some. I walked back and got a couple of sets. A fair way from the water's edge are a few canopied shelters for sun shade, mostly in use. I asked a young couple if I could leave our bags and towels nearby, they agreed and I went back to the girls. Both had already been in the sea and Susie is eager to use my camera. When I took my turn with a snorkel the reason was obvious, lots of large fish were lounging lazily close to the ridge in the deeper water and shadow of the boats.

At camp the loft tent is erected and the van part prepped for sleeping. Damp towels and swim wear pegged out on Susie's travel washing line, stretched between a fence and a small tree. One at least surviving my parking skills! The girls had discussed cooking arrangements. Tonight's menu, steak and jacket potatoes. Here the camp kitchens also had outdoor electric powered barbeque facilities, unfortunately the hot plate on the one nearest to us wasn't working. So Chris took responsibility for the potatoes in the very busy kitchen and Susie volunteered to cook the meat on one of the working grills near the front of the site. I went to see how she was coping, she was OK, right in a melee of blokes doing the same thing. Steaks cooked we walked back to our nearest eating area, she had the meat, I carried the utensils.

We sat, had a couple of beers and enjoyed the meal. I gave the girls a verbal ten out ten for effort. Internet is free here, so Susie and I took the opportunity to book our next flights and an overnight stay at an Ibis hotel near Perth Airport. We were all bedded down by 10pm. I noted in my diary 'where did the day go?'

Tuesday March 24th Day 40. To Shark Bay. 600km. Road trip day 8.

Up and out of the van by 6.30am, having slept in periods. It seems sometimes that a previous day's busy events play on my mind. Yesterday had been a roller coaster! After toast and coffee the van was quickly squared away. On checking the utensils a big knife was missing. I walked to the barbeque grill where Susie had cooked, luckily it was there.

Stopping close to the park exit, in reception Susie got the deposit back for the gate key. Ipod music pumping we were on our way at 8.15am, heading south as part of the return journey. The van indicators failed just as we left. Susie made several calls to roadside assist. Their instructions, 'muck about with the hazard light switch' and it worked. Better than a garage visit eating up time. Chris made sandwiches and we ate them, again all on the move.

143

At Carnarvon, shopping and refuel all done by 1.30pm. My driving shift over, Susie now at the wheel, me then getting kip in the back of the wagon. I must have needed it. Chris had been driving for two hours and I woke as the van was being taken in for fuel, the second time today.

Entered the National Park area at about 3.00pm, stopped at a couple of places for photo opportunities. At the last making a driver change, I'd take us into Monkey Mia and we were there by 4.00pm. Chris and I waited in the van while Susie got us signed in for two nights. The campsite was jam packed, fortunately ours being a small van we were allowed to park on the edge of the camp's internal service road. As a bonus the nightly fees included the price of a meal for each of us in the fast food restaurant.

Parked in between other vehicles and with enough room to put the loft tent and ladder up. We were very happy. The girls wouldn't have to cook and the weather was superb. Evening was arriving, the sun dropping on the horizon, so had a quick look around to get our bearings. This place is one hundred percent a holiday resort with two storey motel accommodation and from ultra-luxury motor homes down to one man tents pitched on grass. At the beach only a metre from the water's edge we could see dolphins swimming. What a place! I thought to myself why would anyone coin the name Shark Bay for somewhere so beautiful?

Sat at one of the picnic tables we treated ourselves to some beers and talked. The sun was close to the sea now so we decided to eat and used our meal vouchers to order food. Me, beef and ale pie, Susie, chicken and salad, Chris, fish and chips, with of course, more beer.

All of a sudden some excitement near the food counter, a member of staff had seen a snake. A big one! A good thing about Australia is that most folks have an affinity with wildlife but the snake was in the wrong place and it was soon caught in a pool leaf net. Being one of the smallest and lightest on scene I was bodily bumped over a six foot fence into the bin storage area, took the net and a good look at the Rock Python, then handed both over the barrier to other helping hands, mostly men's. A volunteer offered to drive a distance out into the National Park and release the reptile. I would have love to gone with him but dinner was on the table!

As a group we'd talked too long, drunk that little bit too much and still had the van to arrange. Not only that, we were booked for the 'Dolphin' feeding session at 8.00am in the morning. So in the brightly lit campsite we all sorted the wagon's sleeping arrangements. Although exhausted and beer affected, I wrote my diary, finishing with the note, 'what stars Chris and Susie have been, I will never forget these days' :)

Wednesday 25th March day 41. Monkey Mia. Road trip day 9.

All up and about by 6.30am. A quick coffee made and had. We head to the shore and pier for the dolphin experience. Annexed to the campsite is an Ecology Centre run by Park Rangers and staffed mainly by volunteers. We lined up single file on the shore and pier with many others, men, women and children. Through a loud hailer a lady tells us that over the recent years a study has been made of the ocean dwelling dolphins that freely visit this bay. They are a wild natural pod, not pets. The family groups have been identified right down to individuals, including parents and children. Only five mammals are fed on any one day to ensure they remain self-sufficient. My feeling is that this going to be a bit of a tourist show. Having watched many educational television programmes I have come to have a great admiration of these creatures. By day's end I will have revised my opinion to an even higher level of respect.

As the running commentary continued, several staff members each holding a stainless steel bucket containing fish, entered the water to about knee depth. The audience is told that the dolphins are just out of sight and would

145

soon come to shore and be fed. Sure enough in a short while there were fins and the shiny backs of these mammals breaking the surface of the water. At the same time they are being introduced by name, this one is 'Lucy' over here is 'George' and so on. At such a shallow depth they must have almost been touching the sea bed.

A call is made for volunteers to do the feeding, mostly children are selected from the many hands raised. They went in to the sea and stood next to the bucket holders. Under strict supervision a fish is put into small hands. Watching a fully toothed dolphin take the offering gently and carefully using the side of its mouth is a wonder, no biting and no snatching. Total discipline and I instantly knew who was in control and it wasn't the Rangers! Another round of hand feeding to be done and Susie fortunately is enlisted. My camera ready, took the shot and was very pleased to get it.

No cooking breakfast for the girls today. After the show we ambled to the restaurant and had bought ones served. We chatted, I expounded and even questioned my own new opinions about dolphins. Wild but organised creatures. How did the queueing 'Pod' decide whose turn it was to come and get the free feed on any one day? Whose turn would it be tomorrow? It certainly wasn't being influenced by the Rangers. Why didn't sharks take advantage of the free food? That would be fish 'and' fingers! I joked that the family groups would argue in dolphin language, eventually laughing at the poor animal chosen to go in, eat dead fish and entertain us humans. After all these beings are perfectly capable of hunting their own breakfast, they've been doing it for millions of years. It isn't our bay, it's theirs, even though they may have to share it with sharks!

After ablutions the girls did some laundry, then we all prepped ourselves for a day on the beach. Plenty of sun tan lotion required, today is a scorcher. Using purpose built decking we walked through the sandy scrub and settled on the shore in front of the campsite. There were others here but still plenty of space. Our towels were laid out, water and a few snacks in our bags. Susie and Chris many times sniggering, reminding me of the possible visits by sharks. I was OK, just don't pee in the water, I've read the books, seen the films!

The sea is warm, with a current but not strong enough to cause concern. No more than a metre or two from the water's edge the occasional dolphin or sometimes a pair patrolled the shallows. A few small cabined motor boats were moored, others came and went. Some fishing, others just cruising the bay. A pelican was also resident, it either sat on the sand or paddled, either way if you got too close it clacked its beak as a warning. Chris also saw a turtle. We three swam, paddled, floated or sun bathed. Simply wonderful.

I walked for a while and met a fellow traveller, Johan from Czechoslovakia, he spoke good English. In less than half an hour we'd discussed world history from the dawn of time to present day, politics and the state of European football.

While in the sea, at one time my eyes fell upon a true beauty, probably unique to this continent. A creature of which I was spell bound for a few moments as I marvelled, thinking of the genetics, the thousands of years of development. OK, so I couldn't help noticing an absolutely gorgeous young woman wearing an Australian flag bikini. Yes, call me an old pervert, my wife and daughter did and the berating I got for taking the photograph was harsh but as the advert says, 'she was worth it.'

Always looking for an opportunity for an underwater picture of a dolphin I had my camera strapped to my wrist and set ready. A pair went by and I clicked several times in hope of the elusive 'look what I got shot.' Stood in the water thigh deep, shading the camera screen with one hand was checking the pictures for quality or not. Then bump!

Something in the sea had hit me, not too hard but enough to buckle my knees. I looked up as a dolphin only a couple metres way was certainly looking back. I swear it was laughing, it must have heard the girls talking. No way this wasn't a deliberate act, these mammals have sonar. I imagined that it was now on his way back under the pier to meet friends and tell the story of how it had just made a human think that a shark had attacked. How its mates must have laughed when it described the shocked look on my face.

At one time a large ray slowly passed by, its shadowy shape undulating in only a foot of water. I came to understand why it was here. On return from boat fishing, some anglers would clean and gut their catch close by, entrails and unwanted bits thrown back into the sea. Free food, this just reinforced my theory that almost for sure, sharks would definitely be about somewhere.

After the beach it was time for some personal grooming, I hadn't often had the chance for a proper head shave. All cleaned up by 5.30pm. Chris and Susie played some cards then we went to dinner at the Monkey Bar, vouchers used for food, cash for beers. Three different meals, ale pie again for me, Chris had lamb curry, Susie a pizza. We were joined at our table by some interestingly coloured large beetles.

Retired to the van at about 9.30pm. A storm is brewing out at sea, some terrific lightning flashes in the distance. I wrote my diary and noted 'this two night stay has been worth its weight in gold.' A poor description, just being sad about leaving tomorrow but I knew what I meant.

Thursday 26th March. Day 42. Towards Perth. 8 hours 500k. Port Dennison. Knobby Head South. Road trip Day 10.

Chris and Susie berthed in the loft tent overnight, I was in the van. Unfortunately we'd all had a broken night. It rained heavily about 3.30am, although the storm had been mostly dry and noisy. During my toilet breaks I'd seen the most spectacular multi coloured lightning.

I boiled water and roused the girls at 6.30am. Even now there was the occasional rumble of thunder and distant lightning flashes. Flies weren't yet about but they soon would be. Susie packed the loft tent while I sorted the van. She and Chris then made our breakfast of poached eggs on toast in the camp kitchen and we ate there. After ablutions I picked up an abandoned baseball cap in the shower block. It had been hung on a mop handle since we'd arrived. Waste not want not! The girls collected our laundry from the nearby washing lines. Amusingly the mother emu that wandered the camp with her three big chicks ambled by without a care. We were soon on the move, out of the site by 8.15am.

A long way to go and our first destination would be Denham, because a day ago I'd noticed some severe wear on the outer edge of a rear tyre. Susie had made a couple phone calls about this. The hire firm's suggestion was for us to change it for the spare wheel. No chance of that, a six inch wrench and my muscle could never compete with wheel nuts previously tightened by an air powered driver. A tyre fitting workshop was needed.

A slight detour and we didn't have the full address of the workshop but the satnav got us to the road. On arrival the fitter completely agreed that a new tyre was necessary, he made a phone call to the van hire company, price to be agreed I supposed. Job done. Next stop Geraldton, here we refuelled, got food, beer and some cigarettes for me.

We were on the main road route for a long while, sometimes close to the sea other times more inland. Lunch was made and eaten in the van. By now Chris was expert at preparing rolls on the move.

Susie suggested a visit to a place of interest on the coast. 'Stromatolites,' supposedly living rocks, bacterial single cell microbe organisms. I checked the fuel gauge, for the first time in our journey it was showing near reserve and I didn't like it. I'd rather have got to the next fuel station than see bacteria! We were definitely taking a chance of having enough petrol but at the signed junction turned off the main road, an information board showed the distance as 14 kilometres.

There were a few other vehicles in the car park including a tour bus. A short stroll over rough ground took us to a purpose built wooden curving walk way. This goes across and above the shore then over the shallows so that the stromatolites need not be disturbed. Strategically placed information panels explained historical and scientific details. Personally I only remember the sulphuric smell.

Visit over and after Susie having a quick bush p**s, left us with a tense drive back to the junction turn off. I spent more time looking the petrol gauge than the road. Fortunately we made it and rolled onto the forecourt of one of the very few service stations to refuel. We'd been here on the way up the coast. At that time it was full of massive road trains.

The weather remained dry but very overcast, it was hard to establish if we were heading into the brewing storm or away from it. As late afternoon arrived so did the rain. The Indian Ocean Drive sometimes took us into, other times out of the down pours but as we approached the coast they stayed with us. It was about 4.00pm and still raining when we left metalled road for graded track. There were several options for overnight camps, all the bio toilet type. The first we pulled into was empty of travellers but there was an old caravan with a make shift canopy, the whole lot had been converted into static living accommodation. Leaving the girls in the wagon, I wandered over and approached an old chap who was watching cricket on a mobile TV. I asked his opinion about the weather situation. According to him it would remain wet and windy and the storm brewing out at sea would arrive during the night.

Had a three way discussion in the van, should we stay or should we go? Decision, left the site and drove for a short while further along the coastal track and turned into another slightly larger camping area. There was one big touring wagon already parked up. We'd stay here, during the last half hour the rain had stopped and the wind dropped to a breeze.

The van was set up for overnight use, stools and table placed outside. While Chris and Susie were busy prepping a chili con carne dinner I wandered down to the rocky shore. Mother Nature was still giving a free lightning show. On the horizon purple and red flashes pierced the dark clouds, looking like distant artillery fire.

Making the meal was under control, the girls played cards and we all had a can or two of beer. On the scene arrived an older chap riding a purpose built three wheeled motor bike. The panniers and basket contents easily identified him as a fisherman. He accepted my offered beer, taking the can in a hand having fingers the size of big red bananas. A few friendly words turned into a good chat. He had a good moan about the recently imposed quotas for fish catches and also mentioned that at his age of seventy years the fly plague was the worst he'd ever known. Something to do with the recent cyclone maybe? He heard Chris sneeze and asked, "Your missus got the wog?" My look of surprise brought an explanation that the last word was a local colloquialism for the flu bug. I won't be bringing the phrase into common use in England. He left as darkness fell, we sat and ate our dinner. At dusk another vehicle arrived, an estate car with three women passengers. I thought we'd struggled with a camper van, they emptied the car of all luggage and bedded down inside.

Before retiring I took one long look out to sea, in the blackness the lightning show was even more spectacular. I had a thoughtful reflection.

Friday 27th March. Day 43. To Cervantes. 150km. Road trip day 11.

Awake and out of the van at 6.00am. Lightning flashes had been occurring most of the night. There are dormant flies everywhere, on the van body and even all over the dash board. How the f*** did they find their way in? So before the sun woke them we decided to get away as soon as possible. Made and had a quick coffee. Those with need visited the bio toilet. The van was prepped and we were off by 7.00am. Susie consulted a map as we drove and selected a little place called Leeman's Cove, so I head there following satnav instructions and drive with all windows open. As the flies woke they were thankfully sucked out of the van. Within an hour arrived at the small cove and parked under trees in a delightful furnished picnic area a few metres from the water's edge.

A breakfast of eggy bread, tea and coffee made as the little town was just waking up. Nearby a few boats were being launched from trailers.

Our next stop would be the Nambung National Park, here are rock formations called The Pinnacles. We first went into the visitor centre, then in blazing sunshine took the one and half kilometre signposted walk around these fascinating naturally formed structures, hundreds of them. If imagination is let loose, shapes of animals, dinosaurs and all manner of objects can be seen. From here, drove and parked at Hangover bay. Made and ate sandwiches for lunch. Then onward to Cervantes, where by early afternoon we'd booked into a coastline campsite actually called the Pinnacles, this having full facilities, kitchens, shower and toilet blocks.

After setting up camp we ambled into town. A cute little place, not much to offer but has a small parade of shops. I bought a dustpan and brush to clear the van of sand and other debris. We also purchased a little treat, choc ices and ate them on the way back to camp.

Susie and Chris took a walk along the shore, had a paddle and chatted. I started to clean the van. For me a harsh reality was kicking in and I supposed it would be the same for the girls. The West Coast road trip was coming to an end and we're barely 200 kilometres north of Perth City. By now I am almost a feral outback boy, having only worn a vest and swimming shorts for the best part of ten days. I swept more sand from the van interior, almost as if I was sweeping away what had been such a fantastic experience. I wiped down the van windows, washed the bonnet and front grill, clearing dead bugs and other insects. Victims of the thousands of kilometres travelled.

The girls played cards, the game was called sh*t head, I never could understand it so didn't bother. After taking showers we all went to the camp kitchen. I tried to do some internet research for a trip out of Alice Springs. I knew Chris and Susie had been discussing plans for further ahead, Fiji. I'd take that on board gratefully, as and when. We ate the fry up dinner at a kitchen table. Soon it would be sleeping time. Chris and I both noted in our diaries that being with Susie on this journey had been an 'emotional experience.'

Saturday 28th March. Day 44. Return to Perth.

Awake at 5.00am, still dark. Out of the van and I decorated a wheel for the last time, a front one just for a change! For the first time in days I was cold, so got back under the thin blanket and tried to get another hours kip but last day blues prevented that. Got up properly at 6.30am. Everything left hung outside is wet, towels, clothes, etcetera. Water boiled, woke the girls and served tea and coffee. The sun is coming up so I spread the wet stuff out to dry. Poached eggs on toast breakfast made and eaten in the camp kitchen. Ablutions done and back to the van. It, the fittings and utensils as ready as they are ever going to be for returning to the hire company. We're loaded and ready so hit the road at 10.00am. The sights on the way back in are oddly familiar and we're all in a strange mood, even the ipod road trip music anthems don't lift us.

On the outskirts of Perth we hit a traffic jam. Susie uses phone mapping because we need to find a shopping centre with a camping store. One located and here we purchase head wear mozzie nets and repellent sprays, essential for mine and Chris's visit to the Northern Territories. That done, guided by the satnav head for the Ibis Hotel near Perth City Airport. Arrive at about 2.00pm. Already booked online so just a matter of checking in. While at reception a taxi to the airport is confirmed for tomorrow morning. Fortunately we're allocated a family room on the ground floor. The three person arrangement being a double with a bunk bed over. Ibis International hotels are a failsafe. I'd used them before in Brazil, they give exactly what they describe. Here, free tea and coffee is also available in the lobby.

Baggage is bumped from van to the room, Chris would stay, Susie and I taking the van back into Perth City, me driving. It's Saturday, the Wicked Camper people wouldn't be on site this afternoon and they'd given us a gate entry code. There we parked the van, gave it one more wipe down and brush out, then locked it up and dropped the key into a metal letter box. We'd either be charged the cleaning fee or not, by now I didn't much care. Although I hoped they wouldn't notice the additional damage caused by the jumping tree in Kalbarri, which could theoretically end up costly.

Susie was clever enough to negotiate the bus routes back to the hotel and we're safely in the room by 4.00pm. It certainly wasn't a campsite and although no one would admit it, we were definitely down in mood. Susie predicted being back in a city would hit hard. It had! Chris drew a sad face in her diary.

Using the ipad for reference and Susie's cell phone, I was attempting to book a three day two night trip out of Alice Springs. I'd found two companies, the most likely to provide being called Emurun Tours. It could satisfy the desert destinations we hoped to visit, including the famous Ayer's Rock. I wouldn't know if I had been successful until early morning, a representative would call me as soon as confirmation was available.

Meanwhile Susie and Chris did more planning for our visit to the Islands of Fiji. Mine and Chris's entrance and exit flights for that trip were already booked.

There was to be no camp cooking tonight now that we were interim city dwellers. Having taken turns to use the bathroom facilities, me shaving my head as a bonus, we dressed, almost as civilians. I was back in a shirt and long trousers, albeit safari type. On the bus ride back to the hotel we'd seen some fast food restaurants dotted along the very wide and busy main road. The MacDonald's was chosen. In the glare of street lighting we trooped along and went into this fast food outlet. It has the most modern computer driven menu selection, push the buttons on screen, hey presto, orders made. We all ate a burger of some sort with a beverage of soft drink or coffee to finish.

Back at the hotel we tidied and part packed our bags. In what sockets were available, phones and ipad were charged overnight. All of us were in comfy beds and between clean sheets by 9.30pm.

Sunday 29th March. Day 45. Perth to Alice Springs. North West Territories. Qantas Flight QF1938. Dep. 12.25pm Arr. 4.35pm. 2,000km.

Woke at 6.00am. Had a reasonable night's sleep. We're in the hotel breakfast room helping ourselves to the buffet selection, when the first phone call from Patrick of Emu Run tours came at 7.30am. He took some of our personal details, gave us trip details and the probable address of our Alice Springs accommodation. A confirmation call awaited and that came at 8.40am. Sorted!

Taxi for three to Perth airport. Susie said we could have walked or bussed, my daughter has always been careful with money! She's now going back to Sydney. At departures we separated to obtain our respective boarding passes. Her flight was first and we said 'au revoir,' we'd meet there soon. Chris and I sat, had a coffee and checked email using the free wifi.

Having rearranged our baggage we went through the security procedures. As it's an internal flight, no customs desk. Aeroplane boarded, I was soon asleep. Lunch was served, afterwards I slept again while Chris either read her 'kindle' or listened to music. When awake I wrote my diary.

Landed on time. Not a big airport. Went outside, found and booked a shuttle bus. A short drive later we're dropped off at the Alice Motor Inn, 25 Undoolya Road. A fenced and gated property with a small planted courtyard. Nobody is about, the reception is closed and locked. Nearby we spot a box with a crocodile lid. In it is a key and note! We have a room, number thirteen. More motel than hotel. Very clean and has everything needed, including kettle and cups, so we made a brew. Knowing the Alice Springs exit date I immediately set about booking a flight and back packers hostel accommodation in Melbourne. Easier said than done because Microsoft has f***** me over again and it takes two hours to unblock my email. 'I hate these a******s!'

While having a cigarette outside I meet Kevin. From Eastbourne, recently widowed, seemed a nice bloke. He had the room next door, we chatted. He's on the mini-bus with us for the tour and actually knows tomorrow's pick-up time. We decided to walk in to town later as a group to get dinner. Chris and I showered and changed clothes. Dark now, at 6.00pm we three wandered about a kilometre down to the high street, found a decent pub, Todds Tavern and had a few beers with a good fish and chips meal. Talked all the while getting to know each other. Alice Springs looks a fairly quiet town but we'd been warned to be wary of Aborigines because many have issues with drink or drugs. They're not welcome in pubs and sometimes pester tourist to buy alcohol for them. We didn't come across this problem.

Back at our room, Chris and I selected what clothes and kit we needed for the trip and put it all into the canvas holdall. We'd take our small day bags, the back packs and top coats would stay in the room until our return. I charged all of the electronic devices overnight, the camera as a priority. In bed early 9.00pm, alarms set to 4.30am for tomorrow's 5.45am pick up.

Monday 30th March. Day 46. Alice Springs. Emu Run Tour day 1. Ayers Rock Sunset, overnight 'swag' camping.

Up at 4.00am. Chris made toast and coffee in the self-service complex kitchen. We sent a couple of Whatsapp messages home, letting folks know our condition and position. Dressed appropriately in safari shirts and trousers, we're collected at 5.50am. The mini-bus driver-cum-guide introduces himself as Eric. Tall chap, an ex-patriot Canadian about thirty years old. The vehicle is towing a large roof racked and sectioned closed trailer. Our holdall is loaded into it as others would be. He drives around Alice Springs making quite a few stops, collecting other tourists at various accommodation addresses, hotels, hostels and bed and breakfast types. One group aren't ready. Annoyingly we have to return to get them at the end of the pick-up run. Eventually extracted, a trio of bleary eyed Hong Kong Chinese, early twenties, two men and one woman, she pulling a wheeled pink hard shell suitcase case and dressed more for a night club visit than to the desert.

More people are collected at somewhere else I can't remember and the last few at the airport. Eric now having a full complement of passengers started the 450 kilometre drive to Ayers Rock. He uses the on board microphone to further introduce himself and explain the tour itinerary. Complimentary breakfast snacks are handed out. It's a long way, an all desert landscape, reddish brown, mostly flat with scrawny thin trees and twiggy bushes. Apart from some toilet breaks and photo opportunity stops, very dull but I managed to get some sleep.

Other than us, Kevin and the Chinese group, the group consisted of several more nationalities. I only remember some, mainly those who made an impression. In no particular order, Mr & Mrs Canada, age late forties, he knew everything and his wife took charge in the kitchens! Mr & Mrs Spain, nice couple, late thirties with son of about nine years old. I had my photograph taken with the lad, him being the youngest, me the oldest. Mr and Mrs Sri Lanka, early fifties, him a writer, her a teacher, lastly, Mr and Mrs France mid-thirties.

We drove quite a distance in the Uluru National park before pulling into a gated and fenced campsite at about 11.30am. Here are many buildings, mostly cabin type but also brick built toilet and shower blocks. We're parked in a sub-divided area of the site, a compound for the particular use of EmuRun Tours. Other similar plots are being used by different companies and organisations.

All out of the van and Eric started to organise us. He unlocked the doors to a roofed, wood built unit, the walls such as they are being framed wire mesh insect screen. Inside are sinks, cooking griddle, kettles, pots and pans and general paraphernalia for meal preparation. Stretching almost full length of the hut are two large wood refectory tables with fixed bench seats on both sides. All bags are taken from the trailer and placed on one. We're all then instructed to pass the parcel with the 'Swags,' these probably rolled and strapped by the last users are stowed in the trailer's roof. Eric passed them down, us 'campers' bumped them into a small lockable shed near to the big hut but within the small compound.

A large 'eski', a polystyrene cool box was brought in from the trailer. This contained plastic dishes, bowls, plates, cutlery and all the food stuffs to make lunch. Eric grilled burgers, bread rolls and salad were prepped by volunteers. Jars of relish were placed on tables. Coffee and tea was available on a do it yourself basis. Chris and I sat opposite Mr and Mrs Sri Lanka, her opening gambit "have you tried the sweet chili sauce?" Hard to answer, as my attention had been drawn by the noise made as the Chinese sucked their burgers. Do they ever chew?

Lunch over, volunteering hands did the washing up and packing away. With everybody's gear left in the hut, we all board the wagon, get out of camp and back on the road. Next stop the Uluru Cultural Centre. A purposely architecturally designed and built place. A walk through experience, every single exhibit and display dedicated to Aboriginal culture, history and tradition. This whole area is now under the administration of the senior and better educated ranks of these indigenous people. The land recently repatriated by the modern Australian government, its guilt of previous year's treatment seemingly unending. As an outsider and having been to other museums which also expounded this unfairness I found it difficult to comprehend. In the seventeenth century many other of the world's continents were being explored, even ravaged, at the same time as Australasia. The aborigines, as found were a stone-age race of people, slow to adapt and probably were exploited, but if they thought it had been tough in the coming years' maybe they should take a look at the history of the Americas.

It's of course, very, very hot. Eric forcefully impresses the need to drink many litres of water. In the back of the bus is a big plastic drum of the liquid. He wasn't happy that the old orange juice bottle I was carrying only had a 300 millilitre capacity. I explained quite honestly that I knew my needs and had done for a long time. If I drink two litres of liquid, I pee the same amount. I rarely perspire, even when playing sports and need only a few sips of water to replenish. I wasn't sure that he actually understood.

Eric drove us around the rock, parking, then we walk at various points of interest. He reeled off lots about aborigine history and myth. It's a once seen and done experience with lots of pictures taken. Our head fly nets

160

came in very useful. Only so many of these insects can be swallowed, inhaled, wiped from eyes and extracted from nostrils. Flies target the head because they are after liquids, water, sweat, saliva, they'll take what they can get. Afterwards we drove to a parking-cum-view point and along with hundreds of others watched the 'magical' sunset and enjoyed cheese and biscuits accompanied with sparkling wine served in plastic cups.

Night time, back at the campsite. There are dim lights on lampposts marking walkways. The refreshments hut is opened. The swags are extracted from the shed and laid out on the ground in the compound. Eric explained the basics. It looks like a body bag, a thin padded ground sheet with a stitched polyvinyl top cover with zipped sides. Inside is a removable sleeping bag of standard design. I'd seen them used on other campsites but with hoods offering total enclosure. The type here were open at the head end. Chris and I mused about sleeping out on the open ground, 'this should be interesting.' It had been a very sweaty, tiring day, we walked to the bathrooms and showered. I hung our towels and our rinsed underclothes on the shed walls to dry overnight.

By now Eric, driver, guide and chef, had started to prepare supper! Chicken stir fry. Some willing hands pitched in to help, there were quite a few happy to avoid. It was a bit of a bun fight getting somewhere to sit. It's amazing how in such a short time little cliques start to form, those who did nothing sat at the bench table chatting, while those that helped had to squeeze in where possible.

While sat at the long table Eric suggested that everyone should introduce themselves, giving names and a short profile, who, where from, what age etcetera. What you didn't find about the other passengers now there was no knowing unless a personal conversation was struck. In three days with one almost over there wasn't going to be enough time to develop long term friendships.

Grub finished, washing up packing away being done, it's easy to spot the worst shirkers. The Hong Kong Chinese group, busy with iphones. At about 8.00pm Chris and I wrote our diaries. Needing to be on the road by 5.30am to see the sun rise at Uluru, Ayers Rock, Eric announced a 4.00am start.

9.00pm, the swags had been laid out in a sort of circular fashion. If anybody had any dignity left, they'd soon lose it in the compound. Dressing or not for bedding down was here and now. It's still hot, underclothes seemed the best idea and making sure drinking water was close by if needed. My day bag used as a pillow I slid into the sleeping bag already inserted in the swag. Zips were being pulled up all round. Next to me, Chris did what was necessary for her own comfort, bra discarded at least, no babying here. Kevin was close as well. The dumpy git laid on his back and asleep within minutes, snoring, keeping me awake for ages. I got up for a p*** and went behind the same shed I'd hung our washing. On the way back I clipped his swag with my foot. People don't snore when they're awake! Call me a mean b*****d, I don't care, I'd slept in dormitories during all male fishing trips and knew the rules. Although hot and uncomfortable I did drift in and out of sleep, when awake looking at the stars in the night sky. Chris noted 'they were absolutely fantastic, not only bright and big, seeming so low that you could reach up and touch them.' Clear cut thoughts, we hadn't even had a beer. The site was dry due to the proximity of Aborigines.

Tuesday 31st March. Day 47. EmuRun Tour day 2. Ayers Rock sunrise.

Woke at 4.20am. It was still dark. Others were stirring, some still asleep but it wasn't long before everyone was up and about, busily rolling and strapping the swags. Responsibilities took a natural unordered role, mainly males piled the swags into the shed. Females were setting out the kitchen area, kettles boiling water, sliced bread thrown in toasters. Breakfast was going to be a snatched affair at best. Selfish it may seem, my priorities as always, coffee, cigarettes and a bathroom visit. Chris had to do her own thing!

Mini-bus seats filled, we're out of camp at 5.30am. A short drive to join the many parked buses, coaches and hundreds of people at the viewing platforms, all here to see the sunrise at Uluru. It was in fact a special sight and I took some pictures for the album.

From here it was onto the 'Domes' at Keta Tjuta, another but more spectacular rock formation. The walk around and through was about 7 kilometres, the sun high in the sky and temperature hot. From here back to camp to make and have lunch. All this achieved by 12.30pm. It seemed a rush because it was. The hut was cleared up, locked, trailer loaded and off we went again. Intended destination a campsite near King's Canyon. We'd driven for a while then the wagon was pulled in at a service station. Eric refuelled while some folks picked up snacks and drinks in the shop. Some like me got a few cans of beer to enjoy tonight, these were placed in the eski.

On we went, quite a few kilometres in fact, but it quickly became apparent that Eric was struggling. Better put, the van engine wasn't running very well and losing power. Fortunately it remained drivable, although poorly, to reach a place named Curtain Springs Station.

These fairly isolated outback farmsteads are all called 'Stations,' a throw-back to early pioneering days. This one had been long established, family owned for many years. Now a small village comprising fuel pumps, limited garage mechanic facilities, shop, restaurant, bird breeding, overnight parking with toilet and shower block and so on.

Eric pulled the van up and did the macho man bit by crawling under it trying to find the problem. Unfortunately he didn't have a clue. We weren't going anywhere. After many years in the motor trade I had an opinion and was forthright in giving it. An obvious a fuel problem, starvation, dirty or similar. Kevin chipped in. At the last stop, from the bus window he'd watched Eric fill the van with petrol! Eric was taken aback, his face drained, white as a sheet. The vehicle was diesel powered. While he searched for the pump receipt I popped the filler cap, a gentle sniff confirmed. The document became academic proof.

By now most of the other passengers had used the toilet facilities, found their way into the shop and were indulging in snacks, drinks or both. Only me, Kevin and Eric remained with the mini-bus. I put out a suggestion. If we could borrow a length of tube the tank could be easily syphoned, emptied of petrol then any residue diluted by fully topping up with diesel. It's been done a thousand times but Eric would have none of it and started making phone calls. What happened next would be an 'office' decision. I'd said my 'piece.' In my head a couple of words floated around, like 'wanker' and 'bottle-less tosser.' It wasn't my problem anyway!

A couple of hours passed. As a group we made small talk while sitting in the shade of the restaurant canopy. Eric made and received more phone calls. The upshot, await a replacement bus, sounds easy but Alice Springs is at least three hours distant. By 4.30pm I'd retrieved the beers from the eski and shared them with Chris, written my diary and had also dished out some gentle stick to Eric. I was now buying fresh beers in the station shop. Worse than anything that could be possible they didn't have cigarettes and I was down to about six, so gave them to Chris for rationing!

Eric had been force fed instructions from the company's office. It had been arranged that supper would be prepared and taken at the station. It having an outside benched seated eating area with gas fired cooking griddles along with so many other marvels. The chaps carried the cool boxes to this area as the females generally organised. At the same time, about 6.00pm, its trailer unhitched and left in the car park the broken van was pulled onto a breakdown truck. Eric took charge of cooking kangaroo steaks, sausages and chips. Bowls of salad, breads, potato chips and sauces were passed around. We ate well.

The substitute mini-bus arrived sometime after 7.30pm, just as we were clearing up. Trailer hitched, kit loaded and passengers boarded. Eric now had the responsibility of a night drive to Kings Station. Total darkness only pierced by the van headlights. At one point he hit the brakes very hard, some horses had just wandered from the verge straight into the path of the wagon. A very near miss!

Approximately 9.30pm. Arrived unscathed at the station camp, this with similar facilities to the one used in Uluru. Eric parked in the company's section of the compound. Another screened walled hut was opened and the box of utensils, plates etcetera were brought from the van to be washed up. Swags were dropped to the ground from the trailer roof rack. Tonight though, we'd be using them inside permanently fixed tents. There are plenty of these in rows near and at the back of the hut, so no sharing necessary. I picked up two swags and our holdall then put them onto the wood floor of the nearest tent available. Then we went and did our bit for the team, wiping up and packing away. Dirty water was drained into slurry containers, these had to be emptied on the ground away from the hut. I did this with one other chap. Meanwhile the Chinese busied themselves getting cables plugged in to charge their heavily used iphones. I boiled water and made me and Chris a coffee.

In the tent Chris and I searched for our head torches, found them and hitched one to a post just inside the door flap. The other being used in hand while laying out the swags and sleeping bags. Who'd used these last night or the days before was anybody's guess. A 5.00am start is agreed for the morning so no time for showers. For us it was teeth cleaning only. Into the swags at 10.30pm.

I noted in my diary, 'Tonight should have been the camp bonfire party. Not to be but still a cracking day of improvised entertainment.'

Wednesday 1st April. Day 48. EmuRun Tour day 3. King's Canyon to Alice Springs.

Chris and I got up at 5.00am, we'd had a fairly rough night. I didn't go to sleep until past 11.00pm because the Chinese group had been chit chatting loudly in the kitchen hut. I rolled and strapped the swags. We packed the holdall and day bags. Breakfast and coffee was taken in the hut. Van and trailer loaded and by 6.00am we're on the way to the valley of Kings Canyon for the 'rim walk.' About three hours and 6 to 7 kilometres.

Arrived at a carpark at 6.30am. All out the van and gathered around Eric. He pointed out the walkway up to the top, an unmade path of rock and clay, it's very steep and known locally as 'heart attack hill.' The question about water surfaced yet again, I reaffirmed that what I carried would be more than enough. To prove the point, Chris and I made short work of the hill climb even though it was a near seventy five degree incline in some places!

Mr and Mrs Sri Lanka were last to the top, already suffering from swollen feet and ankles, she did really well.

There were several groups with guides already up here. Etiquette dictated that a sensible gap be kept between each so that all could enjoy the sights and take photographs at specific viewpoints. Eric led the way, indicating this and that as the scenes of an almost out of this world prehistoric landscape unfolded before our eyes. Deep gorges, sheer rock faces that in places were leaning perilously out of vertical. Fly catching birds came out of holes made by weather and wind. Down in the gorge we visited the Garden of Eden, a pool sized water hole surrounded by tropical trees. Definitely a land that time forgot. Our insect head nets were on and off as required. Of the three places visited, this the last, was definitely the most spectacular.

Walking down to the parked van is a gentler affair although care is still needed, a turned ankle here could prove disastrous. I had drunk only a few mouthfuls of water and had to pee three times during the walk. Proof positive of my theory!

All safely in the bus we left the carpark. Drove a while and then stopped at 'Ebeneezer's Road House.' I bought cigarettes for me and coffee for both of us.

On the way back towards Alice Springs Eric made a fuel stop, several of us closely double checked that he selected the correct pump! We said goodbye to a few people as they were dropped off at various places on the way into and around town, to the rest when we arrived at the Motor Inn.

After arranging to visit the pub later with Kevin, we had well needed showers then part packed. Did some picture transfers to the ipad and posted a few notes with photos to Facebook. In town I shared fish and chips with Chris, nice, but better was the four pints of lager. Back to the Inn, very tired, 10.30pm to bed.

Thursday 2nd April. Day 49. Alice Springs to Melbourne, via Adelaide. Virgin Airways VA1740 Dep. 10.05am. Arr. 4.55pm. 2,225km.

Both up at 6.30am, made coffee in the room, ablutions done, then had breakfast in the kitchen. Checked into today's flight online. Noted that my email account is again blocked but I have to move on from that. It's a travel day with targets to be met. Shared a taxi with Kevin to the airport. Through security, got boarding passes then some coffee. Just enough time to drink that, have a handshake and say a quick goodbye to Kev. We boarded the plane. I checked that my Gmail account is working and decide I will have to use that if Microsoft keep f*****g me over.

Arrived Adelaide, clocks are forward an hour. While in the lounge I seem to have sorted Outlook. Got a phone text giving a code to access my email account, I'm still p****d off though. The second leg of the flight is a fifty five minute wait and I make a silly mistake!

Although I'd been using a nicotine inhaler my tobacco craving got the better of me and I decided to exit the building for a smoke. Stupidly, instead of dropping my backpack, day bag and leaving them with Chris. I walked to one of the auto exit doors carrying them. No sooner than had I stepped forward and the doors opened I realised my foolishness. They hadn't even closed as I tried to spin on one foot to stay inside but was spotted by a guard, pulled to security and made to run my bags through scanning. The she wolf SS officer found and confiscated my tiny watch maker screwdrivers! What an idiot I'd been. Chris agreed wholeheartedly when I related the sorry tale.

Anyway, routine restored and the next flight made we arrived in Melbourne at 4.00pm. Clocks forward another hour, so now 5.00pm. Outside the building I smoked a couple of cigarettes then found a shuttle-bus.

One hour later, $50 poorer we were in St Kilda and outside the Oslo Hotel, 38 Grey Street. First impressions an old colonial era hotel or private house. I couldn't tell. The first and second floors at the front aspect have full length balconies, vertically panelled with a handrail at waist height. I imagined that this had been grand place at one time, now it looked sad. I'd already booked so we had to take it as found. Inside at reception, (actually a hole in a wall similar to a dining room serving hatch), next to a locked door, a strange bloke with a pseudo French accent dealt with our checking in. It's a pay up front job. So I did, for the key deposit and a basic three nights with a proviso that we could extend. I couldn't help seeing into the 'office.' It was like a junk shop, kettles, fans, pillows, umbrellas and all sorts of paperwork strewn everywhere. There are plenty of 'do this' and 'don't do' notices pinned or sticky taped to grimy walls. The few young folk in the area were either stretched out on old sofas watching television or using laptops. We hadn't attracted such strange looks since India. Was it because we were old enough to be their grandparents?

I noted in my diary, 'What a slum, a backpacker's pigsty but we'll make the best of it.' I found out later that Susie had stayed here back in June 2014!

We'd explore the kitchen later. So having been given a key and directions to our first floor room went up the furry, fluffy carpeted staircase and found it at the end of a corridor. A communal bathroom is directly opposite our door. The room is large. French doors opened onto the balcony, furnishings, chairs, table and wardrobes are vintage and very tired. There's a fridge, microwave oven and kettle. The bed had old tatty blankets and pink sheets. We'd use our blow up cushions to bulk the pillows and cover the cases with our own towels.

Left our padlocked baggage and went out, just down the road to a British themed pub, the Elephant and Wheelbarrow. Drank beer, ate a meal and talked. We're both tired but need to get things into perspective. In a new place and fresh situation. Discussions about what's been, seen and done can wait. We're in a city, a big one, fresh priorities are forefront. Left the pub and went to a local supermarket, shopped for tomorrow's lunch and breakfast items. Bought plastic cups and other odds and ends. Being realistic is actually horrid so we went and had another beer before going back to the Oslo! In the room, checked the web and made coffee. After being in the high temperatures of the Northern Territories we were both cold. With absolutely nothing planned for tomorrow, went to bed at 11.30pm.

Friday 3rd April. Day 50. Melbourne. St Kilda Beach, Port Philip Bay, Albert Park Lake.

Got up for a toilet visit about 8.00am. It wasn't the best bed in the world but I got back in. Almost three weeks of travelling had taken a physical toll. Both needing rest we dozed for a time, surfacing properly at 10.30am. It wasn't quite as cold as last night. Showered in the communal bathroom, each taking turns as security. In the room, boiled water for coffee and micro waved 'choc au pan' as breakfast. We had a lot to talk about, unfinished discussions from last night. It was just me and Chris, "me and you, you and me," often quoted when vital decisions had to be made. There were a couple to be sorted and quickly. The Oslo is certainly far from ideal accommodation, just being in the room standing on the stained carpets is a stark reminder. Should we stay or should we go? The price met our loose budget terms, that same cost got us five star hotels in India but we're here and now, Melbourne with Australian prices.

The weather brightened, we dressed, consulted a basic tourist map and decided to go for a walk to explore the local area and make decisions with clear heads. About midday went down stairs and inspected the hostel kitchen. Should we utilise it? The grime made our minds up in a micro-second. Not!

Left the building heading toward Port Philip Bay, St Kilda Beach and its pier. Wandered for several hours, looping around Albert Park and Lake. Calculating our normal walking pace of four kilometres per hour we'd probably exceeded ten. Not exactly the relaxing day needed but by the time we arrived at the 'English Pub' all vital decisions had been made. Neither of us would 'bottle it.' We'd agreed before leaving England to take the rough with the smooth, anywhere, anytime. Very proud of my missus today!

So regardless of it being s***hole we'd remain at the Oslo, arrange an exit flight to Sydney and extend our stay to that day minus one! I'd find an 'Ibis' Hotel, book a room and we'd overnight in comfort before flying out of Melbourne. Sorted!

Back to the hostel, through the clanking iron panelled gate picking our way to the door through the bottles, cans

171

and fag ends in the forecourt. Late afternoon. In our room I did Skyscanner and Booking.com searches. Paid for a flight to Sydney and booked another back packer's hostel for the 7th of April. We took a couple of hours sleep and woke early evening. It was cold again. I went down to reception, a different bloke was at the 'hole' in the wall. I paid for the extra nights required. He gave me a pair of 'Myki' cash top up cards for use on the city's public transport system.

The weather here is hot during the day, cold and windy at night, so dressed in fleeces and top coats we went to the pub. It was well populated with a two man band playing. We had fish and chips for dinner with a couple of pints. Talked, double checking and qualifying our plans. I was as happy as I could be, exit and entrance strategy done and should relax. While getting beers I noticed a poster advertising an AFL game at the Melbourne Cricket Ground, so asked the barman if tickets were difficult to obtain. He said it was easy, pay at the gate. I suggested to Chris that going to the match would be a good idea and a reason for visiting the city centre. She agreed.

About 10.30pm. The end of Good Friday. We walked back to the Oslo. Nearby are several pubs and a couple of other hostels. People are milling, chatting and drinking at the entrances. The smell of cannabis strong in the air. Back at the room we readied for bed.

In Perth, Susie had warned me that after the road trip, then being in the outback with its wide open spaces and fresh air I would find it hard to adapt being back in the city, any city. How right she was!

Saturday 4th April. Day 51. Melbourne, AFL at MGC, Eureka Viewing Tower.

We didn't get out of bed until 10.00am. I felt as if I'd wasted some hours. While Chris made coffee I told her that I got up during the small hours, had a smoke on the balcony and in the semi darkness I'd watched a couple of men climb the garden compound fence in front of the ground floor male dormitory. They searched the ashtrays for doped cigarette butts then checked cans and bottles for any remaining drink. I watched them leave, same method. It's a sick place in a sick area!

We ate croissants for breakfast and confirmed to each other that going to the AFL game wasn't just last night's beer talking! By the time we'd showered and not knowing kick off time or how long it took to get into the city, a bit of a panic ensued. Left the hostel about 11.30am still having to find a local 7-11 store to top up the Myki cards. Shop found, cards loaded, we got on a tram headed for Finders Street Station. A sort of interchange for road and rail services. To get to the MCG it was easier to follow the crowd. While walking we talked with a father and his young son. The dad informed us that this was the first game of the season. His home side hadn't won one of these in ten years.

Continuing through the landscaped park we arrived at the internationally acclaimed stadium. What a place. We'd heard about it, seen it on TV and here we are for Melbourne Demons versus Gold Coast Suns! Outside the ground it's a family day out, very friendly with both side's colourfully shirted fans mingling. I had my picture taken with some away supporters.

Inside and before the main event. On the full sized cricket pitch, lots of mini goal posts had been set up and children played a non-contact version of the real game. Both sets of supporters sang their respective team songs, naff but amusing. Obviously Chris and I had heard of AFL, even seen clips on TV. Although 'Association' football fans we were looking forward to seeing a live contest for the first time. We certainly weren't disappointed. The basic rules are easy to follow and tactics can be understood. Athletic, very muscular players in skimpy shorts and tight singlets fully commit in both tackle and running. During half time, at a superbly

173

organised food outlet I bought beers and the famous 'beef pie' with chips.

I'd previously had the temerity to dismiss this sport. Here we'd been thoroughly entertained. After the game, which the Demons actually won, I promised never to be dismissive again!

Left the stadium at about 4.00pm. Before walking back to the city centre, checked the tourist map and noted an interesting place advertised. The 'Eureka Tower,' famed for its high level observation platform. With time to spare we decided to visit. The tallest skyscraper in town, tickets cost $27Aud. A superfast elevator took us to the glass enclosed viewing storey. Truth had been told, the vistas are fantastic.

Daylight fading, evening is fast arriving. I was pleased we'd achieved so much here on only our second day. Took a tram ride back to St Kilda. Shopped for beer and food stuffs. Went back to the hostel, showered and dressed, ready to go for dinner.

Saturday night, it's busy but still manage to get a table at what had become our local pub. Had a meal, a couple of beers and discussed what to do tomorrow. Back at the hostel readied for bed. Clocks back an hour tonight. Daylight saving even takes place here in Australia.

Sunday 5th April Day 52. Melbourne, Victoria WW1 Shrine and Museum, St. Pauls Cathedral and the Docklands Development.

Surfaced about 9.30am. Coffee and microwaved croissants for breakfast. Chris made up some sandwiches. Online, I booked a room for tomorrow night at the Ibis in the CBD (City and Business District). Financially the extra cost of staying there is balanced by cheaper transfer costs to the airport. While on the internet, I posted a few pictures and messages to Facebook.

Took the number 16 tram to Finders Street but got off the stop nearest the Victoria State Shrine of Remembrance.

174

Situated atop a small hill, a beautiful deco period building serves as a memorial to those who gave their lives in war. We explored the basement which has a wonderful informative military exhibition of wartime artefacts. Afterwards and with other visitors attended a short service conducted by a uniformed Army veteran. It's called 'The Ceremony of the Sun on Love.' Very emotional. The finale, a shaft of light falls upon a plinth carved with the phrase 'Greater Love Hath No man.' This represents the sacrifice of human life for the sake of Australia and the World.

Events such as these help put any problems that have or may occur into a sensible perspective.

Chris and I sat in the quiet landscaped grounds, talked out our thoughts and ate sandwiches for lunch. Afterwards got back on a 16 tram, its route should take us close to the Ibis Hotel. We got off one stop too far, walked back a little and found it. Makes it easy to do tomorrow. A quick look at the map and head for the main streets near Federation Square. All of the roads leading to it are full of shops and even on an Easter Sunday many are open. In one, a camera-cum-electronics store, I found a little device that transferred data from a memory card direct to an ipad. I wanted one! Especially if it alleviated the aggro I've been through using a wireless transfer method. At only $10 it was cheap but I wasn't sure, so didn't commit.

The doors of St Pauls Cathedral were open, we popped in for me to have a quick word. An Oriental Priest was giving his take on Easter as a sermon to the few folks in the pews.

Many trams here are vintage and free to use around the city centre. We took one to the Docklands. A very modern, shiny development but with many empty units. The sky was grey, the wind blowing cold so after a wander got on another old tram and went back to Flinders Street. Next door to the station bought coffee in a café. A weird place doubling up as a betting shop, also has slot machines and even sells beer. Australia!

Tarried for a while in the square. Street artists, jugglers, comedic magicians were entertaining people, tourists and locals. Dark by 5.30pm. We left. Back at the Oslo by 6.30pm. In the room, drank a few beers and wrote our diaries. The timed light switches in the communal bathroom proved a nuisance, especially if using the toilet. We had to have our torches handy! To round off a pleasant Sunday we treated ourselves to beef and lamb roast dinners at the pub. About 10.00pm, took to bed for our last night in the Oslo.

Monday 6th April Day 53 Melbourne, move to the Ibis Hotel.

8.30am, coffee and breakfast then started packing. Last night I posted a scathing revue of the Oslo to my tripadvisor account. Now as house rules required, stripped the bed of linen such as it was ready to take to reception. Shouldered our bags. Dumped the bedding next to the hole in the wall, got our key deposit back and checked out.

Took a tram to the modern Ibis Hotel, 15/21 Therry Street. CBD. A kind receptionist allowed us to check in early to a lovely room. We both showered. Chris volunteered to do some laundry, so I located the floor with the coin slot washing and drying machines.

1.45pm and we're not sure what do for the rest of the day. Checked into tomorrow's flight online then had a nap. Chris was ironing when I woke. She'd done well and noted in her diary 'it was nice to have clean, pressed clothes.' We repacked our bags then made coffee. I love the Ibis!

4.00pm went out, although knowing it will be dark soon. We're local to the street market area, University buildings and student accommodation. The North Melbourne district seems very oriental, lots of Chinese and Korean folks. With fast food restaurants catering for that type of clientele. We walked and shopped, bought some tinned lagers then found the camera shop. I couldn't resist and bought the connector. Back at the hotel, used it to

176

upload some photographs, so easy, I'm very happy. It's the simple things in life!

There's a Bistro in the basement of the hotel. We went in for burger and chips. A good wifi connection here so Skyped and talked face to face with Angela, our eldest daughter. In the warm room, before going to bed between clean sheets, we had coffee and watched the TV round up of today's AFL games. I'm a fan now!

Tuesday 7th April. Day 54. Melbourne to Sydney. Virgin Airways VA845 Dep 1.00pm. Arr. 2.25pm. 900km.

7.30am, woke with bad belly ache and stomach cramps. Chris had similar symptoms during the night. Dodgy burger, dirty glass, who knew? Amazing! Travelled for so long and neither of us had experienced any food related problems and didn't expect this surprise. Managed to eat some buffet fried breakfast then wished I hadn't. Smoked just one cigarette before the first of several uncomfortable bathroom visits.

By 9.45am, packed and checked out. Used two buses getting to the airport. Usual routine once there. Sat in the lounge waiting for the flight, needed to eat and drink so bought coffee and steak pies.

In Sydney, we'd be meeting up with Susie and were looking forward to that.

The flight only took an hour and a half, I slept for most of it. Shared an Airbus shuttle from the airport, $15Aud each and were dropped off outside the hostel. Sydney Central Inn, 428 Pitt Street. An old building. Entrance lobby is a small ground floor space with desk, tourist leaflet stands and stairs at the back wall. Neighbouring is a large pub-cum-nightclub. After the Oslo experience I was wary, asked questions of the Thai girl receptionist, requesting to see the facilities and room. These are reached by the classy old original stair case and on the first and second floors that span over the bar next door.

177

Our billet looked fine, a shared kitchen and bathroom on the same landing and in good order so I paid for a three night stay. We were given clean towels, free of charge, unusual for a hostel. A nice touch.

Didn't hang about, it's still daylight. Went out not only to explore the local streets but find a supermarket to shop for food and drink. Checked out a pub as a possible to get tonight's dinner. It's very cold and windy. The area is similar to the one we'd just left in Melbourne, tall buildings, offices and some residential. At pavement level mostly oriental small fast food outlets and shops. The roads are very busy with traffic. Night had arrived by the time we'd dropped the shopping back in the room. Back out, up the road and found the pub. Far from busy, we had a couple of beers and meals of chicken parma. I was still getting belly pains, I'd had them on and off all day and hoped they'd be gone tomorrow. Beer cures everything! Later, in the room, sent Susie some messages, studied maps, leaflets and planned tomorrow's sightseeing. Very tired we hit the sheets at 10.00pm.

Wednesday 8th April. Day 55. Sydney Harbour.

Got up fairly late, after 10.00am. The bed had been comfortable. We'd obviously needed the rest. Across the hallway in the kitchen, Chris made coffee and toast with marmalade. Last night I'd researched the 'Blue Mountains' and had decided to move there for a three day break. As travel manager I announced my intentions to a very surprised wife during breakfast. She'd have some of this evening to read about the trip! So before sightseeing our first job today would be ascertaining train schedules to and from Katoomba, which is some eighty kilometres west of this city.

Chris made some sandwiches to take with us then we walked down the hill to Sydney Central Railway Station. A fellow in one of the ticket booths was very helpful. Travel arrangements established we then made a long walk north, heading for Sydney Harbour. Through Hyde Park, past the Anzac memorial and all the way to the Opera House. We strolled around this famous building and the sea walls while taking in the magnificent views of the bay and bridge. The weather overcast, windy and threatening rain but we still took touristy photographs! From here we went into the Botanic Gardens. Paths led us to Mrs Macquarie's Chair, a sandstone feature on one of the shoreline peninsulas. Headed back to the city centre. Took a look inside St Mary's Cathedral, it would have been rude not to. Skirted Hyde Park using main roads and made it back to the hostel about 6.00pm.

I did a little more research about touring in the Blue Mountains. While online I found a hotel that would suit us, so booked it.

A lot to talk about when we met Susie later tonight. We'd been having discrete text message conversations. Its Chris's 60th birthday on the 14th April and we're planning a special day. I hoped to get a few minutes of private conversation tonight.

Met at about 9.00pm outside a pub called the Albert Hotel near the railway station. It had to be somewhere mutual, Susie's still living and working in the city and would need to get home at a sensible time. Faris was with her. In England he'd been a long term boyfriend, now an 'ex' but they are still very good friends. Everyone needs them.

Inside the pub was very loud, more with raised voices than music. After ordering food and drinks we did our best trying to have a four way conversation in the noise. It was great to meet up. The upshot, Susie and I agreed a 'Sydney Harbour Bridge walk' as the birthday highlight. I was also informed that as a gift, Angela is to pay for me and Chris to have a three night stay in a posh hotel. Also agreed with Susie was that some of our time in Fiji would be at a 'homestay.' Lots sorted in a very short time and we'd had a beer or two!

As couples we parted company at the railway station. Chris and I walked back through a badly lit little park close to the bottom of Pitt Street. Here the people that couldn't afford a hostel were dossing in tents. They'd be cold tonight.

Thursday 9th April. Day 56. Sydney.

Didn't get up till 9.30am. I'm very tired, it must be the weather and distances we're walking. We both had showers after breakfast. I made more efforts trying to link Hotmail to Gmail, only time will tell if I have been successful. I must admit that having been so angry and frustrated with my email account I would have willingly got on a plane to California, burned down the Microsoft offices and inflicted physical damage on Bill Gates.

At 1.00pm we left the hostel. Yesterday while walking we'd picked two sites that deserved proper visits. First, the Anzac Memorial. Another beautiful 1930's building. It must be our age, Chris and I are emotionally drawn to such places. 'Lest we forget,' the lives sacrificed giving us and others the opportunity to do what we do now. Stayed quite a time and bought poppies as we left.

Next the city's Natural History Museum. Old people get concession prices, we must have been lucky, didn't even have to show Chris's passport! A fantastic place with so many brilliant exhibits. Spent too long here and at about 4.00pm bought coffee in the roof top restaurant, great views over the city. Naughtily we ate our own sandwiches.

Trailed our way back through the city streets to the hostel. On the walk, bought a couple of microwavable meals. Back in our room, listened to music, made plans, drank some tinned lager, ate 'shepherd's pie' and reflected on the day. Another good one.

Friday 10th April. Day 57. Sydney to Katoomba. 102km.

Up at 7.30am. Ablutions done, breakfast eaten, sandwiches made and bags packed by 8.15am. Checking out is 'leave the room key in a box' at the unattended reception. Back packs on and make a fifteen minute walk to the station. Tickets bought and at 9.18am we're heading out of the city sat in a wide train carriage with a double deck of seats. It makes lots of stops. We enjoy the views from the windows, little townships and homesteads.

Arrived in Katoomba at 11.30am. The weather bright but cool. Walk up a ramp to get out of the station and see the town for the first time. Not very big and on a hill. The main street is quite busy with people and vehicles. Using written directions taken from the internet, we walk fully laden, downhill to a valley road. On a junction is the Clarendon Guesthouse, 68 Lurline Street, 2780. Chinese family owned and managed. The building is quite old, probably 1920's, reception and lobby area walls are covered in old posters and adverts for musical acts that probably performed here in times gone by. We're too early to be allocated a room but are allowed to leave our bags in a large room that was once a restaurant.

Katoomba, normal residential population two thousand, swollen on any given day to seven thousand people, mainly tourists and here they are well looked after. Getting to, from and around the sites and viewing points in the Blue Mountains is best done by bus. The most popular company uses double deck London style. $35Aud per person, including a sixty years of age discount, buys a booklet map which also serves as a three day ticket. This entitles a holder to hop on or off at any of the indicated stops. The buses run a looping route and are guaranteed to be at any one stop at thirty minute intervals. Brilliant!

So it's just after midday and one of these stops is just outside the hotel. Day bags with us, top coats on, we catch a bus and buy tickets. The driver is very chatty and informative, he knows his job well. We find they all do. Each new passenger is questioned politely and then introduced by country of origin to those already on board.

We intended only to travel the looping route as a test drive but got off at 'stop one,' access to Katoomba Falls. From the driver's commentary we already know that 'katoomba' is an aborigine word meaning 'tumbling water' and that the Blue Mountains are so called because of the haze of sap rising from acres of Eucalyptus trees.

On foot, we're at the edge of the heavily forested mountain range and start our first hike using tracks dotted with old sign posts, the poker seared lettering barely readable. Steps and paths, broken, solid, wet, dry and overgrown in places! What more could we want?

After nearly four hours of trekking, getting on and off of buses, following the guide map and trail signs, we'd visited The Falls, Echo Point, Honeymoon Lookout and Leura Cascades, had been up and down the gorge, above and below spectacular waterfalls, traversed rock pools, stood on the sheer edges of cliffs, ducked and dodged branches in woodland so thick that the sky couldn't be seen and even spotted a Lyre bird! We'd experienced a whole gamut of weather, sunshine, drizzle, a downpour of rain and our coats had been on and off. We'd been amazed and overawed. Now we were definitely tired.

4.30pm, back at the guest house. Reached by a wide creaking staircase our second floor room was ready. Clean and compact, single beds with electric blankets, a corner sink, dressing table, kettle and cups. Just down the hallway a shared fridge, further along is a bathroom and toilet. Ideal, nothing more needed.

5.00pm. Walked up hill into town. Found a supermarket and liquor store, bought lunch foods and beers.

Earlier I'd explored the public areas of the hotel. There are many not in use. A large basement with dance floor and stage, now just storage, a games room in the same condition. This must have been the place be to be in days gone by, lively with entertainment.

Knowing that the restaurant or bar aren't in service, where to go for dinner? Asking at reception we're told that the 'Club' just down the road would welcome us. There we'd find out why the demise of services in *this* guest house became inevitable. We showered, dressed, listened to music, had a beer and readied to go out.

Dark, cold and damp when we left the hotel. A hundred metres down the road, past a big carpark is a modern complex of brightly lit modern buildings. On a plinth close to the main entrance an old artillery piece dripped with rainwater. In the reception area, a smiling official welcomed us and issued temporary free memberships to the RSL Club, (Returning Service League), an Australian equivalent of the British Legion. Just inside there's a slim glass fronted wall cabinet with a display of militaria. Letters, books, badges, a couple of bayonets etcetera. Mainly items from the Southeast Asia campaigns of World War Two.

More of the place came into view. A modern open plan lounge with upholstered chairs and sofas, a drinks bar, games area with snooker and darts, a side room full of coin slot gambling machines and several wall mounted televisions. Floor to ceiling panels screened off a small theatre. Most noticeable and accessed through doors is a massive Chinese restaurant with seating for at least three hundred people.

At the bar we ordered beers, pints! Obviously subsidised prices costing about the same as a pub served mid-size schooner glass.

The first lagers went down well while chatting to a young ex-serviceman. He gave us the story of the club. Originally formed in a 'hut' by World War One veterans in 1920. Now a fully developed business. We took our second round of beers into the restaurant. Choices, a la carte or buffet, deciding on the menu we ordered T bone steaks with trimmings. I felt a blow-out coming. Correct assumption, ice cream desert followed. All too much? Not really, it had been another brilliant day, the Blue Mountains, now this place. The meal was 'icing on the cake!'

Back at the guest house by 10.00pm. Chris noted in her diary, 'knackered, straight to sleep, separate beds.'

Saturday 11th April. Day 58. Katoomba, the Blue Mountains.

The hotel breakfast room is part in the main building and a 'planted on' conservatory at the front aspect. Plenty of people here, including families with children and it's tight for sitting spaces. Food, crockery and utensils are all set out for self-service, so a bit of a bun fight to get anything

184

on a plate. Making toast is a trial, multiple plugs in a single power outlet causing several outages. The Chinaman and his wife did their best in topping up foodstuffs.

In the room. Chris made up filled rolls for lunch. With them, afternoon snacks and water bottles packed in our day bags, we boarded a tour bus. At about 10.00am got off at the Scenic World stop. This is the most popular, largest and industrialised tourist visitor centre. It offers not only cable car rides across and down to the gorge but also has a superb viewing platform. Many folks will only ever come to the Blue Mountains once, so there are lots of coaches and mini buses delivering and collecting organised tour groups. Most people are here for photo opportunities. Many are oriental so there plenty of cameras with long lenses, others are neck hung and some on sticks.

Studying the booklet map I'd noted that a path from here led down the gorge all the way to Katoomba Cascades. I assumed that not many of the tourists that stop here would be walking this track. I was correct. Hardly used, the start was difficult to find but we did. Chris and I used tracks formed of fallen branches in puddles, encountered plenty of mud, difficult root strewn areas and there were wooden steps, sometimes up, sometimes down!

On occasions it was so foggy visibility was only two or three metres. Sometimes we arrived at a place seen yesterday but at a different level or the opposite side. We saw some visitors crossing barriers, taking liberties with their lives to take photographs while stood on the spill plane of a waterfall, the drop being hundreds of metres! By the end of our five hour expedition we'd been to Gordon Falls, Narrow Neck and several other viewing points, also taken countless photographs.

Back to the guesthouse at about 5.00pm via a short shop for supplies in town. Later we enjoyed the facilities at the RSL Club. A few lagers then a fine Chinese meal of pork chow mein and mixed rice.

Sunday 12th April. Day 59. Katoomba, the Blue Mountains.

8.30am, a big, white, cock parakeet woke us with loud calls from just outside our room window. This morning the breakfast room is even more crowded. A lot of guests arrived while we were out yesterday.

The sun is shining. The map has been examined. For our last day in the mountains we selected a new expedition route. First to Gordon Falls, next, to all three levels of the Siloam Pools, then onto Lyre Bird Pool. We bussed to the start point. This trail is very Jurassic, thick undergrowth with ferns and water dripping from overhanging rocks. Hardly an easy walk, very steep and slippery in places, often broken or no path at all. We didn't meet any other people while trekking. Made several stops to admire the views and take fantastic pictures.

I noticed that being in the sun Chris's face has come out in freckles on some of her fine wrinkles, so a new word has been invented, 'frinkles.' I'll be punished for that!

We didn't want our last day to be too hectic, came out of the gorge, onto the road and took a bus into to Leura Village. A small two road size place. Had a wander about. Being Sunday it was busy with both tourists and locals. Bought coffee, sat on a bench and ate our rolls. About 2.00pm, bussed back to Katoomba and bought some take-away beers.

Showered and dressed. Spent the late afternoon and early evening sat on comfy chairs in the hotel lounge. Wrote our diaries, Chris sent messages home through her phone, I transferred photos to the ipad. Spent time on the web researching and speculating what to do in New Zealand. It's probable that we'll only have time to visit one island.

Hanging on the walls of this room are pictures of the hotel in its days of grandeur. Now it's a wobbly place, no straight lines, cold but cosy. The friendly Chinese owner informed us that he'd been a tenor opera singer and had bought this place for his retirement years. While we were in the lounge a group of folks in the breakfast room were plucking violins and playing pipes. Maybe as the early settlers did in Australia? Odd, the music reminded us of a film, Last of the Mohicans.

To the club tonight for the last time. Had beers and Malay style curry. Afterwards, thanked the reception staff for their kindness and hospitality. This will never be forgotten.

Monday 13th April Day 60. Katoomba to Sydney. 102km.

Up at 8.00am. Packed. Chris made up filled rolls then we had breakfast. In the lounge afterwards used the ipad, found and noted directions to the hotel in Sydney. We said thank you and goodbye to the Chinaman. I'd loved this place, had even found my own private toilet in the basement!

Fully laden we did the uphill walk to Katoomba railway station. Ate our rolls during the two hour journey to the city. Arrived just after midday. With back packs on we trekked up more gradients to the hotel. The Cambridge, 212 Riley Street, Surrey Hills. No meals included but a three night stay somewhere posh! At check in there was some confusion, Angela's credit card hadn't been cleared for the deposit so I had to use mine. I told Susie by text, she was fuming. We were to meet here at 3.00pm and before arriving at our room she'd resolved the matter and not only that, had also obtained three pairs of breakfast vouchers as compensation. Well done for that!

After a good catch up chat she left and took our laundry back to her house. She'd come here again later this evening before we all go out for dinner.

From the eleventh floor are stunning views across the city. They are even better at night. The room is plush, furnished in a black and white theme, king size bed, sofas, chairs and table. There's a balcony, very handy, I can smoke on it. This building is just across the road from a low rise sprawling concrete construction, the Police Station, built much like a fortress. Chris and I took showers.

Susie was back by 7.30pm. We talked and had a couple of beers. She'd planned tonight's pre-birthday visits. By 8.15pm we're in a Pub, a sort of pseudo western bar but didn't stay long. Via a liquor store to buy beer and wine, we went for dinner at an Italian restaurant. A bring your own drink place. Discussions continued during the meal, Susie giving up work, plans for Fiji and what to do tomorrow? Dropping hints at the possibilities for the 'birthday girl.' 10.40pm we left, Susie to the station us to the hotel. Chris noted in her diary 'Bob put a lovely message on Facebook, almost had a 'moment.' Pasta for dinner and shared a bottle of red with Susie, first wine I've had in months.' All true!

Tuesday 14th April. Day 61 Sydney. Happy 60th Birthday Christine! Bridge Climb.

8.30am, we're both up. Slept well except for being disturbed by a strange vibration noise. The building's central core contains the air condition ducting. Poor design, even the receptionists know about it.

In the ground floor restaurant we enjoyed our first free breakfast. After that Susie arrived at our room. She has birthday cards and token presents for Chris that have been sent from home. Her biggest gift today will be the 'Sydney harbour Bridge Climb.' The secret is out.

Unfortunately I got a present that I didn't need! The ipad has stopped working, it could be disastrous.

The man upstairs and Mother Nature have collaborated to bless the birthday girl. Fine weather. The sun is shining high in a clear blue sky and the wind is just a light breeze.

A taxi ride to the Rocks Area near the harbour. The 'Bridge Climb' centre offices and shop are built into to sub-structure below the road. It all starts here. We have some nervous tension, the arch is very high. Watching from the shoreline we'd seen people doing the climb. Being early, we went up the steps onto the pedestrian walkway. The road is hectic with vehicular traffic. Took some photographs of the towers at this level. Back down, entered the centre and presented ourselves at reception. Susie had paid for our tickets online.

We three are allocated into a group numbering ten people and meet the others in a waiting lounge. There's a lot to deal with, all in a serious but relaxed attitude and each section by a different person. A video watched, an induction talk and completing medical forms, then it's further into the building to an area fitted with changing rooms and racks of equipment. Our possessions are put into lockers. Nothing personal except spectacles is allowed to be taken on the climb, no wrist watches or cameras. Everyone is introduced to Tyson, our climb leader. We're issued overalls, once changed into those we're then given arrest restraint belts and hard hats. Every item clips on to one or each other, hankies, head phones, even spectacle arm tabs. We're shown how to attach the restraint clip to a 'running wire' and all get onto a metal stepped frame for a practise climb. Fail on this you don't go onto the bridge. Phew!

Tyson's commentary starts as we clip on to the safety wire for the proper climb. For now we're all still inside the building. Using a tunnel constructed through one of the towers he leads us out into the underside of the bridge!

We're now below the road and very high above the streets that serve the harbour. The wooden plank walkways aren't that wide but I feel very safe. I suppose my experience of working from ladders and scaffold gave me confidence. Seeing the riveted girders close up is good. We hear Tyson through headphones, he reels off statistics, history and other details. Exiting from the underside we head upwards using steps and ladders toward the arch through the fretwork of steel. Soon we're above the main road and can see the roofs of moving cars, coaches and lorries. There are other groups doing the same, a sensible gap is kept between each. Only the guides have cameras and they make strategic stops to take photos. As the climb to the top of the massive steel arch is made the views over the harbour district are magnificent. At the top, close by an Australian national flag flutters. A crossing is then made to the other arch. At this junction, each pair, group or individual gets to say something into the camera set to video mode. A steady climb down is made back to the centre facilities. Here we shed ourselves of all the equipment and dress in our civilian clothes.

It's been grand three hour experience, not cheap but worth it. Annoying though, is knowing that the photos and video will now be charged as extra. Fortunately we had a secret weapon, Susie, our technology aware daughter. By the time we'd left the complex with our climb certificates and souvenir caps she'd managed to obtain the media on her phone. Clever girl!

Just over the road is a pub, very handy. Feelings of achievement still high we trooped to it, ordered beers and mix of snack foods to share. Free wifi here. Breakfast time in England, very convenient so we made a video skype call to Angela, then connected with Charles, Kerri and the Grandchildren.

Afterwards we walked through the city back to the hotel. Showered, had a couple of lagers then went for dinner at a pub just across the road, The Porterhouse. We ate rump steaks and drank more beer. All of us were eventually fighting tiredness. We walked back to the hotel, Susie went home.

Chris noted in her diary, 'had a great day, I won't forget my 60th birthday anytime soon.' I should hope not!

Wednesday 15th April. Day 62. Sydney.

9.30am Breakfast. I probably had too many celebration beers yesterday and was still slightly fuzzy. Today I have to prioritise. We need to shop for a few items but top of the list is to take the ipad to the 'Apple' store on George Street. Fortunately all of the trip photographs so far have been uploaded to the 'Cloud.' Although I have most of the trip documents printed, the device holds all of the back-ups and a lot of other vital information, and it's essential for making flight and accommodation bookings as we move regions. I know I can use internet cafes and public computers in hotels but with the hassle I've had so far with Microsoft, this fills me with dread!

The Apple store is an ultra-modern glass fronted building. Even more of the material used for construction inside, amazingly including the stairs. The ground floor is where devices can be tried or purchased and it's very busy. The second floor is where the tech guys do their bit solving problems, here it's even more hectic. It seems company policy is connect faulty device to a computer, click on a few keys, if resolved fine, if not 'here is your replacement.' A chap gave me an appointment for 2.30pm. So time available for some shopping. Looking for padlocks, bags and device connection cables, we tramped the streets. I hated it, even bought and ate a sandwich while on the hoof. One stroke of luck though.

Tucked away in one of the many arcades we happened upon a jewellery repair workshop. Had Chris's St Christopher medallion reattached to the neck chain with a new jump ring. Cost two dollars, actual value, absolutely priceless!

Not quite 2.00pm and back to the Apple store. It's next door a busy MacDonald's so we had coffee. After that Chris and I separated, she continuing shopping, I joined the queue for technical help. My turn, I'm called and I sat at a long counter. The techie introduced herself and I explained the ipad problem. Unfortunately while staring, fixated by her facial metal piercings. One in her nose, a hoop with ball ends fascinating me. She knew her stuff though, connected the ipad to a computer, at the same time firing questions. I answered as best I could. Her explanations, it could be reloaded and I'd be in possession of what would basically be a recondition device. The alternative, I'd be given a new one but it'd be empty. F**k me, I had concerns here, big ones! Five minutes later, success! Thank you young lady.

All I had to do know was reload the applications. I'm not the quickest presented with such a challenge. Having builder's thumbs I elect to do this while in the store, my thinking being if I cock up I can at least beg for help. I found the whole operation very stressful. Sat on a hard bench for nearly an hour. Skyscanner, Booking.com etcetera, only one app failed, Lloyds banking. By now Chris had found me, I wasn't in a good mood and having what is best described as a 'Snickers' moment. We left the store, I bought one and ate it. Better now!

Success and failure with shopping. Couldn't find a pair of flip flops for Susie but did get some luggage carabiner clips and spare device charging cables.

At the hotel I completed the loading of the banking app then checked that the ipad was working in all other functions. We did some pre-packing for tomorrows exit. Susie joined us at 5.00pm, she'd had plenty to sort out for herself. After leaving her job here in Sydney she'd travel and be with us in Fiji. From there she'd go to meet a friend in New York and afterwards fly back to England. Later we all had dinner and drinks at the local pub, excitedly discussing the prospects for the Fiji trip of which she elaborated. The day of arrival we overnight at Nadi, next morning move to the 'homestay' village of Namatakula. Three nights here and then go back to Nadi for one night. The next day we'll sail by ferry to the Island of Mana for a four night stay in a resort complex. At the end of that return to Nadi. For us just a one night stay before flying to

New Zealand. For Susie it would be two nights, her flight to New York being a day later. Simple!

We parted company at about 10.40pm, a little late considering tomorrow's alarm was to be set for 6.15am. At the room I had a coffee and cigarette on the balcony. Took a last look at the night sky over Sydney. A storm brewing out at sea, flashes of multi-coloured lighting tinting the heavy cloud.

Fiji, Bula and phewee!

Thursday 16th April. Day 63. Sydney to Nadi, Fiji Islands.
Fiji Airways FJ910 Dep 1pm. Arr. 6.50pm. 2,630km.

6.15am, packing completed. Nerves twitching and adrenalin racing, I smoked several cigarettes while stood on the balcony. Text messages are sent to Susie confirming our status. Chris sent 9th birthday greetings to granddaughter Zoe in London. Breakfast, bacon, egg and toast. We made some 'take away' sandwiches for Susie and slipped them in our day bags, with some cakes, croissants and fruit. The room cleared and inspected, checked out at 8.00am, wait in reception for Susie. She arrived in a taxi at 8.30am, along with her worldly goods. Safely at the airport by 9.10am.

Completed immigration exit cards and Susie's flight is first. We say 'ciao,' we'll be a group again in a few hours. Chris and I stand near the queue as she checks in at the Fiji airways desk, then watch her disappear into the departure lounge.

It's our turn an hour later. Unfortunately the woman on the airline counter has just been given a hard time by an irate female passenger and we get served the overspill. First by having to prove that we have exit flights from Fiji, without them you can't get onto the Islands. Then the weight of our back packs comes under scrutiny. We're told they should be checked in as luggage. At 9kilos they are over the limit but I'd hoped that the size would see us through. I explained that we have actually paid for hold luggage but would prefer the bags to be carried on. We get the OK for that. Thank goodness.

At security I suffer the indignity of losing my decent pair of long splinter removal tweezers. Oh well, at least they never found the smaller pair hidden in my razor case and the two gas lighters! It'll happen eventually.

Boarded by 12.15pm. A big aeroplane but only ninety passengers, almost two thirds empty. In between sleeping, writing our diaries and eating airline food, more forms arrive for completion. One for immigration, the other a 'Bio declaration' that we are not taking any vegetable or organic matter onto the Islands.

The rest of my time is spent reading a magazine article about Fiji. Useful, as I knew nothing about the country's history except it had been part of Britain's Imperial Empire. I'd swot up later using the internet but for now I knew several things. During WW2 the island of Espiritu Santo had been a major USA military base. After the war lots of equipment including tanks had been dumped into the sea, the area is now a diver's paradise. The nation feels that it suffers undue political influence from Australia and New Zealand, although many people from these two countries visit as tourists.

More importantly in the late 19th century, Colonial Fiji's population had been bulked up by Indian immigrants, brought in to supplement the labour force. After independence and in recent years the awkward mix of indigenous and Indi-Fijian has created many periods of instability, resulting in many military and political coups. Fortunately mostly bloodless.

The almost six hour flight arrived at Nadi about 4.00pm Fiji time. Chris and I passed through customs and other checks, got some cash from an ATM, then met Susie just outside the airport terminal. We watched and waited for a shuttle bus. It being sent as part of our one night accommodation package. One hour and several phone calls later, it arrived. Our luggage loaded, we're on our way to the Tanoa Skylodge Hotel, Queen's Highway, Namaka.

After a short drive, enter the grounds of the lodge, pass many chalets and stop at reception. Checked in we're then driven back to one of these buildings. Our cheap, cheerful but tired room with two beds, an ensuite bathroom and a small kitchenette. There are about four more of these self-contained units in the same block.

Chris and Susie are first to use the bathroom facilities. I stepped outside to smoke, stood in the light of a lamppost. A taxi drew up and stopped very close by. From an open window the driver asked if I needed to go anywhere. I replied that I didn't. His next words were a request for a cigarette. Having plenty I offered for him to take one from my packet. He did. From the passenger side of the car a slim, good looking, black girl got out. 'Femme fatal?' Her slick hairstyle immediately reminding me of Betty Boo. She asked, "Could I have one of those?"

I replied "Of course." And proffered the pack. Being tired I didn't think any more of the situation being other than a chance friendly meeting.

Her next question. "Are you going somewhere? I replied "No." Following immediately with "I'm about to take a shower."

When she said "I'd like to take one with you," the penny dropped. With a smile I stated that it was a lovely offer but my wife probably wouldn't be too happy with me. I bid them both goodnight turned and went into the room. I related the event and conversation to the girls, we all laughed.

Clean and dressed we walked through the grassy grounds of the complex. Frogs were hopping everywhere. All paths led to the bar and restaurant. Table selected, beers and food by way of curries ordered. Most of the talk was speculating about what we'd find at the homestay. How good it will be to contribute to the local economy, not just put coin into the pockets of the already rich. After eating we mixed with some other guests, chatted and played a game or two of pool. The bar had long closed when we left for our room and bedded down at 1.00am. It had been a long day.

Friday 17th April. Day 64. Fiji, Namaka to Namatakula Village.

Up at 9.00am. Ablutions and packing done, leave our bags in the room and walk in oppressive heat to the reception area. Susie takes the lead in sorting transport to the homestay in Namatakula village. Estimated price quoted for a taxi, up to $130 (about £40) Susie wants to bus. I prefer a cab. Leave the woman at the desk to make some phone calls and we go to the bar area for breakfast. Unknowingly while eating and still discussing the ride options and costs it seems the situation has been resolved. In fact, made for us. At 10.15am we're told by staff that a taxi is outside waiting, our luggage already in it. Fare $100, I'm happy. So having checked that all of our baggage is present and correct, get in the twenty year old Toyota and off we go.

Before leaving the city boundaries we request to get some supplies, there are no shops in the village. The driver makes a stop at a supermarket. A purchase of three days beer for all of us and cigarettes for me. Shopping done! The cabbie is a nice fellow, a Hindu, third generation Indi-Fijian. I'm in the front passenger seat, conversation soon flows. From him I learn more about current affairs of the country. Native Fijians are still mostly involved in agricultural pursuits. That Indi-Fijians are restricted from buying land and can only lease buildings or property and something that becomes obvious during our stay, how the latter are so much more industrious.

The approximately 100 kilometre drive took about an hour and a half. Not totally a coastal route. Scenery is beautiful, varying from lush forest to grasslands. We see isolated homesteads, plenty of plantations, mainly of sugar beet. Quite often mountains are in the distance.

Susie had sent a text message to Tupou, the 'lady' of the homestay, informing of our estimated arrival time. She's to meet us at the village bus stop. The car rolled passed a sign indicating Namatakula. The driver slowed and sure enough into view came a lone woman sat in the poor shade of an artisan constructed bus shelter made of two posts, some branches and dry leaves. She knew this was the taxi and stood up almost at the same time of our approach. We stopped.

There was very little introduction. Within seconds she'd joined Chris and Susie in the back of the cab and instantly gave directions. The car turned off of the tarmac road onto a muddy, puddle, rutted and branch strewn track. The driver easing slowly between trees, shacks and huts, some part built and others falling down. My thinking was that this isn't the place for an old Toyota saloon and we'll likely bottom out axle deep, but no! He did well and the car was stopped near a clearing. Tupou got out and dragged away a small fallen tree, allowing the car to be parked on a firm grassy area. I paid and congratulated the driver. The mud spattered car looked as if it had just completed a rally course. Tupou went through a gap in the trees and quickly reappeared with a stockily built youngster. I thought this maybe her son, especially so when managing to walk away carrying two of the backpacks. How wrong could I be? This was Lisa her daughter!

Carrying the remainder of our kit, Susie, Chris and I followed them through the trees and other low hung, very wet foliage. Squeezing in between two timber framed buildings we popped out and found ourselves in front of the 'homestay' site. There are no marked boundaries. It would be unfair to call this an organised complex and with the current weather, a lie to call it paradise. To understand where we were takes some explaining.

Beyond a big sand bar the ocean can be seen in the distance. The immediate shoreline which comprises of sand, stones and mud is being lapped by a fast stream of fresh water flowing from the hills. Not powerful enough to break through the sand and shingle bar and get to the sea but forced to turn and rush past the homestead. Here it becomes narrow, concentrated and washes away parts of the fragile edge of the shore. There is plenty of evidence that major erosion is taking place. Several trees with shallow roots fully exposed lean precariously over the stream. Other palm tree trunks bereft of branches lie in the water looking like unfinished beaver dams. The river meets the sea just past another smaller land draining creek and before a sloping promontory. The eroded material ends up here. The landscape is more estuary than bay. Twice a day, as the ocean tides dictate, the sea floods over the shallow end of the sand bar and reaches in, taking its turn to reshape the shoreline. Which includes demolishing washing line posts and removing plants from the area.

It's not cold but under a grey sky and in drizzling rain, we're introduced to the buildings. Corrugated tin roofed huts of varying size placed on stilt posts or masonry block piers. They are nearly in line, set back about ten metres from the water's edge and barely visible in the heavy vegetation.

Mine and Chris's accommodation is to the left of the much extended family lodge, to its right is Susie's. Two huts have rickety timber steps leading to the entrance doors. Ours has loose concrete blocks. There are no paths leading to anywhere, just gaps in the trees and bushes for access.

Further along is the ablutions lean to. Comprising two sections, theirs and ours, both similar. Concrete floor with plastic curtained shower areas, a toilet pan, cistern and an old sink with a cold water tap.

Our minds are still computing the new surroundings as we're invited into the dimly lit family lodge. At the back in one corner is a kitchen area bounded by a counter. This is cluttered with utensils, crockery and other cooking paraphernalia. Nearby there are two tables and chairs set out lengthways in refectory style. Next to the door leading to the host's quarters stands a tall fridge, importantly now cooling our beer cans! Some artisan carpentry work has provided a waist high room divider, in this area are some lounge seats.

Tupou serves coffee and a lunch of pumpkin and tuna curry. She joins us, we sit and talk.

Afterwards we all go to our respective huts. Susie says she's taking a 'nap' at hers. An often heard quote when she wants to be on her own to think things through. Chris and I inspect ours. Two beds, one with mosquito netting, on the other we put our luggage. There are two plastic chairs and a small table, handy for night time water bottles.

Chris is invited by Lisa to join her in cutting some cassava leaves, she also knocked a green skinned orange fruit from a tree. They don't come any fresher!

The wife and I take an exploratory walk. Local children have obviously finished school for the day. Regardless of the weather and the fast flowing water, the shoreline and rivers edge is their playground. They are in and out of the creek, jumping from the part submerged trees.

There are several places to sit, mostly saturated. A random log forms a seat, a wood picnic bench table that's seen better days, exposed rusty nails tell where the missing parts used to be. Folks are coming home from work. Rubber wellie boots a popular footwear for those who make a living in agriculture. It's almost surreal watching a native man wearing oversized boots cross the river riding a bare back horse.

Before nightfall I took the opportunity to clean up. Rinsed hands, face and brushed teeth. That'll do! Followed up with a generous application of insect repellent. I've no doubt that being at the edge of a rain forest and so damp it will soon be mozzy central. Even if you were dry, getting anywhere through the bushes made you wet. I'd only been here for a few of hours and was slipping easily into 'outback boy mode!'

Late afternoon, dusk and evening all rolled into one. The girls had to wait until after 6.00pm to take showers because of several power outages. Tupou said that these are caused by works on the main road. My opinion was that this little homestead didn't have the wiring necessary to cope with more than a couple of light bulbs.

After night fell we grouped at the tables in the lodge. More talking as dinner is being prepared. We had coffee, then a couple of beers while Chris and Susie played cards. Here we meet the man of the house, 'Sake' alias Danny, 49 years of age, unfortunately not a perfect specimen, looks and acts much older. He wears a woollen hat and jumper. Almost certainly diabetic, the black skin on one swollen lower leg even blacker and he struggles to walk. It hadn't looked like he did much maintenance or repair around the home and garden. Now I knew why there was such disarray. Even the 'Danny's Homestay' sign, its posts rotten, had wilted into the bushes.

He likes a chat. When given a snippet of information seems astounded and every time retorts, "phewee my brother." I sat with him in the 'lounge area.' We talked for quite a time. Among other things he reckons the weather will improve. He should know surely? Our conversation is audible to all. He is worried about erosion of the shoreline, Chinese investment in the Islands and even admitted that he may have to sell up if the land around his was sold.

He confesses that when his wife told him that us as new guests were in our sixties, he was worried that we may not be able to cope with the hut steps. Laughable if he hadn't been so serious, especially as by now Chris and I were 'fit as butcher's dogs.'

Heavy rain can be seen and heard belting down at the open doorway. We sat at the table with Lisa while Tupou served an extensive dinner. Fresh mango juice, beef noodle soup, chicken curry cooked in coconut milk, cassava, rice and potatoes. Sake didn't indulge. While we ate he'd been joined in the lounge seats by a 'brother.' A distant relative, eventually introduced as a pastor. Me oh my, did this man have some stories!

After the meal, the girls and Tupou played cards. Susie and Chris introducing her to the delights of 'Rummy.' I sat with the men for man talk! Discussed everything, politics, religion, world affairs and taxation. Nothing was off limits, including the Syrian crisis. On this subject the Pastor introduced a very interesting anecdotal story. "Quite recently in the Middle East, some peace keeping Fijian soldiers had been kidnapped by Islamic terrorists. Government officials here negotiated with leaders of Fiji's Moslem community for their safe return, suggesting that if the captives were not released the indigenous population may just resort to some bad old ways. Cannibalism! This insinuation seemed to work as the soldiers were quickly repatriated." It was either a good story or just bull sh*t, I'd be checking my feet on the way out!

9.30pm. Dinner, drinking and conversation is over. We've planned tomorrow's events. Chris, Susie and Tupou will travel into Sigatoka, go to the market and get supplies. On their return, we as a group will attend a traditional Fijian funeral service being held for her aunt.

Rain is still pouring. We're given some anti-mosquito smoke coils. Using our head torches and getting very wet on the way, we make final bathroom visits then go to our huts. I have already decided that a night time toilet visit is not a viable option. Door open and water the plants the solution for me, Chris will just have to ache. I lit the mozzy coil, set it on a plate placed on the floor, the smoke is reassuringly thick. Carefully lifting the insect net we slip into bed. It's damp. 'Phewee my brother,' what a day it's been!

Saturday 18th April. Day 65, Namatakula.

The noise of wind, rain and roaring sea had us awake several times. During the night from the doorway I added to the moisture a couple of times. 7.00am, we're both up. It's still raining in fits and starts but Chris has decided a shower is in order. I'm still only thinking about one. At the lodge we're served a breakfast of pancakes, banana and beverages. By 8.30am, Susie, Chris and Tupou have left by bus to Sigatoka. I showered and was mosquito bitten almost immediately. It won't happen again, showering or being stung!

Outside the toilet block a female cousin of the family is doing the laundry. The soap and wash board reminds me of India.

About three hours later. After their ride in a noisy old bus packed with villagers, shopping in the market and a taxi drive back, I'm reunited with wife and daughter. For expediency lunch is do it yourself sandwiches with a filling of onion and tuna. Tupou informs us that the funeral visit itinerary is to be reduced. Auntie's body will have been disposed of during the morning, so we will only be attending the wake in the village hall and the communal feast thereafter. Sake and his bad leg have decided not to go. Chris and Susie dress in smart clothes, I put on a clean shirt and Tupou assists me in putting on a traditional Fijian man's skirt. I look a picture, plenty are taken!

At the wake we're supposedly going to drink 'cava,' a mind numbing drug derived from the root of the plant. Very popular in Fiji. Rumour has it that it's the thing to do at this type of event. Getting comatose on this stuff doesn't sound like a good idea. Haven't they heard of Stella Artois?

Tupou leads the way. Using fallen branches as footfalls we cross a muddy drainage ditch behind the homestead and are soon in the mix of tumble down shanty huts that form this village. She points out buildings while telling of which relative lives where, fifteen cousins in that family, ten more over there! Many doors are open, squalor aplenty but evidently no one starves, most Fijian women are large to say the least.

We arrive at the communal hall. People are milling about, talking and exchanging greetings. 'Bula' is the welcoming word. Outside and under a lean to roof lays a headless butchered cow's carcass with skin on. The cuts being legs, haunches, torso and neck. Blood is still flowing onto the concrete floor slab, being diluted by the heavy rain then running to the grass verge.

Sitting under a canopy, visible a short distance away, women are obviously cooking using several giant white metal crucibles. Set on stones over open fires, steam and smoke rises, billowing into the driving rain. Quite a sight.

Following Tupou we enter the hall and are invited to sit crossed legged on woven straw floor mats, joining the many people already there. Some ceremonial actions are taking place. At the back of the hall, men are mixing the pummelled cava root into water then straining it though cloth into large plastic buckets. It's not long before we are offered some. Tupou declines outright! Encouragement is given to those imbibing. The crowd claps, a slow start rising to a faster pace, louder and quicker as a wood bowl is lifted to any mouth. Susie and Chris each take sips from a small dish. I've been given a man size container and the clapping started. I'd watched the routine, swill the bowl then down the contents in one gulp. So I did! Tasted like a muddy puddle with a touch of dog sh*t. I had several bowlfuls, the effects on me were only a slight numbing of lips. Too much weed when I was younger has probably made me immune.

The funereal process continues. Adult males from the bereaved family sit at the top end of the hall. One chap has obviously had too many Cava's and is fully stretched out, no longer 'compos mentis.' A big fellow wrapped in a robe looks like a witch doctor. He rattles a string of whale or shark teeth while speaking or chanting. Some folks make replies, many just carry on talking among themselves. Cava is being downed all around. We Cooke's didn't have a clue about what was going on.

4.00pm, Tupou has had enough. I couldn't work out whether she was just bored or just not bothered. We follow her lead and leave the building, so it seems that the feast is also a non-starter. We trudge back to the homestead being met by more 'cousins' on route. Lots of in-breeding in this village. A genetic defect is definitely being passed on, the dropped bottom eyelid evident in Tupou's niece notable in others. Especially during the school visit that we make later.

The weather is still grim, not raining but very overcast. Susie takes one her famous naps. I change out of my skirt. Chris and I decide to go for a walk. It's low tide, so we plod across the sand flats towards the promontory. We find lots of coral and large sea shells, mainly halves that have been washed in.

About 5.00pm, at our hut Susie tries to sort out the Telstra roaming facility on the ipad. No luck, it's a shame, I'd have like to have found out the FA Cup semi-final results. In the lodge the girls play cards while tonight's dinner of rice and lamb stew on the bone is being prepared. Susie also informs us that we're actually booked here for four not three nights! With the weather and limited facilities my heart sinks. The thought of extra time here is daunting. F*** me, we only brought three day's supply of beer and I'll soon run out of smokes!

While the girls play cards, Tupou now being taught 'trumps,' I chat with Sake and ask if he goes fishing. After all, the ocean is on his doorstep and even closer at times! He says we will do some tomorrow. Hand lining for sharks. The blood and entrails from the slaughtered cow will have been dumped in the sea, drawing the predators towards shore. This sounded good, although I'd have preferred at least a rod and line.

8.30pm sat in our hut, wrote my diary. There are a few old travel books lying around in the lodge, I'd borrowed a volume of Lonely Planet and before going to bed I read more about Fiji. 'Mana' our next island destination is described as divided, either resort complex or backpacker. No mix.

Chris noted in her diary, 'hope we have a nice day tomorrow, I think we're all a bit fed up with the rain.' 'Phewee my brother!' An understatement surely?

Sunday 19th April. Day 66. Walk to Mango bay

Woke about 9.00am. It had been night time take-two. The sea and rain had been very noisy, we'd had very little sleep and I'd watered the plants several times. This morning everything is damp, clothes, bed and me. F*****g inside and outside, damp! The sun is hiding again. We're all very quiet at breakfast, Fijian doughnuts, Paw-paw and coffee. Chris has got lots of bite spots on her legs, Susie gives her an antihistamine tablet and supposes bed bugs. I reckoned mosquitos. Who knows?

It's Sunday. What to do? Fishing is out of the equation, Sake and his bad leg put paid to that. Suggestions from the hosts are the Church service or the low tide walk to Mango Bay. The latter entails crossing the river, going over the sand and shingle bar, turn southwards, edging along the shoreline and around the rocky headland. We know that locals working there do it and have seen them. The big questions, when is high tide and if trapped how do we get back? Looks as if we'll need a three head discussion. Susie went for one of her famous naps. Back in the damp hut after ablutions, Chrissie and I talk. In the background we can hear the church congregation singing. So surreal. It's not raining outside but still overcast so we talked and walked up to the sand flats. Watched some hermit crabs queuing and exchange their shell homes, fascinating. Importantly, we'd decided that the river crossing *must* be made.

We all met at the lodge for lunch. Beef, vegetables and noodles. Susie was a definite for the Mango Bay walk. Rain or not we'd do it, after all, the worst case scenario would be a taxi ride back to this village!

I carried the empty holdall. Put cigarettes, lighter and money in my shirt pockets. We waded into the river and although it's flowing, didn't get washed away. Made it to and over the sand bar then walked up to the start of the headland. Time taken fifteen minutes and the tide was still ebbing. Rain spat a couple of times but this isn't a beach comber's stroll. Picked our way through the rocks and pools, rounded the head and were in the bay. Mostly flat sand with boats on long rope moorings and only a few hundred metres from the small 'Mango beach resort.' Traversed the wet sand, up a grassy slope and arrived. Not many holiday makers about but we're obviously noticed by the staff. I went straight to the bar and bought beers for me and Chris, Susie abstained. Talking to the barmaid, the surprised look on her face spoke volumes when I told her that we were staying at Danny's homestay. She said we were welcome to use any of the facilities. I bought the essential supplies for this evening, more beers and cigarettes, loaded the holdall and we made the return journey. I'm sure the sun tried to shine.

After a mid-afternoon coffee and the girls had showered, we grouped at mine and Chris's hut to play rummy. 7.00pm, went to the lodge for dinner. Beef stir fry, veg and chicken. Afterwards the girls and Tupou played cards. I entertained in the room with the invisible ball and bag magic. One of Tommy Cooper's gems. Toss an imaginary ball into the air, pretend to catch it, at the same time clicking a crispy paper bag. The noise makes it seemingly being caught inside. Timing is everything. Susie knew the trick and joined in, throwing the 'invisible' ball from long distance. Tupou and Lisa sussed it but Sake and his Pastor mate had no idea. It was good fun with lots of laughter. 'Pheweee my brother' I hope they don't voodoo me!

Monday 20th April. Day 67. School visit and to Mango Bay.

Up late at about 9.00am. No rain but it had been an odd night. Lights had stayed on in the lodge till way after 11.30pm. The Pastor and Sake had a loud conversation. Breakfast, dumplings made with coconut milk and flour followed by coffee. Ablutions done and at about 10.30am Tupou takes us for a visit to the village school. This caters for mixed gender, aged from pre-infant to sixteen years, the pupils seemed very happy.

Chris was soon in her element chatting with both children and teachers. Facilities are organised but basic. English language is taught and there is an IT room.

Walking back through the village the near third world poverty is very apparent. Piglets living in little more than crates, toddlers playing on the pathways while chickens wander about. The shanty huts and bure's that families cram into are in awful condition. I never established if there is a proper sewerage system. Many places do have an outside cubicle, some soil pipework is visible, but where the waste ended up is a mystery.

The sun is out and it's hot. After a light lunch we three repeated the walk to Mango bay. This time doing some beach combing. In the shallow rock pools finding some marine life, a blue star fish, crabs, sea cucumber and tiny sea snakes. At the resort we sat for a while, drank a single beer, bought some to take away and watched a few guests enjoy the small swimming pool. In bright sunshine and blue sky the river crossing and walk had been good. Such a shame that the weather had been so bad for the previous days.

Back at the homestay we had lunch. Tuna, potato and rice. Tonight's main event is a traditional 'Lovu' dinner. Tupou and Lisa were preparing for this. We watched, so did Sake and his bad leg, sat in a plastic chair under shade of a tree. First a hole is dug in the sand. In this some branch wood and leaves are used to make a fire with large stones being heated for the cooking process. Once the flames reduce to glowing embers the foodstuffs wrapped in tin foil are placed on. A topping of leafy branches is added and covered with an old tarpaulin sheet, the whole lot then buried. Results later!

The sun is still shining, the man upstairs finally helping out. Near the shoreline I smoke a cigarette while sitting on a collapsed tree. At the dodgy picnic table Chris and Susie are teaching a young girl 'snap' with playing cards. We found out later that this nine year old was Tupou's step sister. Should have guessed, her dropped bottom eyelid was a clue.

At dusk the girls had showers. In outback mode I opted for rinsing armpits, hands and face, plus a further application of insect repellent. Once bitten twice shy, the phrase must have originated in the jungle!

While grouped at our cabin, on a wall we spotted a giant spider, big enough to carry a backpack. There was no way we could relax until it was outside. I grabbed a towel and edged close to attempt a trapping manoeuvre. The arachnid was quicker than a Porsche! For every move I made, it reciprocated, fortunately always toward the exit door and out it went. I checked my bags, I'm sure it had stolen money.

Played cards and drank beer until 7.40pm then moved to the lodge where the Lovu dinner was being set out by Tupou. At the table we were joined by Lisa and the niece. In the lounge seats, Sake was again being lectured by the Pastor. The food by now was on serving dishes and much to Susie's annoyance he decided bless the meal. A feast, lamb and chicken on the bone, rice and vegetables. It was very good, a welcome meal but again not very hot. Chris noted in her dairy, 'fully stuffed, reckon I've put on half a stone in four days.' Best not tell her that it shows!

During the meal Tupou quietly informed that her husband, who hadn't joined us is to give up meat for fifty days. A penance because his leg won't heal. Medicine is the answer not pseudo Christian witchcraft! The Pastor obviously has his own take on Lent. She is also supposed to adhere to this instruction but has refused. This must have been the upshot of last night's heavy discussion. I really don't like him and I knew Susie had taken an instant dislike. She has facial 'tells.' This big man, who in his own story of experiences in the mining industry and serving on cruise ships is also highly opinionated but has little or no sense of humour. Last night he couldn't suss the ball and bag trick and got annoyed. Anyway, we'll be gone tomorrow so left kind notes in the visitor's book.

Susie went to bed at 8.30pm. In our hut, Chris and I did some packing then drank beer and played cards for a while. Chilling before sleeping. 'Phewee my brother' day of days, thank you Mother Nature.

Tuesday 21st April. Day 68. Namatakula to Nadi.

Fully awake at 6.30am, we got up. The night had been a succession of strange noises early on, then wind and rain. By 7.30am ablutions done and 99% packed. It was very quiet at breakfast. The sun is up, I took a short walk and watched the ocean tide come in take some more of the foreshore away. Sake and Lisa are nowhere to be seen. Fortunately, goodbyes to them were given last night. Back at the hut I close the bags, symbolically ending the four day homestay experience.

At 9.00am we have our back packs on, day bags shoulder slung and other items are clipped on. Tupou leads us through the village to the main road, lots of 'Bula' greetings from people on the way. It's hot and there's no shelter. We drop our bags and wait for the 9.30am Express Coach. 10.15am, still not arrived! Lots of cabs, mini buses and other passenger vehicles have passed us. A truck with four men even tried to pick up the girls, mmmh I wonder why? One cigarette left and no gum, I have that smoke. Our single deck bus arrives, we load the hold, give last goodbyes and hugs to Tupou. She works her socks off and deserves better. Susie pays the fares and we're on our way back to Nadi, via Sigatoka village. Here there's a twenty minute pit stop. I bought some smokes.

At Nadi bus station we're immediately targeted by Indi-Fiji taxi touts and for only $10 on our way to new lodgings, via one stop for more cigarettes and insect repellent. By 12.30pm we've checked into the Wailoaloa Beach Resort sited directly under the nearby airport's flight path. There's a swimming pool. We've a shared room, two beds, fridge and ensuite bathroom. Total luxury compared to what we've just left. I eventually access the free wifi and open a Telstra account. The Australian sim card is still current and I'm hoping to get use of the roaming facility.

We get busy with our own needs. Personally, by 6.00pm I've had beer, taken a swim, eaten lunch, shaved, showered, cut my toe and finger nails and drunk more beer! Basically I'm in heaven. Susie also booked our places on the ferry to the Island of Mana.

7.15pm at the resort's bar, beer for me, cocktails for the girls. We meet an Indi Fijian of sixty seven years old, well educated, he stayed in England 1979-82 and visited again in 1990. Our conversation covers many things, we agree on much. Especially that Fiji is still not quite grown up as a country. Dinner is ordered at the restaurant, Chris and Susie share a bottle of wine. The food is good but a long time coming. I went to bed soon after eating.

Wednesday 22nd April. Day 69. To the Island of Mana.

Susie and Chris came in for bed later than me, had a night cap I presumed. I was awake several times during the night, once from being cold, uncovered, Chris had coiled in the sheets. 8.00am, it's going to be a busy day. First ablutions then a buffet breakfast of coffee, eggs, toast and fruit. During which I use the ipad, continuing the search for a first place to stay in New Zealand and I have one identified. While online I try and fail to pay an important domestic insurance premium. The company's site is s**t so I leave an angry message. 10.00am, we're packed, checked out and waiting in reception for a shuttle bus to the ferry port.

Foolishly I've been angry with Chris over a simple division of expenses. I shouldn't have because she's been good in most things. I'm probably stressed. Maybe when we're back to being a pair I'll be able to get the trip finances back on track. The shuttle arrived, luggage loaded, we went about a kilometre to the Mercure Hotel, transferred to another coach then onward to the port. Susie collected the pre-booked return tickets and checked in her big rucksack. Chris and I wear our backpacks. I bought some fruit and crisps as snacks at a local shop. We queued then boarded the catamaran ferry 'Cougar II.' Took seats at the stern top deck. In bright sunshine we left port. Some brilliant views on the way out. The ferry makes several stops at smaller islands, it didn't anchor but drifted, allowing smaller shuttle boats to come astern to disembark passengers and luggage. Even in a calm sea it was fascinating watching the crewmen deal with this. Some of the islands we passed seemed so small that a decent size wave might swamp them. Odd though, each had a white fluffy cloud above it, even those visible in the distance.

1.30pm, last stop, the Island of Mana. The ferry moored alongside a purpose built timber pier on the south beach. A group of men in traditional costume are playing guitars and singing a greeting. Disembarked we're soon in a magnificent reception area checking into the sprawling Mana Island Resort. The complex is in work, making improvements and has slightly diminished facilities. Susie had found us premium priced digs at heavily discounted cost. Such a clever girl! A Buggy driven by a big Fijian fellow takes us and luggage to our 'Bure.' A timber building on stilts, one of quite a few large chalet's overlooking the north beach.

Designer built, big, spacious and luxurious accommodation. Probably could use a few more superlatives. Beds, settee, chairs, fridge, mini bar, ensuite bathroom and a terrace with sun beds. It's about 2.00pm we drop our bags and walk back through the grounds and take lunch in the resort restaurant. Sandwiches had with one small beer each. The bill arrives, very expensive, it won't happen again, after all, we are self-catering!

Afterwards Susie decides we're to explore the island, at least the coastline. No denying the girl is keen. The tourist map suggests it's walkable? So we head off east along the south facing beach, past some accommodation probably built for locals, shore side restaurants and then the ramshackle back-packers huts. After about fifteen minutes we round a headland. Hoping to hit the north beach at the back of the resort where our cabin is situated, we walk westward. The ground here is rocks, sand and washed up sun bleached coral. After two hours we reach a high rocky promontory and need to get up, over and around it to reach the shore! Easier said than done. The girls are wearing flip flops. Another snap decision needed, if we walk back, it'll be dark before the pontoon is reached. Glass half full or half empty?

Susie would be OK but should two sixty year olds being doing this? A reasonable clamber got us to the top, but on rounding the point climbing became dodgy. Sharper, steeper and downward. Foaming waves break below us, quite scary in places especially on the wet boulders. We edged very carefully, sometimes with bare feet for better grip and passing footwear by hand. Made it safely onto the smaller rocks and wet sand of the beach, heartily congratulated each other at the achievement. A stroll now, over the dunes, nipped into our cabin, changed into swimwear and went to the resort pool for a dip. Here in broad daylight we watched bats the size of seagulls flying, landing then hanging upside down in the trees. Back at the cabin we all showered, ipod music played, 'The Killers' booming from the speaker dock. Diaries are written, emails checked, photos are uploaded. Why aren't there thirty hours in a day?

7.30pm, walked out of the complex up the south beach to an artisan restaurant. Ordered large beers and food. The girls shared dishes of sizzling prawns and chicken, I had a burger. So much cheaper that some of the resort's oriental clients were here! On leaving we bought some large beers for the chalet fridge. The Mana complex has nightly entertainment, on the way back we briefly visited. A traditionally grass skirted song and dance group were performing. Touristy, naff, but hey ho, it didn't hurt to take a look. In the cabin we indulged in a tot of whisky, one of Chris's birthday presents. The girls played cards,

Johnny Cash sings 'Hurt' through the ipod speakers. I stood outside on the terrace watching the colours of the night sky. A good way to reflect on a superb day before writing my diary and I quote exactly as written:-

'So Day 69 Closes, I have lost weight, belly fat gone and muscles in my upper body have wasted slightly, although smoking too much, I'm mostly good. Susie and Chris are as fit as fiddles but both admit to have put on a little weight. I have jested that they'll be Fijian in size if they are not careful. Since the Oz road trip I am mostly covered in mosquito repellent, a good lathering every day. Most days we've been in bed between 9.30 and 10.00pm, only a few times later. Personally, I find it odd not being 'on the move,' being in the same place for more than two days gives me concerns that I will lose my 'edge.' Web access also has become as important as food and toilet. Oddly I have been in the Fiji Islands for 7 days and still not been any deeper in the Pacific Ocean than 40cm. Hopefully I will do better tomorrow. Bruises, I have done well to avoid until today, picked up a nasty stain on my right wrist, how, I don't know. Enough for now, I'm going to have a smoke and crash 10.55pm. The Ice Gel is ready! (Susie is run down, close to the w*g!) Notes:-Large 600ml Beers are $8.50 =£2.60--------20 cigs, B&H $10=£3.00, no wonder the AUS/NZ allowance for import is only 50.'

Thursday 23rd April. Day 70. Mana, Fiji.

Swimming in the Pacific for proper today! All of us are up about 8.15am. A good comfortable night for me. Big bed, plenty of space. Ablutions, then walked to the 'not' resort bar and had breakfast, variations of egg, toast, bacon, hash. Small meals but enough. At the resort store we signed for three sets of snorkelling gear. By 11.00am had sun beds on the north beach. We all swam for a long time, the tide is not quite full so rocks and coral are in the shallows. Safe for me. I took pictures, in, out and underwater.

Later I walked west to the cove headland, took photos of live coral and some fish stranded in pools higher up in the volcanic rocks.

I took the snorkel kits back at 4.00pm. Bought ice creams and took them to our pre-arranged meet at the swimming pool. In the distance we watched small reef sharks, their dorsal fins a giveaway as they sliced through the surface of the water.

5.30pm, at the cabin. Having a beer while readying to go out. We walked along the south beach to the farthest 'non-resort' bar restaurant. This one is backpacker heaven! Ramshackle the best description. Full of what Susie describes as rich kids slumming it on 'daddies' credit card. She has more experience of travelling than us and we're not so judgmental. Tonight's madcap entertainment includes hermit crab racing, with prizes and a dancing competition Fiji style. It's fun to watch the antics of both organisers and youngsters!

Here at the 'Mana Lagoon Backpackers' sharing the buildings and beach tables there's a small independent restaurant. Ravi, an Indi-Fijian, owner and chef introduced himself, seems a really nice chap. We order some cheap 600 millilitre bottles of beer, they'll go down well tonight! Dinners are arranged. For me curried beef, Chris gets steak, Susie has fish. Ravi sits and joins us. Conversation flows during which I mention a fishing trip, he says he can organise one, also reckons he can arrange cheaper massages for the girls. I think they will stay with the resort booking. He's a Hindu married across the religious divide to a Moslem woman. They have a son, a toddler with the most beautiful eyes. Ravi has some interesting takes on life and believes in fate lines. That alone is enough for us to get on well. By 10.30pm, the beer has taken a toll. I need bed!

Friday 24th April. Day 71. Mana, Fiji.

I'm supposed to meet Ravi at 8.30am. No chance. Woke up with hangover at 8.00am. Eventually get to his bar at 9.30am. Very few back packers about at this time. We order breakfasts. Ravi has news, he's arranged a fishing trip for tomorrow, cost $80. I'm to meet him here at 5.30am.

11.00am, settled on sun beds at the south beach. Sign out a two man plastic kayak, life jackets are compulsory, great fun for an hour, took lots of photos. Later, using snorkel kits we're all in the water exploring the coral for the first time in this area. In the sea my confidence is growing and I take some good underwater pictures. Chris noted later 'have never seen so many beautiful fish in one place, it was like swimming in a tropical fish tank.....first time kayaking.'

2.30pm, the tide has ebbed. To protect the coral, resort staff ask people not to snorkel in an area between two buoyed and roped off lines. An American couple ignore the request and deservedly get rebuked. Chris and I stand in the sandy shallows watching some tiny fish build a nest. Schools of larger types dash about near the surface, their shadows on the sea bottom easier to see than them.

Later we all walked to Ravi's to get dinner. Entertainment tonight is Fijian fire dancing. We're all sensible enough not to over indulge in beer, me especially. Left at 9.00pm. At the cabin I crashed early, the girls played cards for a while.

Saturday 25th April. Day 72. Mana, Fiji. Anzac day. Fishing trip.

Being awake before the 5.00am alarm was easy. I was excited and looking forward to some sea fishing, I hadn't been out on open water for years. Got up without disturbing the girls, my kit was ready, swimming shorts, hat, sun glasses, cigs, lighter and a $50 note. Quietly left the cabin. It's still dark, the only light coming from the resort lamp posts. A few people were about in the grounds preparing flag staffs for Anzac day. Walked barefoot out of the complex then along the south shore sands, being careful not to trip over any mooring lines and was soon at the backpackers huts. I could hear snoring from one of the reed huts and there were a few bodies dotted around sleeping. Carrying a pair of fishing rods and a bucket of tackle Ravi arrived minutes later, part opened his kitchen and we had a quick coffee.

He tells me that things got a bit hectic at the 'party zone' last night. Worse for drink, some of the backpackers decided to skinny dip. The village elders aren't happy and he has to be back ashore by 10.00am to lay down the 'law' to the miscreants.

A fibreglass open boat, about three metres long arrived at the shore. Ravi secured his kitchen. We walked down the sand, stood ankle deep in water and loaded the gear. As we stepped on board I was introduced to the skipper, John, a weathered Fijian sea dog. He didn't hang about, the outboard motor was kicked into life and off we went into the darkness.

The sun still well below the horizon, the sea black as ink, only John and Ravi knew where we were heading.

Time ticked by, we're still on the move, the light improved and silhouettes of other islands came into view. A dawn sunrise over open water can only be described as spectacular. This one was!

Before we started, as many fisherman do, a friendly wager was struck. $10 for the first fish caught, same amount for the biggest and again for the most.

The first angling method tried would be trolling. The boat on the move as lines towing lures are run out, hopefully to attract fast swimming fish such as Tuna. Did this for quite a while, at one time thinking we'd strike lucky. Close to the lures a good size fish leapt clear of the surf but no joy. Small flying fish also came out above the waves, often an indication of being hunting from below. The boat was anchored, John needed to top up fuel. All three of us are smokers, so as a concession to health and safety we refrained from sparking up. A fifty litre petrol explosion is best avoided!

We tried bottom fishing, then pumping a lure up and down. Again no luck, not a single bite! So back to trolling. The clock was running towards the end of the mornings fishing. As for the bets, anything caught now would win all three. I would have happily paid up to see a catch but it wasn't to be and we made our way back to Mana. I had thoroughly enjoyed the experience. Fishing in the Pacific Ocean, a box ticked big time!

I'd been up for over five hours. Walked back to the cabin. Made coffee, ate crisps and biscuits for breakfast. Spoke to the girls before their appointments, they'd done some laundry at the complex facility. I collected that at midday just before they came back very happy. Chris noted 'the best full body massage I've ever had, even had my feet done.' Not my thing, never had one, the only person that touches Mr Cooke is Mrs Cooke!

On the south beach we got sun loungers. The girls were soon snorkelling. I tried to sleep, couldn't so I signed for a one person kayak. The surprised look on their faces when I paddled up to them was brilliant. My floppy hat proudly displaying a poppy as an Anzac day tribute.

We lounged in the sunshine. Nearby a party of six oriental guests settled themselves around a pair of sunbeds. They must have arrived on today's ferry and hadn't wasted anytime in organising some snorkelling. Most were wearing swimming shorts, life jackets and long sleeved shirts, seemingly paranoid about skin sun damage. The sea remained untested as they posed for their numerous cameras and cell phones whilst fully kitted in masks, flippers and breathing tubes. In that their similarity to intrepid underwater explorers ended. We three sat watching, barely able to resist the urge to laugh out loud as they attempted various entry methods. Walking forward like penguins, trying the correct backward steps and falling over into six inches of water. Others crawled, making it to the buoyed line and hauling themselves into a foot or two of water. At times face down sometimes up, snorkel tubes often held in hands as dysfunctional arms and legs flapped or splashed without rhythm. Snorkelling it certainly wasn't, hilarious it definitely was. All too much for us heathens near to stitches.

At 2.30pm, leaving Susie and Chris on the beach I went to the cabin for a coffee and a sleep on an outside lounger. They woke me on their return at 4.00pm. After dressing for the last supper we drank beers and talked about the South America leg of our trip.

For dinner the girls shared a sea food platter, I had fish and chips as a consolation prize. Ravi and I bantered about the angling trip. To prevent a late bet winner I reckoned he'd made the skipper move the boat too fast on the final trolling runs, making the lures skip the sea surface. He didn't deny it!

Sunday 26th April. Day 73. Mana to Nadi, Fiji.

Woken at 9.00am by knocking at the door. A staff member wanting to check the chalet mini bar contents, at resort prices these of course had been unused. Coffee made and packing started, tidied up the room, baggage collected at 10.15am. In reception Chris paid the account and checked us out. Had breakfast at Ravi's, said goodbyes to him and family, we'd stay in touch through Facebook. After resting for a while on the south beach decided to wait in the resorts reception where it was cooler. Took time to double check that all of our luggage was on the pier ready for collection well before boarding the 1.30pm ferry.

The return only took an hour and a half, not many stops for passenger pick-ups. Disembarked and took a taxi to the Wailoaloa Beach Resort for the second time, just overnight for us. This is a comfortable place with cheap food. Dropped our kit in the room then went to the pool. Later in the afternoon did some online work, banking mainly but also booked a place to stay in Christchurch tomorrow. The forecast temperatures on the South Island New Zealand are eighteen degrees centigrade daytime, down to five at night. It could be a shock.

Readying for dinner we found that the mozzy spray had run out. I took a walk in the dark, found a shop and replenished. We ate and chatted, quite a lot about Susie's post New York plans. She's returning to England and then staying with Angela in London for a while. I'm devastated when she restates that if a decent job doesn't turn up she'll go back to Australia. I beg her to at least go to our house where she can live for free and not make a final decision until we return in mid-July. This and our forward travel plans don't make me the best of company. Tired, emotionally drained, I crashed and burned about 9.30pm.

Highs and lows in New Zealand.

Monday 27th April. Day 74. Nadi, Fiji to Christchurch via Auckland, New Zealand. 1st leg. NZ.553. Dep. 2pm. Arr. 5.05pm. 2nd leg. QAJXJH. Dep. 7.35pm. Arr. 8.55pm. 3,135km.

I didn't sleep well, today's travel plans were running through my head. Got up, had breakfast, packed and organised our places on the airport shuttle. Susie has one more night here, I help carry her kit to a dormitory. She has been great company. Having had such a fantastic time and shared so many experiences we will miss her badly. 10.30am, checked out. Confirmed online that our flight is happening so it's waiting time. 11.00am, the shuttle arrived. So did the inevitable tearful goodbye to Susie. All of us cried. Red eyed and tearful Chris and I got into the mini-bus.

The airport routine wasn't too bad. By filling our coat pockets got the backpack weights down to 7 and 7.2 kilos respectively. Waiting for a gate number we ate pies, drank coffee and bought sandwiches for the flight, which took off on time. Slept until food was served and immigration cards needed completing. Arrived Auckland, North Island. Disembarked, it took an hour to get through the hoops of immigration and bio security.

Walked 900 metres from international to the domestic terminal. Had a smoke on the way. Found the check in, then had coffee. More security for the 2nd leg to Christchurch South Island, boarded, off on time 7.35pm. Arrived 8.55pm. We came out of the building, f*** me it was dark, cold and p*****g with rain.

Took a shuttle van to a suburb a few kilometres from the city centre. We didn't have any food supplies. When asked, the driver was kind enough to cruise past a few shops. Being after 9.30pm it was like a ghost town, nowhere open and we'd suffer the consequences. We were his last drop off. At the City Worcester Hotel, Worcester Street, Linwood, we checked in. The young Chinese or Korean manager gave us a complimentary 150milliltre bottle of milk. At least we could make coffee using our sachet supplies but all we had to eat was a Snickers bar, which we thinly sliced and shared! Although a heater was turned on the room was cold. The bed felt damp and the electric blanket only worked in one half of it and now I had the trots! After trying to research road trips online and unblock Outlook Express email yet again, at midnight we went to bed, wearing clothes! In my diary I wrote, 'again I have spent an age on the web or phone trying to unblock email and too much time on booking and research, I'm hating it.'

Tuesday 28th April. Day 75. Christchurch.

Had a rough night, woke up still with bad guts. Managed a coffee. Went out and shopped locally for breakfast foods. I normally starve myself if I get a bad belly but needed to eat. Chris made poached eggs on toast. Only having ten days to play with, decide we'll explore the parts of the South Island that can be comfortably achieved in that time. I also need to book an exit flight back to Auckland and afterwards take an aeroplane trip across the Pacific Ocean to South America. Simple!

Online, found 'Unique Car Hire.' Very local, in fact around the corner in Fitzgerald Street. So we put coats on and wandered there. Met Geoff, born Essex England, has been here for many years. We talked, asked advice on the best places to go in the limited time available. His suggestion, point the car and drive, he didn't turn out to be wrong. An automatic Nissan four door saloon was arranged for $30 per day, collection on Thursday morning.

We intended to do more but I was far from top form. Decided to go back to the motel and have some lunch. Chris made jacket potatoes with ham and cheese.

Afterwards we intended to complete the exit strategy and properly plan a road trip.

Online, I enter details to Skyscanner for a flight from Christchurch to Auckland. Happy with the one I find, book and pay for it. What a w****r! I double checked and realise I've booked a flight to Sydney, Australia! Although cancelled within minutes I've probably lost my money. D**k head! So with my guts even more chewed up I have to book the correct flight and an Ibis Hotel near Auckland Airport. Chris sat with me, treble checked everything, no mistakes this time. Now we had to get the road trip planning done. My belly had been growly all day, I didn't want to eat or drink but eventually we walked to the Indian owned mini-mart and bought soup.

From about late afternoon to 7.00pm had maps laid out, permuting possible destinations with stop overs, calculating distances, timings and making notes. So much, that I was totally p****d off with it. Had soup about 7.15pm. Hadn't even washed or managed a shave. It had been planning or the toilet. I certainly didn't have food poisoning but was shivery and had cramps, symptoms of a stomach chill. The electric blanket had been switched on for hours. Before going to bed at 9.45pm I noted in my diary. 'So fed up, almost don't want to be here anymore.'

Nevertheless a round trip driving plan with destinations had been made. Leave Christchurch on Thursday and overnight at Greymouth. Move on to Franz Joseph, stay for two nights. Continue south and stop for the night at either Lake Hāwea or Wanaka. The next day, if possible, drive all the way up the West coast to Kaikoura. This would leave us an easy run back into Christchurch. We'd search for possible accommodation as and when we could, keep note of at least two addresses at each place and enter them into the satnav on arrival at the town or village. Easy!

Wednesday 29th April. Day 76. Christchurch.

10.00am, apart from a couple of pan sprays I'd slept for twelve hours. Outside the sky is clear. Chris made breakfast, coffee and toast, then some sandwiches for the day out. She's been a star, good back up in all aspects. I actually feel marginally better, not so chewed up. Just after midday we're ready to walk to the city centre. We need to find a chemists and get antihistamine cream. One of the insect bites Chris got in Fiji has become spread and inflamed. Map in hand we walk out, the sun is shining but we wear coats. I'm happier, we've achieved so much in such a short time. All is good until we realise we're striding away from the centre!

Felt a total idiot but didn't panic. Took a bus ride! Entering the city centre, evidence of the devastation caused by the 2011 earthquake is still apparent. Derelict and empty plots, lots of construction work and acres of scaffold erected. Buildings and businesses did survive but in many of the cleared areas, converted shipping containers single or stacked, serve as cafes, boutiques and shops. We bought a take-away coffees, sat on a bench, ate our sandwiches and prioritised sourcing essentials. Going high into the mountains, especially the glacier area we speculated that obtaining an extra layer of warm clothes would be a sensible idea. In a discount warehouse we bought very cheap fleece waistcoats, woollen gloves and beanie hats. Elsewhere we purchased antihistamine cream and a microwave meal. Heavy rain driven by a strong wind arrived suddenly so we took a taxi back to the motel.

Picked up a couple of cans of beer at the mini market. At the room I shaved my head and showered for first the time since Fiji. I feel better in myself and regret yesterday's low point. There had to be one at some time. No reason be down now, I've got an indoor hat!

Thursday 30th April. Day 77. Christchurch to Greymouth. 350km.

After breakfast Chris made rolls for lunch then we went to pick up the hire car. Met Paul, Geoff's business partner, they really are nice blokes. Checked out of the motel, loaded bags and got straight on the road heading towards Hanmer Springs. Here we stretched our legs and took a look around. Then it's to and through the Lewis pass. In the sunshine the autumn scenery is stunning, often with distant snow-capped mountain tops. Clear roads through the Victoria Forest, rivers and creeks crossed using skinny bridges, verges with steep drops into gorges, wild double bends with low speed warning signs. I nearly lost control on one! Made several photographic stops. The car handled well up or down the mountains. Chris had her first New Zealand driving experience and she'd get more!

4.30pm, rolled into the coastal town of Greymouth, found our accommodation of choice. The Motel on High Street. A nice place with parking outside the cabin. New owners, they're keen and making improvements. Chris and I are allocated a family sized unit, kitchen, two bedrooms and refurbished bathroom. Walked to a local supermarket and bought some victuals. Took showers, afterwards, online I booked a backpackers hostel in Franz Joseph, drank a couple of beers while doing so. Had dinner at a very quiet local grill restaurant. As strangers in town our waitress took an interest in us, we had a nice chat. A dark, cold, windy night, even from inside our lodge the sea could be heard smashing the coastline. Being well fed and tired from the day's travel we slept easily.

Friday 1st May. Day 78. Greymouth to Franz Joseph. 180km.

Up 7.45am, Chris made breakfast and rolls for daytime snacks. Left the motel at 9.15am. Visited the supermarket, did a beer and food top up. Before leaving town we parked up and took a stroll to the coast. Well the worth a look, grey sky and a sea to match. Man killer waves breaking over rocks. So powerful that whole trees had been washed up on the stony beach.

A short distance outside of Greymouth we made a detour inland to visit 'Shanty Town.' A reconstructed 19th Century gold miner's village. The sun is shining when we arrived. A very interesting place with lots to see. Spent quite a time here. Walked in the wet forest, took a short ride in an old steam train with plenty of Chinese tourists on it. Even found a spec of gold in the panning sluices! Bought coffee, sat at a picnic table and ate lunch before moving on.

Travelled up, down and around mountains. Split the driving duties. The smile and concentration on Chris's face said it all, exciting and exhilarating. Scenery on route was fantastic, very changeable. We made stops at two beautiful lakes.

3.45pm. Arrived at an overcast Franz Joseph. Checked into The Montrose hostel for two nights. A bargain, $60 for a modern second floor room with ensuite bathroom and central heating. Put our foodstuffs in one of the fridges in the immaculate communal kitchen then walked out. Explored the town and picked up some information leaflets about trips to the glaciers.

Had showers, drank lager and discussed tours, hiking, maybe even a helicopter flight. Decided on the latter, if the price and more importantly the weather was right. Later, ate and drank at The Alice May restaurant, reasonable meal but the barmaid just moaned about drunkenness in town. Afterwards, made coffee in the hostel kitchen.

Before going to bed 9.30pm I asked the man upstairs for a good day tomorrow. What's being greedy wanting two in a row?

Saturday 2nd May. Day 79. Franz Joseph Glacier.

After a superb ten hours rest, up at 8.00am. Chris made breakfast in the kitchen. Here, mostly stainless steel surfaces, superbly clean and a credit to the hostel. Today we'd decided to do the walk to the glacier face and if possible, a helicopter flight. There are several companies operating, so I went to reception and asked for a recommend. The manager was on the phone in milliseconds. Brilliant, we were booked, the one o'clock slot, $150Nzd, the cheapest trip, once over the glacier and back.

The rest of the morning is ours, we jumped in the car and drove ten minutes from town to the free carpark. Sign posted paths led out to the ravine, follow these and other walkers all the way to the glacier face. There and back in an hour and a half. Mostly over rocks, some loose and with a few tricky gradients but not too difficult. The main track runs alongside the raging River Waiho, there are also waterfalls. As human beings it's impossible not to be humbled by the sheer scale of the prehistoric mountains and ice flow. Awesome!

Had time to eat our rolls before heading back into town. 12.30pm presented ourselves in the main road office of Glacier Tours. A very helpful chap went through the do and don'ts. Next, without coats on we're weighed. Chris was heavier than me and wouldn't admit the figure, "sod off," her hissed retort when I asked! We signed our lives away on the disclaimer form. Then a bonus came to light, we're informed that the chopper is now fully booked.

Chinese tourists have taken the three spare seats and paid for the full Monty. The flight is now over both glaciers with a landing on Mount Tasman! Not only that, the weather is superb, sunny skies, no wind or rain. I wonder who organised that.

While waiting on the other passengers we had a quick coffee in the café next door. At 12.50pm, as a group we're escorted over the road to the helipad. Chris and I are like excited school kids, we've never been in a helicopter. It was waiting, rotor blades whirring. We ducked, got in, took the back seats behind the pilot then as instructed put headsets on and buckled the safety belts. Up it went smooth as silk, we didn't know what to expect but there was no vibration, almost as if we were in a fast rising balloon. I just kept taking pictures. The pilot's commentary came through the headphones. From the air we could see the glacier that only a couple of hours ago we'd walked to. Through the clouds into the pure blue above and the helicopter was landed on a flat area of Mount Tasman. Everyone got out. Without being asked the pilot used my camera to take shots of us as we posed. He pointed out Mount Cook, its white topped peak piercing the clouds below us. Treading into the crispy, white virgin snow we were allowed to wander but no further than a thin stick marker. Who'd want to fall from here anyway?

Back to the aircraft. The pilot gave us the front seats, we had premium views for the flight back to town. I switched modes on the camera, took video of the approach and landing. Describing the experience as awesome is an understatement!

Later went for beer and curry at The Tiger Mountain. Didn't stop talking about what we'd just done. What a day!

Sunday 3rd May. Day 8. Franz Joseph to Lake Hawea, Queensland. 275km.

After breakfast, boiled some eggs and made luncheon sandwiches. Loaded, drove then fuelled the car just outside of town. In bright sunshine head off for the Lakes of Hawea and Wanaka. The route taking us through the Haast and Huart passes. Made lots of stops. A coffee break at a working salmon farm and later, parking high up on the Shore Mountain Lookout. Here the Tasman Sea stretches uninterrupted all the way to the Antarctic. At Thunder Creek Falls we walked on rocks and watched the fast flowing foaming river dash by. Views approaching the lakes are superb.

Arrived in the village at 3.30pm. Shopped. Bought some beer, big potatoes and locally produced rump steak. Checked into The Lake Hawea Hostel, a good backpackers place built in grounds at the back of a big pub-cum-hotel of the same name. Facilities, outside toilets and shower block, communal kitchen and lounge. Our room is Spartan but clean. Left the kit inside then took a walk along a stretch of the giant lake. Lovely, calming, watched fish breaking the surface of the quiet waters.

Early evening, Chris cooked dinner. A few other guests were there, I hoped they weren't vegetarians! A German woman and a French couple were playing Trivial Pursuit. During the game I overheard a question regarding London's Nelson's Column. No one knew the answer. I very much enjoyed informing that it celebrated one of England's greatest heroes and the victory over France at the Battle of Trafalgar!

With jacket potatoes, the steak was cooked to perfection, a superb meal. Well made, Chrissie!

Wifi is good here so I did some research about Lake Tekapo north from here. We still hadn't made up our minds about tomorrows destination. Looks like we'll wing it!

Monday 4th May. Day 81. Lake Hawea to Kaikoura via Lakes Tekapo and Wanaka. 625km.

Breakfast had, lunch made. 9.30am, car loaded, off we went. Stopped briefly at Lake Wanaka. Here we bought a pack of beers for later, coffee for now and ate our sandwiches. It's a beautiful place but we'd seen one earlier!

While sat in the motor, the 'winging it' came into play. We decided to drive the full distance north east to Kaikoura. A long way and we'd have to be careful how many times we stopped. Unfortunately some of the vistas in in this beautiful country are hard to resist!

We split driving duties. Chris making the final run towards the town. By now the sun had set, all grim grey sky. She did a grand job taking the car down the last of the winding mountain roads, around the cliffs and through tunnels close to the rocky shoreline.

Arrived just before dark and found the backpackers hostel, the Kaikoura Motel and Holiday Park, again with Chinese or Korean owners. I only booked for one night just in case. The family size cabin allocated was dated but fine. Had an ensuite bathroom and several bunk beds. We showered and cracked a couple of beers. I transferred some photographs from the camera. Wifi here is useless, so intending to get a better connection near the reception I stepped outside into the night. F**k me, the ipod slid out its case, hit the concrete floor and the screen went black. I thought I'd throw up. Back in the chalet it was even worse. The screen had cracked in several places and glass was missing from one corner. My stomach churned. Our lifeline to the world f****d!

I did the 'push both buttons' reset. Nothing! Connected to power and did the same. Jeez, the broken screen lit up, a couple of taps and there were functions, eventually working in all aspects. Someone is definitely looking after me. I searched and found my tiny roll of masking tape, made some emergency repairs and that would be how it stayed overnight.

About 8.00pm, still cursing my foolishness we wandered into town, found a pub, ate and drank. Afterwards in bed by 10.15pm. It's been a 'funny' old day!

Tuesday 5th May. Day 82. Kaikoura, Whale watching.

7.45am, a grey morning followed a very cold night. Not enough covers on the bed. After a homemade breakfast we walked to the Whale Watch Centre and asked for the trip price, its $300Nzd. So went outside to talk about it for a few minutes. We'd spent quite a lot of money so far! Would we ever do this again? No! So booked it.

Drove to a supermarket and bought foodstuffs for the next day. At reception got another blanket and booked the room for another night.

10.00am at the Whale Watch offices. Signed in then joined other folks and are given a safety talk before a bus ride to the boat. Arrived at the harbour, about forty people including us are boarded and seated on the vessel. In clear sky we left the dock and out to sea. The crew are very informative and explain their roles. A big screen educational video is shown. We're told that no whales have been seen for two days and to remain seated until called to the viewing decks.

First encounter! A crewman reckons it's a pod of about four hundred dolphins. It's the ocean deep, who finds who? Show offs! Close to the boat they're definitely performing for us. Why else would they do back flips, super high leaps with twisting spins. Such agile magnificent creatures.

A woman stood aft, with camera and mobile phone in separate hands, the boat lurched, the phone slipped from her grasp and slipped silently down the stern into the sea. The look of surprise and shock on her face went mostly unnoticed. I had no doubt that our dolphin friends will be adding that device to their undersea collection of human memorabilia!

The vessel is in constant contact with others in the area. They all use underwater microphones to listen for the sound of whales and share information about where and when one of these mammals may surface. The boat is let to drift. We all stare out, eyes searching for a tell-tale sign. Metres away an Albatross flies by, just above the waves. Eventually luck comes our way. During a period of less than an hour, two whales surfaced for air, their blow holes spouting spray. Of course most of the enormous animal is below water but their dive is spectacular. A giant tail the last part of the beast lifted high before disappearing into the depths.

2.30pm, back to port. The trip has been well worthwhile. At the car Chris and I check the tourist map. Just north of town a seal colony is indicated, surely worth a visit? We park up close to a section of rocky headland. Nearby, probably an ancient rock fall from the mountain opposite, piles of grey boulders are all the way down to the breaking waves, A few other people are here, there's some pointing of fingers. Yes, there's a seal in among the rocks well away from the water. I crept closer, camera in hand ready for that elusive picture. Oh no, not just one seal, many! At first hard to see, their skins providing perfect camouflage, but when big daddy raises his head and gives me the 'look' it's time to leave.

An information sign tells of a seal 'nursery' across the road. Over we go into the forest. There's not much light here. A tricky, slippery, tree strewn, mountain path follows a waterfall that spills into pools at several levels. In these, young seals in different stages of development are learning future skills. It's fascinating being allowed so close to nature.

3.45pm, fuelled the car on the way back to town. In the chalet drank a few small tins of 'Speights' lager before going for a pub dinner. We have to be early! Everywhere closes by 9.00pm. Wifi is free in the bar, so along with planning for tomorrow I searched and found an ipad repair shop in Christchurch. Bed by 10.00pm. Chris noted in her diary, 'a day of firsts.' I second that!

Wednesday 6th May. Day 83. Kaikoura to Christchurch. 180km.

Including making rolls for the journey we're ready to go by 8.30am. Before leaving town, went to the local supermarket bought food and some wide 'sellotape.' I'd decided that time is too short to find a computer technician and to make a more permanent artisan screen repair myself. Programmed the satnav to take us to the motel we'd previously stayed and take a chance there'd be a room. Stopped many times to take pictures during the three hour drive.

The South Island road trip was over and thoroughly enjoyed. We'd travelled 1,510 kilometres, spent $236Nzd on fuel, $224 on car hire and had seen a small portion of this wonderful country. Back at the Worcester Motel there was a spare first floor room available so we checked in. Took the car back, paid for the hire time. Couldn't thank the guys enough but I was still willing to take a liberty! Spoke to Geoff, asked if he'd be interested in being paid $25 to collect and take us to the airport tomorrow. The kind man said he'd be happy to do it for free. With the rest of the day free of commitments Chris arranged for some laundering to be done by the motel staff and we caught up with some personal grooming. During the evening I did some research about South America, especially Peru and the City of Arequipa. Chris made dinner which we enjoyed with a couple of beers. Bed early at 9.00pm.

Thursday 7th May. Day 84. Flight: Christchurch to Auckland. Jetstar JQ250 Dep. 12.20pm Arr. 1.40pm. 765km

7.30am, breakfast of cereals, coffee and for me with travel nerves jangling, too many cigarettes. Final packing done very carefully, coat pockets being well used. Jetstar Airlines have a serious attitude to hand luggage in weight and size. Geoff arrived as we were bringing bags down the outside stairs. A fifteen minute drive to the domestic airport drop off zone, for which he accepted heartfelt thanks but declined payment. Nevertheless I left the cash in the car's centre consul telling him to put it in the 'tea boat.' We parted with handshakes. His and Paul's kindness just about epitomised the friendliness received here in New Zealand.

Had a sandwich and coffee while waiting for the flight. At the airline desk I took the opportunity to have a word with a receptionist about my booking error and was told that there is probably a Qantas enquiry point in Auckland airport. Bought t shirts, one for each of us, wearable and as souvenirs. The woman serving dropped her spectacles, a lens popped out, I made a repair, she was grateful. For me it was a touch of 'good begets good.'

The midday flight was on time, we landed at 1.35pm. I went directly to the international terminal and found the Qantas desk and told the outline of my mistake. The lady gave me a phone, a direct line to an office. Made the call and to an agent named Mary fully explained how while quite unwell I'd made the woeful error. Sympathy wasn't her immediate response. Not many people know that Jetstar is best part owned by Qantas, fortunately I did and suggested that she had the facility to confirm my story online. Although I was admonished for not being more careful, she agreed to authorise a refund. I expressed my gratitude. Airline companies being what they are, quite honestly, I never expected a good result. This had been a real bonus.

Carrying bags, I want to time the walk to the Ibis Hotel. The building can be seen from outside the terminal. If it's easy, I'll know that we can manage the same tomorrow morning and save a taxi fare. Done in fifteen minutes. Checked in and given a room on the 6th floor. Left Chris to organise, went back down and out had a few cigs. Later went to a bar next door with free wifi, had beer and food. A nice place as is all of NZ. Back at the hotel there's no one about in the kitchen so I made a couple of coffees and took them up to the room. Such an early start tomorrow, bed down at 8.30pm, ipod on playing 'David Grey.'

Had some thoughts, I was looked after today, probably have been all trip.

Friday 8th May. Day 85. Flying across the Pacific Ocean, Auckland to Santiago Chile, via Sydney. 23,500km.

Phone alarm sounded for 4.30am. It's going to be a long day! The airport lights are on and can be seen from our window. Packed the last of the kit. I went to the ground floor and got coffees. Had to pay this time! Back packs on, walking, we're soon at the terminal and checking in. Jetstar also issued the second leg Qantas boarding passes. That would be a time saver.

Flying over the great expanse of the Pacific Ocean. How to explain the day? Just getting my head around the plus and minus time zones, along with the fact we'll also be crossing the date line has my brain in knots. Leaving aside the normal airport routines. The details. Depart Auckland NZ at 7.35am for a 3 hour 40 minute flight. Arrive 9.15am Sydney Australia. Here a 3 hour wait. Depart 12.25pm on a 13 hour flight. Arrive Santiago Chile at 10.30am.

We gain some 14 hours. Taking the time differences into consideration we land in South America the same day but an hour earlier than leaving Australia. I'm still confused to this day! But I can say in one word how Qantas Airlines look after their customers. Excellently.

Bienvenido a Chile, América Latina

10.30am, Santiago. We're through immigration and customs quite quickly. Outside the terminal negotiate a set price taxi ride into the city. Mid-morning traffic is heavy, in the low mist buildings look as grey as the sky. Paulo the driver spoke very little English, my Spanish is marginal. The Travesia Bed and Breakfast, Jose Arrietta 83, Providencia, tucked away in a side street, hard to find but he got us there. I took his phone number, we'd use his services for the return journey.

I'd pre-booked this place while in England and had several email conversations with Christian, the owner. He was waiting for us. He'd spent many years in the USA, speaks almost perfect English, is eager to impart advice and marks places of interest on a tourist map, all within minutes of our arrival. The B&B is his pride and joy, he'd spent a small fortune in refurbishing the old building into a quaint boutique affair with antique furniture, bric-a-brac, pictures and sculptural artwork. Varnished wooden floors and creaking stairs a testament to his dedication! We're allocated a comfortably furnished first floor ensuite room, given a front door key and the wifi code. Come and go as you please!

By 2.30pm, Chris and I had walked around the block to acclimatise, searched out restaurants, picked up some cash Pesos at a supermarket ATM and eaten a 'cold' Salsa hot dog with a cup of instant coffee in a local café. Only been here for three and a bit hours and we're almost Chilean!

At the room we showered, wrote our diaries and took an hours nap. The long day had taken a toll.

6.30pm, went out chose a bar, had dinner and a couple of beers. Intending an early night we wandered back at about 9.20pm. Christian was in the breakfast room with other guests. A young couple and a pair of slightly older women, all Brazilians. We're introduced, invited to join them and partake in a glass of wine. Surely rude to decline, so didn't. We sat talking about many subjects until 11.00pm. Welcome to Chile, Latin America!

Saturday 9th May. Day 86. Santiago, Capital of Chile.

Having enjoyed the trip so far day by day, week by week, we arrived here in South America with the flimsiest of plans. Only the exit from Chile to Peru and homeward flights from Brazil were definitely booked. I'd hoped by now to have at least put some dates and stay durations to the hand written list of intended destinations, unfortunately the calendar spreadsheet remained with just approximations. So all future accommodations and travel arrangements will have to be booked as and when needed. Entry and exit strategy will be paramount for every individual place or country. This would become my mission on the day of arrival at anywhere new, once achieved the relief is actually palpable.

Last night we 'hit the sack' and slept instantly. Up at 8.30am and neither of us is completely recovered from yesterday's travelling, jetlag I presumed. Downstairs, Christian is fussing over breakfast, small tables already set and other guests seated. Coffee, toast, cheese slices, pots of yoghurt and peaches. Nice enough, but we'd eventually get bored having the same every morning!

Our time in Santiago will be treated as a cultural 'City Break' and we'll start the day with a visit to the centre. Use the tourist map, pick places to see and walk to them. Our day bags are clipped to trouser waist belt or loops using carabiners, something we do almost automatically. Snatching them would be a problem for any chancer.

Out we go into the mix. Plenty of new and old buildings, the latter influenced by the Spanish colonial period. Being on foot helps to becomes familiar with a new environment. It's Saturday, plenty of traffic, busy with local shoppers and tourists. Chileans enjoy visits to their own capital. We arrive at 'Cero de Cristobel' (St Christopher's Hill) a very popular attraction. A funicular railway provides a ride from bottom to top with a midway stopping point for those wishing to visit the city zoo. There are also steps, tracks, paths and a road to the apex. Fitness fanatics cycle, run or jog these routes. We, at sixty plus years old show our passports, negotiate the concessionary rate and let the train take the strain!

At the top station is a crowded viewing platform and café area. From here steps lead up to the statue of St Mary of the Immaculate Conception and garden sanctuary. People come here to reflect. It's quite emotionally moving to see the candles lit and expired along with many hand written notes posted, these either giving thanks for their child or praying for one. Chris and I sat for a quiet moment in the chapel.

After taking in and photographing the super views of the city we bought lunch in the café area. Coffee and empanadas. I warned Chris about the un-stoned olive found in these pastries, one bite and a tooth broken for sure! We purchased some note books and pencils as souvenirs for our grandchildren. Also picked up some postcards. Sat on a bench in the bright sun we did the true tourist bit and wrote them to friends and family. The first time we'd done this!

Following a map, we strolled paths at the top of the hill. Supposedly there were other places to see but they weren't notable. Back at the B&B, left our bags and coats then did some shopping locally. Topped up the supplies of sun tan lotion and insect repellent. Didn't need those here, the pack of beer we did!

Sunday 10th May. Day 87. Santiago.

The Plaza De Armas, (Place of the Warrior) every South American City has one! Sunday, a family oriented day out. A public place, there's a small police presence to keep order. The sun is shining on a busy square with lots of trees and bench seats. There is a vociferous God squad. A man stood on a box in speaker's corner loudly hails his opinions. A comedian gives a free performance. Of the three we didn't understand a word but the comic did get some hearty laughs. At the central fountain, as well as children playing in the water, a mad stray dog attempts to catch coins in its mouth as folks throw them, its success is rate poor, hence it's soaking wet and shivering from retrieving them, then placing them on the pool rim for no reward or treats, mental!

There are plenty of food vendors at the perimeter. Had lunch stood at a tapas style stall, fixed price for a 'cold' hot dog and a bottle of beer less than £3Gbp. Afterwards we visited the Natural History Museum, far too much to see in one go, we'd return later.

On to the Central Mercado, a sprawl of buildings, one contains the sea food market and many restaurants, no demarcation. In here at a bar we had a beer, asking for the tab Chris spoke her first Spanish words, 'Quenta por favour?' (How much please?) Whence paid, the barman replied "thank you!" She commented later that she smelled of fish. Only her clothes surely?

On the way back to the B&B through the park, we came across a big crowd, families, people of all ages, sat and standing. We joined them watching a hand puppet theatre set up in a booth similar to our own Punch & Judy shows. It was lovely to hear the children's laughter. No need to understand Spanish. Evidently 'he's behind you' is a universal warning!

Monday 11th May. Day 88. Santiago.

Out by 11.30am, back into the Plaza. The Post Office is open today. Quirky South American style 'take a ticket, sit and wait your turn.' Stamps bought and post cards sent to 'Blighty.' We had a look around the PO museum. Very good with philatelic displays and antique telephonic equipment. From here into the Cathedral. A Catholic mass coming to an end, many folks queuing to receive the 'the body of Christ,' a token wafer placed on their tongue by a priest. Christianity is still a very strong religion in South America.

Outside the building, zealots are shouting through megaphones. Two Languages being used, in English it was plain to understand that they were calling for the church to do more. More what?

Having visited the fish market yesterday our minds were made up to have lunch at one of the internationally renowned restaurants. In the 'Donde Augusta' we enjoyed a platter of sea bass and sword fish with mixed salad. £25 cash, served with a smile, accompanied by folk guitar music, priceless!

The market area consists of shops, malls and stalls selling everything conceivable, from electrical goods to vegetables. There are numerous workshops undertaking repairs, tailoring, electrical and computers. Several did screen replacements for lap tops and other devices. I was tempted to bring the ipad here but thought better of it. I did find and buy a replacement pack of tiny screwdrivers.

Now I'd have to find a way of hiding them from zealous airport security!

Back at the B&B. Chris and I discussed and made a vital decision. We'd definitely not stay in Lima, Peru, just use the airport connection to Arequipa. Online, I booked a reasonable B&B there for three nights. During the evening I attempted some chair high push ups. Disappointing, I've lost so much upper arm strength and will need to work on this. Annoyingly I seem to have developed a slight ear ache. Wax or fluid?

Later Christian was kind enough to phone Paulo to arrange our airport taxi. We wait on confirmation.

Tuesday 12th May. Day 89. Santiago.

Left some laundry with Janice the housekeeper then walked to the Plaza. Visited lots of chemist shops asking for ear medication. No luck. Took a look inside the Basilica and afterwards finished the tour of the Natural History museum. Lunch, empanadas and coffee in a café just out of the square. Later, did some online research about South American mobile networks. We're going to need a sim card eventually.

Wednesday 13th May. Day 90. Santiago.

We've probably been here for a day too long, that's the vagary of guesswork when pre-planning flights. Decided against trying to get an ipad sim card, so walked eastwards for a change. More a business district so not much to see. Doubled back and crossed the river bridge, went through side roads to the lower reaches of the Cero Hill. Took coffee in a small café, the Pino Nino, before walking up to the level containing the zoo. Later went to the same café for a lunch of 'Pescado y Fritas' (fish and chips). Had a good chat about football with the Brazilian and Colombian waiters.

At the B&B I texted Paulo. I had concerns that he may not do the taxi pickup, enough for me to email Christian and ask him to double check. Back from dinner I found he had left me a note, all was OK for the early collection. I went to bed very relieved.

Thursday 14th May. Day 91. Santiago, Chile to Arequipa, Peru, via Lima. 1st leg, Avianca Lineas Areas. AV624 Dep. 7.30am. Arr. 9.20am. 2nd leg, Trans American AV817 Dep. 5.15pm Arr. 6.45pm. 4,400km.

Although my phone alarm was set for 4.00am I'd been awake well before. At about midnight, Chris decided to have a hot flush of near nuclear temperature. Afterwards, sleep had been patchy at best. So as not to wake other guests we crept down stairs as quietly as possible. Unfortunately at this time of the morning the creaking boards sounded like demolition. Just had time to make and have a coffee in the kitchen, then I stood at the front door and had a couple of nerve calming smokes while waiting for the cab. Paulo arrived spot on time.

Today we're using Avianca, an airline service I'd only heard of because of the cheap and advantageous booking made in October 2014. A two part flight, first Santiago to Lima, the second into Arequipa. If we'd decided to stay in Lima we could just have not bothered with leg two! Negotiated the self-check in machine and got boarding passes for both flights. Bought coffee and croissants while waiting at the gate. After a three hour flight we were in Lima, Peru. Same day another country!

With almost eight hours to spare I decided to put some time to good use. Found a 'Claro' phone company booth, had a sim fitted to the ipad and paid the fee for a month. It took ages for the woman agent to make a connection. Just as well it did, because the Arequipa B&B needed confirmation of our arrival for the taxi pickup. In the airport's big ground floor area, who'd believe it, there's a MacDonald's restaurant. We bought coffee and greasy chicken bits with chips. Hot food! I was starving. Hate to admit, but it was lovely.

So far, a fairly good run of luck at airports. It ran out today! Boarding gate number announced we presented ourselves and passes in good time. Unfortunately they wouldn't scan. We're sent downstairs to get fresh ones at the desk, lugging backpacks, day bags against the flow of people. Done. Back upstairs through the milling throng and we queued again. Chris got through but not me. Rejected again! I have to step aside as a supervisor is called. I'm sweating like a drug smuggler waiting one side of the gate while my missus is on the other. Eventually someone manually keyed me in. Phew!

My trial wasn't over yet, at security I almost completely undressed to get through the metal detection, I had visions of the 'blue glove.' Was I glad to get on the aeroplane!

Mountains, Incas and Pachamama in Peru.

Landed in Arequipa at 8.35pm, taxi waiting as arranged. In the dark, a twenty minute drive into town. Normal graduation of building types, industrial near the airport then grotty poor areas with better appearing towards the historic city centre. I should have realised there may have been a problem when the driver centrally locked the car doors at the first set of traffic lights. In many places, groups of police, most with riot shields, seemed to be 'mopping up.' We'd arrived in a city in the midst of a three day general strike, having street disturbances, with a Thursday night riot for a finale!

9.30pm, checked in to the hotel Las Torress de Ugarte, 401-A Calle Ugarte. Chris and I had a rule about not exploring any town if arriving after dark. The receptionist confirmed that it would probably not be safe to do so anyway. Dinner of biscuits and coffee in the room. Bed and slept instantly.

Friday 15th May. Day 92. Arequipa, Peru.

Nice hotel. We had a buffet breakfast. Surprising how much better things are when the sun is shining and your belly is full. Tourist map in hand, out we went. Walked a couple of blocks. Saw evidence of yesterday's disturbances, rocks and stones in little piles tucked into wall corners. Ammunition to throw at any wayward police car.

First visit today the famous Monasterio de Santa Catalina. Incepted in 1650, now a world heritage site, comprising a small walled town built for Nuns. Truly a beautiful place with so much to see. Spent three hours here taking many pictures. For me, the ancient wooden doors are a delight. The cloisters have great charm. In one it was as if we'd stepped back in time, both having exactly the same thought, an 'El Cid' moment. In the film when

Rodrigo de Vivar meets his daughters for the first time. It could have been here!

Afterwards, went to a hole in the wall fast food outlet, dining area with plastic tables and chairs. Mainly used by locals, it served various set priced meals, we had chicken, chips and coca cola. Our first lunch in Peru!

Onto the Plaza de Armas, yes another! Plenty of shops around the perimeter, bought some beer and cigarettes, found an ATM and got some cash. A banner waving crowd were protesting near the Cathedral, a less aggressive continuation of the strike. Policemen hovered nearby. Plenty of touts for restaurants, others plying tours. Picked up some leaflets, we need to get our heads together to sort one out.

At the hotel. Read the leaflets and discussed an exit strategy. Ideal for us would be a road trip that takes in Colca Canyon and then gets us to Cusco. We agree on that so book an extra night here as breathing space. Later, had an expensive drink in a very posh bar then went for dinner. Although night time the streets were quiet and I'd seen enough of the locality to be confident.

Saturday 16th May. Day 93. Arequipa.

Had a restless night. I need to get the trip organised. So as recommended by Veronika in reception, it's to the travel agents to meet Roberto. I outline the details, seems to be no problem just a few adjustments. We're to return at 2.00pm and sign up.

Had cake and coffee as a snack before going on a paid for guided visit to the Cathedral de Arequipa Museum. Very good with many exhibits among them priceless religious jewellery. The tour finished on the roof in amongst the enormous bells and towers. A bonus was good views of the snow-capped volcanic mountains El Pichu Pichu and El Misti.

Because of a power outage, meeting the travel agent is re-arranged for 4.00pm. Just outside the plaza we go to the

Museo Santuarios Andinos to see 'Juanita.' Another paid guide needed. He gives us our first in depth education into the history of Inca tribes. We're taken through dimly lit designer styled rooms with carefully displayed archaeological finds and eventually to the prize exhibit. The mummified body of a girl child sacrificed high in the Andes to the Inca Gods. Her remains now ghoulishly kept in a glass cabinet maintained at below zero temperature.

We're only 2,000 metres above sea level. Vehicle traffic is heavy in the narrow streets and the road around the square. Exhaust fumes make breathing difficult for both of us. We take lunch in an upstairs restaurant called The Balcony,' it overlooks the Plaza. A young Argentinian waiter tells us that here on Thursday a mob was throwing stones at customers!

The later meeting at the travel agents was a success apart from a problem with a card terminal. We'd be visiting the main attractions in the canyon, staying two nights in Chivay and afterwards a coach ride would take us into Cusco. Perfecto!

Susie had told us that there is plenty to do in and around Cusco. Machu Picchu being one big visit! Online at our hotel I booked a six night stay in a hostel. Exit and new entry strategy completed I'm a happy man! Celebration beers and steak dinner later.

Tonight the lamp lit plaza is really nice. Some not so noisy protesters have been corralled into a far corner. Families wander about, children hold balloons and eat sweets or ice creams. Occasionally, vintage cars arrive bringing newlyweds for that special photograph. The brides wear spectacular gowns and sometimes a groom is dressed in military uniform. Their day has been good. So has ours!

Sunday 17th May. Day 94. Arequipa.

After yesterday's accomplishments we're relaxed and plan to keep it that way. In the garden this morning we watched the hotel owner spoon feed a breakfast of melon pieces to 'Lala,' a giant tortoise. The sun is bright and high in a blue sky, almost shirt off weather. We decided to visit the market. As usual a typical South American affair. Massive. The surrounding streets buzzing with people. Small local shops display their goods on already narrow walkways.

In the centre is a high roofed, warehouse type building full of vendors offering everything from televisions to poultry, clothing and other dry goods, wet fish, vegetables and fresh meat. The stalls are mostly next to each other, gangways are only a metre wide. There are lots of flies about but birds swooping and catching are dealing with them. Mother Nature's indoor mobile hygiene service!

Did some shopping back at the Plaza, in a farmacia got antihistamine tablets. Further treatment for my ear problem. It's not wax, with a bit of online self-diagnosis the symptoms are of 'swimmers ear,' decongestants can help dry the fluid. For snacks while travelling through Colca Canyon we stocked with biscuits, bread rolls and crisps. Having decided to chill out in the hotel garden this afternoon, we bought a few beverages.

Sat in the warm sunshine we wrote our diaries, watched 'Lala' the tortoise wander the grounds, drank beer and talked about what we'd done and what we're soon to do. So much still unknown, these are very exciting days!

Later I paid the hotel account and we did some packing. Took our last dinner in Arequipa at a nice restaurant in the Plaza. I had pork ribs, Chris ate Alpaca meat for the first time. She noted that it had the texture of beef steak and tasted sweet.

Monday 18th May. Day 95. Arequipa to Chivay, Colca Canyon. 163km.

7.00am, sat in reception waiting for transport. The big portrait of St Christopher on a wall reminds that we're reliant on others for safe travel. 7.30am, a fourteen seat Mercedes mini-bus arrives. We're first to board and have a choice of seats. The van then makes several other pick-ups in town. Annoyingly, an American and his Latin girl-friend create a thirty minute delay. Obviously couldn't get up in time! Traffic was hectic in the city but we got to the outskirts by 8.30am.

Our fellow travellers are a mixed group, mostly couples, Spanish, Italian, Brazilian, French and some 'tossers' already mentioned. Driver Maximo is introduced by the guide Pedro. Who's next half hour of talk in both Spanish and pigeon English extolls the virtue of chewing coca leaves and their alkaloid medicinal properties as the best preventative for altitude sickness. He does however, forget to mention that the recreational drug cocaine is derived from this plant and its possession is illegal in most other civilised countries. Although when questioned, he does admit that an equal medicinal effect can be obtained through other foodstuffs, some being chocolate, sugary glucose sweets, coffee, tea and believe it or not, tobacco!

Chris and I did buy and try coca leaves, they tasted like s**t and made us feel sick. She'd rely on very dark chocolate and sweets, me on asthma sprays and twenty cigarettes a day. So British!

As the van climbed higher into the Andes the road became quite rough, pitted with small rocks and boulders at the verge. In bright sunshine we could see Arequipa in the lowlands. After passing through a very scruffy village, where caterpillar tracked heavy construction vehicles and a dead dog in the road were the only notable highlights, the landscape became a bleak scrub strewn desert. All the while, Pedro, our coca leaf chewing guide, his cheeks swollen to full capacity, continued his litany of Inca history and economics.

A few stops made, for toilets, to look at small herds of Alpaca and a natural spring. At 4,000 metres above sea level came a coffee break and photo opportunity. Among other snow-capped mountain peaks visible at a distance the Sabancaya Volcano, active with steam and smoke rising. At this altitude we expected to be struggling to breathe, me especially as an asthmatic. Not the case, Chris said that it was slightly difficult to take a deep breath. Personally, I enjoyed the crisp clean air and my cigarettes tasted nice!

The drive continued, descending into Colca Valley. 1.30pm reached the bottom of the gorge and the town of Chivay. A pre-organised group lunch had here. After that, back in the van then up into the mountains using off road tracks to Umara, a commercial venture of weather beaten windowed buildings. Here for the low price of 60 Soles, about £10, with towels and soap included for the shower taken after, we bathed in water derived from natural hot springs. Spent nearly two hours in the hot pool, our skin felt so clean and tingling. Another fantastic first!

On the way back into town, Pedro told of tonight's events and the hour we'd all need to be ready for collection. The van stopped and let passengers out at various accommodations, including posh places for the wealthier. Chris and I were dropped off at the Hotel Terra. Not far from the main square, in a dusty side street with adobe brick and mud buildings. Almost a scene from a spaghetti western. I was fully expecting the shout, "Hey gringo, go for your gun." Evening was arriving and the extreme contrast in hot day and cold night temperatures now became obvious.

The hotel building is reasonably modern, maybe ten years old, empty corridors echoed especially when doors slammed. Our ensuite room is basically furnished but good enough. The bed has a covering of thick woollen blankets. There's a small electric heater, it's quickly turned on.

Collected at 6.00pm. The others are picked up and we're all taken to a restaurant. Dinner and traditional Inca entertainment included in the trip price, beverage costs are extra. Sat eating and drinking, we're treated to an often amusing, sometimes strange, mixture of songs, music and very weird dance routines. Including some that visiting tourists are encouraged to partake and one where a man wearing a ski mask is beaten with sticks by women. Maybe he was a Member of Parliament in disguise!

Tuesday 19th May. Day 96. Chivay.

In bed by 9.00pm last night. Cold enough for Chris to wear pyjamas and me a t shirt. Up early and have a strange breakfast of coffee, 'hot' orange juice, crusty bread rolls and jam.

In the van at 6.15am and out of town onto very rough unmade roads, dust spewing from the rear wheels. A lot of mini buses get this punishment. First stop a village called Yanque. Here indigenous children dressed in Inca costumes are dancing in the square and the souvenir stalls are open. It's not much past eight o'clock in the morning and some of our fellow travellers can't wait to buy some of the tat, purses, woolly hats etcetera. Chris and I took a look at the beautiful 17th century church.

At Maca, the next village, souvenir sellers again! Some locals had captive birds tied to ropes for tourist photo opportunities. I took pictures of a donkey! Soon it's onward and upward, sandy, rubble strewn tracks and through roughly hewn tunnels, still swirling with the dust lifted by a previous vehicle. There are sheer drops at the verges and spectacular views of cultivated terraces rising on the sides of the deep canyon. We arrive at Condor Cross, very popular, mini-buses and coaches parked everywhere. Hundreds of tourists with cameras ready are standing at every vantage point. We join the throng. Sights to behold, in great numbers, Condors with two metre wing span are majestically swooping and reeling.

On the move and Pedro's socio economic commentary continues all the while. We're told that farmers still use a barter system for goods exchange and that many would not survive without receiving government subsidies. Also that many descendants of Inca tribes continue to practice parts of ancient religions, pseudo worship of the Sun and offering token gifts to Pachamama, the Earth Mother.

He was well intended but started to irritate as we travelled back to town. The more coca chewed, the more he prattled, often becoming unintelligible. I was happy when we were all given the opportunity to walk in the sunshine for a while. The van was stopped, high up on a section of crumbling track, a chance to get close to the mountain edge and take pictures of the stunning gorge.

Back at Chivay, lunch was in the same place as yesterday. Just before this, Pedro explained the arrangements for our journey to Cusco tomorrow. The agents in Arequipa seem to have been very proficient. We'd be staying here for another night, so with the afternoon free of commitments we visited the Plaza de Armas to select a place to have dinner tonight. Back at the hotel we showered and caught up on some deserved sleep. I had the last of four short period dizzy spells. Thin air! Nothing more than that.....I hoped!

It's dark when at about 5.30pm we could hear the sound of music. So we walked briskly to the small plaza to find a large procession of partially uniformed children, many just infants. Some were holding candle lit lanterns, others played drums or blew trumpets. They were marching around the square following a carried crucifix. The simplicity of the sounds was so Hispanic. A crowd of adults listened to a speech given through a megaphone. We'd stumbled upon a 'Festival de la Familia.' Poignant and beautiful, bringing a tear to our eyes.

Had a beer in a designer styled modern bar then elsewhere a nice simple meal to finish a good day and were in bed before 9.00pm.

Wednesday 20th May. Day 97. Chivay to Cusco. 435km

Collected by taxi from the hotel promptly at 6.30am and delivered to the 4M bus depot. A tiny office at the front of another hotel. Half an hour later we find that we're to be the only passengers in a fourteen seat mini-bus. Middle aged driver Ricardo is introduced by the young guide Alexis. They are both already chomping on coca leaves. Veterans! It's explained that the 4M Company wants to expand this regular simple bus trip into a proper guided tour, with stops at mostly unvisited places of interest. They have been asked by the owners to request if we would be 'test' passengers and be taken on the first nine hour trial run and then give our opinion of the experience. Quite an honour I thought and agreed immediately.

So we have guide and driver already high on coca and likely to get higher as they replenished their mouths with a handful of leaves. We're given a gift package, water, biscuits, sweets and chocolate. After the road out of town the mini bus is flung about like a rally car, so it was seat belts on! Ricardo didn't muck about, seemed we had a new 'Stig', a Peruvian van driving version. It didn't take long to realise that if stopping places were being added to the journey, time spent at them would have to be made up while on the move.

Driving up the Colca valley we passed through the villages of Tuti and Sibayo. High up in the Andes the van slewed to a halt for me and Ricardo to smoke, and to take a look at the Callalli Castles. Impressive rock formations formed by wind and water erosion. Onward, and Alexis informs us that much of the road is new, paid for by the copper mining companies and mostly used by their giant trucks. We see plenty of them. Evidently it's the mysterious overseas investment and interference along with the displacement of indigenous Peruvians that are the root cause of the recent riots.

A short detour is taken from the main road and we arrive at Kanamarka. A recently reconstructed pre-Inca period village. No souvenir sellers here and we're privileged visitors! As we walk around, Alexis explains more about it. In one stone building we're shown ongoing excavations of what's been mooted as a possible sacrificial burial site.

Back on the main road and we pass a massive working open cast mine. We also see the new landscaping schemes being undertaken to repair the scars of many previous years damage. Driving upwards continued, topping out at a height of 5,000 metres above sea level, 1,500 metres higher than NZ's Mount Tasman! We're briefly stopped by road maintenance work and get out of the van. We're above the clouds. Poking through them in the distance are snow covered Andes mountain tops. Quite an amazing sight.

For a toilet and coffee break we pulled into a recently built and expanding town, here purely to serve the human needs of the mineworkers living in the area. Further on, passed by the Condorama Dam, a mere 4,737 metres above sea level! On clear stretches of road even those with twists, turns, dodgy verges and sheer drops, coca chewing Ricardo kept the pedal to the metal. We're still high up in the mountains when made another brief stop. A cigarette break and for us to take photographs looking down over the impressive twenty five metre long Langui Lake with its mirror like surface.

The winding road descended into Cusco Valley. Now we're below the mountains and they look just as impressive, their folds and creases more apparent, lower reaches covered in vegetation. Tracks snake up them, accessing terraced and cultivated areas. Alexis tells that the planting of imported deep rooting Eucalyptus trees has brought soil stability, helping to prevent landslides.

On the road in the bottom of the valley. Another brief stop at a very tourist oriented café in Sicuani, just to use the bathroom facilities. From here it's a ride of over two hours, through villages and small townships. We eventually pass some ancient ruins, once the arches for gated entry into the Imperial Inca City of Cusco.

The outskirts of the city proper are reached at rush hour. I'm glad Ricardo is at the wheel and has obviously done this trip many times. He and the guide have kept topping up with coca leaf. Their chatting leads to occasional fits of giggles, sometimes laughter. I wonder if this a side effect similar to that of cannabis use. Traffic is heavy in the busy main streets. I've shown the written address of our accommodation to Alexis, he uses phone mapping and gives Ricardo driving directions.

4.30pm, after some crazy driving and an exhilarating tour taking almost nine hours, we're finally in the city centre and parked as close as possible to our new hotel. Our luggage has to be carried up a steep seven metres of stone steps to a pedestrian lane. Alexis is kind enough to help. His job is done, we say our thanks for the safe trip and I give a deserved cash tip for him and Ricardo to share.

Just down the lane we stand outside the Hosteria de Anita, Alabado 525, Cusco 84, use the bell push and are buzzed through an electronically latched metal gate. It's a big place linked by covered walkways, a cluster of smaller buildings with small courtyards. One of these is a planted garden just outside reception. Here we're informed that it's a family run concern and a cash only business. The daughter of the owner signs us in. Someone likes us, we're allocated a large family room. An attic conversion, beautifully worked with polished wood floor and varnished exposed structural timbers. Ensuite and well furnished, three singles and one double bed, a table, occasional and arm chairs. It got even better, dormer windows with excellent views over the historic city, night time now, so it's lit up like a Christmas tree. Did I say perfectos? I'm sure I meant to!

Took quick showers, went out for dinner at the most convenient, nearest, decent looking restaurant. A bit of a designer place, a lot of very rich people come to this city, so it was expensive.

At 9.00pm while walking back to the hotel we saw a perfect example of the wealth here. Outside the main window of an open jewellery shop stood a very large uniformed security guard. On display inside, a necklace, the pendant a spectacular blue sapphire the size of a small meteor. From within, a smiling female shop worker saw and beckoned us. Grinning, I made a sawing motion across my arm. She laughed knowingly so I didn't have to pretend cutting my leg off!

Thursday 21st May. Day 98. Cusco.

After a quality served breakfast we sat in the communal lounge, accessed the internet and researched trips to Machu Picchu. Found out that there is a limit of only four hundred people allowed in on any one day and organising a tour for ourselves was quite complex. The hostel tour desk was fully au fait with the details, as other guests were using this facility we decided to book from here. Arrangements to go were made for Saturday at a cost of 370.Usd each. We also asked them to sort out a bus ride to the city of Puno, our next destination.

Went out, heading down and into the main square, principally to find ATM's and had to use three machines to get enough cash. Cusco as a city is at the thin end of a long valley surrounded by mountains and hills, getting anywhere involves an incline. For example, looking from our loft room windows, the tower of San Cristobel's Church is almost at eye level. A high viewing point in its own right. We made a worthwhile visit there that involved walking up from the Plaza through narrow lanes and streets. Unfortunately, if these routes are wide enough to get a car through, drivers will use them. Traffic here is constant, exhaust pollution is as bad if not worse than

Arequipa. At night a blue haze sits in the cold air. It's not the altitude but fumes that make breathing difficult. I pitied the whistle blowing female police officers on control duties.

Back at the square, Chris was randomly interviewed and video recorded by school children who asked tourism related questions. Because the hostel has only coca tea as a free beverage we bought a jar of coffee in a supermarket. Later we had tacos for dinner at the Inti Pizza, a very small Mexican themed restaurant just down the lane from the hostel.

Friday 22nd May. Day 99. Cusco.

Last night's spicy food had me up early! After breakfast we walked out and talked about an exit plan. Found a bank ATM and got more cash in US dollars.

Wandered into the smaller Espanar Plaza, it's very busy here. We fancied sitting on one of a few benches to enjoy the sunny weather and people watch. The only space available for two people is next to a local man, by his gnarled complexion very much in senior years. I approached and pointed to the empty seat, he indicated for us to sit. I thanked him and shook his weathered brown hand.

We're sat opposite the very old Basilica. On the bell tower, bullet holes around the window told of a troubled history.

After exploring different streets, bizarrely we arrived at the same place lunched at yesterday so had coffee and sandwiches. Pre-empting the trip to Machu Picchu we went to the Museum de Concha, watched videos and studied the exhibits. Afterwards, picked up some beer for the room and pastries for tomorrow.

At the hotel I met with the owner Jose, he had tomorrow's itinerary, quite complex as I'd thought. Transport vouchers, a paper sheet with hand written times for the outward and return journeys. Our bus to Puno was also confirmed, so before we left the lounge, online I booked a place to stay. Took dinner at the Inti Pizza and shared two giant 1100cl bottled beers. We had an interesting chat with a Hampshire born young English couple. He soon to take up residence as a chest doctor in Portsmouth's Queen Alexandra Hospital, his girlfriend in her final year of training to be a GP.

Saturday 23rd May. Day 100. Cusco to Machu Picchu.

Up at 5.00am, very early to the breakfast room and there's not much food ready, but did get some scrambled eggs and coffee. 6.20am picked up by a taxi driver called Aldo. Already a change of plan and take a twenty minute ride to Poroz station. Here we board a special train, its carriages with big scenic windows, side and roof. Seats are allocated, we're sat opposite a Dutch couple who are also travelling many parts of the world. We enjoyed a fine conversation while the train slowly hauled us up the mountain. On arrival at the top station everything is organised, we're directed to the many waiting buses that take visitors the final few kilometres up the narrow winding roads to a very busy entrance zone. Here authorised guides are allocated, ours proves to be quite humorous and informative.

Machu Picchu built about 1450AD, abandoned a hundred years later, re-discovered in 1911 and lots of reconstruction since. The history and use of the place much speculated, possibly a royal estate with some religious purposes? Temples dedicated to the Earth and Celestial Gods have been identified. Many of the dry stone walled buildings are Colcas, larders for long term food storage, so it's likely that the terraces were cultivated. Climbing the steep steps is exhilarating and the views from any aspect are spectacular. The guide's duties over, Chris and I can wander at will, up, down and around. Even at 2500 metres high no breathing problems experienced, the air is so clean. A World Heritage site and totally geared for tourists but actually being here is a privilege.

Nevertheless, Machu Picchu should be considered in the context of world history. Built at the peak of Inca Empire power its desertion is blamed either on disease or possibly the encroachment of European invaders. During its lifetime Tudor Royal families were ruling England. It's certainly made me think!

The bus trip down made. Had time to walk around the village and take coffee. As dusk fell we boarded the train, the return journey plan taking us to a different station. By now it's completely dark. While on the move, passengers are given the soft sell routine in the guise of a fashion show. Rail staff, including one dressed in a grotesque mask as a 'mischievous devil,' entertained by prancing through the carriages. Others wore or displayed examples of Alpaca wool. Very funny at times.

Ollantaytambo is a tourist centre in its own right. Outside the railway station are shops, restaurants, bars and souvenir sellers. It's crowded with people. Many cars, coaches, mini-buses are parked but we still find Aldo and his taxi. Lots of vehicles leave at the same time as us in a sort of night time rush hour. As we hit the outskirts so many headlights pierce the raised dust, it creates an eerie scene. About thirty minutes out and on a gravel track we see three men walking. Without explanation Aldo pulls up and exits the car, our suspicions and nerves are raised. I mention to Chris at awkward times like this that it's better to have a weapon than not. I don't! Having spoken to the men he came back to the vehicle. It turned out that he'd recognised a friend and wanted to know what he was doing out here at this hour. Phew!

After a two hour gruelling and sometimes scary ride through winding mountain roads we were back in Cusco. Had a pizza and a couple of beers locally and were in bed by midnight. A fantastic one hundredth day!

Sunday 24th May. Day 101. Cusco.

Had a good night's rest, got up at 8.40am. Almost a lay in!
Having arranged laundry to be done we put on a
completely fresh set of clothes. Online, I'd been in contact
with a friend, she'd been here and recommended a place
where a good English style fried breakfast could be
bought. Quite a time since that simple pleasure. Only so
much chicken and rice can be tolerated! Found the place
but its small, busy and the queue outside is very long. Idea
cancelled. Back to the Plaza de Armes, the sun is shining,
national flags are fluttering high on their staffs. We sat on
a bench and are immediately approached by one of the
'shoe shiners' carrying his home made stool with its built
in box of polishes, cloths and brushes. We're wearing
trainers, but even a polite 'no gracias' doesn't deter him!
He's spotted a flaw in my toe cap and proffers a tube of
super glue in an attempt to make a job of it. No repair
needed, so with a smile I give him a one sol coin. He's
happy.

Checked the tour map and found a KFC tucked into one
side of the square, decided to treat ourselves there for
lunch. Afterwards strolling through the Sunday artisans
market back to the hotel.

During the afternoon we caught up with some overdue
sleep. Later had beers and a bowl of chilli con carne in a
pub called 'Nortons.' Its balcony overlooked the plaza and
we watched a spectacular night time church festival. A
drum and trumpet band leading ranks of people in a
procession following a carried icon dedicated to Santa
Maria.

Monday 25th May. Day 102. Cusco.

Leaving tomorrow so decided not to do much today. Over
previous days I'd been drip feeding cash to cover the hotel
account, at reception I made the final payment. Went out
got some more money at a bank ATM. Thought I might

shop and find some replacement sandals, so taught myself to say in Spanish, "sandalias y plástico con Velcro por favour?" Visited several shoe shops without luck, probably because there aren't any beaches around here! Wandered the square, took lunch at Nortons. Afterwards, searched out a place to take our last dinner.

Back at the hotel I slept for a while. Chris read and listened to 'Prince' on the ipod. Part packed before going out. On the way, at reception I collected the bus tickets to Puno. Our last few beers and dinner of a shared bowl of curry taken in a very busy and friendly staffed 'Paddy's Bar,' purported to be the highest altitude Irish pub in the world. Couldn't dispute the claim!

Tuesday 26th May. Day 103. Cusco to Puno. 390km.

4.37am, woken by a pre-recorded phone call and a text message, both informing that my Lloyds Bank credit card was used online during the night. The transaction needed verification or denial. I keyed in the latter. Another problem to deal with! Stressing, I opened a window and had a smoke.

Finished packing after breakfast then waited at reception for the taxi to take us to the bus stop in town. Here we board a coach and get another surprise. The ride to Puno is a proper guided tour. A route taking in archaeological sites and more of the Andes Mountains. Visiting the village of Andahuaylillas. Stopping at La Roya, a high point of 4,335 metres. On to Ragen and then with lunch included a stop at Sicuani. A brief museum visit at Pucara then on through the marshlands of the Puno valley skirting Titicaca, the highest altitude lake in the world and every tourist's reason for being here.

5.00pm, after more than eight hours of travel we arrived at the Puno coach depot. Here quite a few touts are pressing for business. We just want a taxi. A man calling himself Jamie and also claiming to be a tour organiser leads us to a cab. I of course still ask for a fixed fare price.

Happy with the figure quoted we get in, so does our man! Clever ploy. During the drive to the hotel we have quite a chat, he tells of the three day general strike starting tomorrow and gives his sales pitch. I take a business card and leaflet but agree to nothing else. Checked in for four nights at the Hotel Hacienda Plaza de Armas, given a lovely room with a small balcony overlooking the square. Another Booking.com bargain!

Before doing much else I need to ascertain what has happened to my credit card. Spend a long time on the web and a small fortune making irate mobile phone to Lloyds. The card has been cloned, used in Nigeria, no longer usable and totally blocked. My immediate thoughts were of the dodgy terminal at the travel agents in Arequipa. I had no proof that a scam was in operation and the bank wasn't interested. What could I do anyway?

I am extremely angry and upset. Calls itself an international bank and offers not one iota of help! I vow to deal with them when I get back to England. Fortunately we have Chris's debit and the two ICE travel cards as backups.

Early evening. We need to eat, so with little exploration choose a busy a restaurant near the plaza. My bad mood is far from improved when the simple meals ordered are served lukewarm on cold plates. I spoke strong, harsh words. The returned micro wave re-heated dinners were just tolerable. We'd not eat here again.

Wednesday 27th May. Day 104. Puno.

Had a rough night. Up several times, a combination of things, indigestion, chewed up with the annoyance about the card problem, hot and strangely struggled for breath. Thin air?

We had things to do, not just exploring! Jamie's tour leaflet in hand, went out intending to find his office. Failed in that so continued walking. Passed by men in discussion, obviously strikers clustered around or sat on benches.

Made the downhill stroll to the lake harbour, had a look around, sat for a while and enjoyed the views. If need be there were plenty of pay as you go boat trips available. Strode back toward the town, the uphill climb not so kind on lungs or legs so hired a cycle taxi. Got off at the edge of the city centre and saw the first group of protesting marchers led by banner carriers, escorted by armed police all heading toward the Plaza.

A hotel receptionist was kind enough to make a phone call to Jamie. We'd meet here later and arrange a boat tour of Lake Titicaca for tomorrow and Saturday's bus ride from Puno to La Paz. Exit strategy sorted!

In anticipation of an early morning start we had a light meal in local bar and brief night time look around the area. Very busy with indigenous Peruvian street vendors and shops, many selling souvenirs and Alpaca wool items.

Thursday 28th May. Day 105. Puno, Boat trip on Lake Titicaca, The Uros floating Islands and Taquile.

Up at 5.20am. Just after breakfast Jamie arrived to confirm Saturday's coach ride to La Paz. A short while later a shuttle bus took us to the harbour. Here we crossed other moored boats to reach the one we're booked on. A purpose built vessel, inboard seating for about thirty passengers, scenic side windows, a small open rear deck and a benched viewing area on top of the cabin. While waiting for all to board an uninvited guitarist serenaded. A little too early for me to appreciate music, such as it was!

Cast off and motoring on the quiet fresh water of this enormous lake with shores in Peru and Bolivia. The sun is shining, it's cold but a beautiful day. The young guide started his commentary, where we'd be going, what we'll be doing and adding interesting historical, socio-economic details of the Uros. A pre-Incan people we'd soon encounter. Within an hour we're cruising close to some of the famous floating islands, these and the homes are completely constructed with 'Totora' reed. Our first stop is one of these.

Tourist boats are already tied alongside many islands. A gentle bump announces our arrival, bow and stern ropes secured and everyone disembarks. Making footsteps is physically weird, as if walking on a mattress. Unfortunately, the next sensation is the stench of fish.

Wearing brightly coloured traditional clothes, families who live and work here are waiting. These ruddy, weather worn, puff cheeked people have souvenirs laid out ready to sell. Children rush to hug the females in our group. Mothers eager to show their homes give invites to view the living conditions.

The guide calls us together to hear a talk by a 'young' male elder who tells that the basics of the island way of life have not changed for millennia and are practised by five families on this one. He explains the uses of the important reed, as a foodstuff, medicine, making boats, fishing etcetera. He doesn't mention that tourists are now the main income. Behind him and leaning against the wall of a hut a young girl holds what at first seems a squeaking soft toy. On closer inspection it's a live scrawny grey furred kitten. Noises emanate as the child either squeezes the body or pulls on its legs!

Talk over. Dropped to the reed floor, the kitten still alive lies writhing next to a very dead plucked chicken and a small terracotta bowl containing a few tiny swimming fish. We tourists are now encourage to pay for and embark on a reed boat excursion. Two of these handmade vessels looking like solid straw gondolas are ready for use. Our group is split evenly to each one and sat on blue polythene sheeting. The boat is 'long pole punted' by a boy of about ten to twelve years old. It seems his two siblings are to be the entertainment. A sister sings her version of 'Frere Jaques' and 'twinkle, twinkle, little star.' A kindergarten aged brother, wearing an infant's overcoat and a pink Winnie the Pooh back pack struggles with the chorus. Not helping is the thick shiny slime of green snot hanging from his nostrils to bottom lip!

The vessel is punted once around the small island. At the back of which I spot outboard motor driven boats covered in tarpaulins. That's progress I supposed. We're a captive audience. The young girl expertly holds her woolly hat in front of us one at a time. Who wouldn't drop in a coin or two? By the time we're being secured to the island the monetary spoils have already been shared. Snot boy is in floods of tears as his sister only gave him one 'Sol.' Never mind, before disembarking there's time for hugs and even kisses. Chris and I were on the other side of the Island before the green slime could get near us!

Back on board our vessel the guide informs that it's a two hour cruise before we reach Taquile Island. The sun is warm through the windows. Coats off, me and some others sleep most of the way until woken by further commentary.

The island, once a prison is now semi-autonomous. Its small population operate the farming, fishing and tourism industries as a collective. The boat is moored alongside a purpose built jetty. While disembarking we're instructed to meet in the main square almost at the top. This involves an upward climb to a height of about 500 metres using steep track, steps and paths, some with a sixty degree incline. All in our own time of course! Many people struggled, pausing for breath after only a few paces. In thin clean air, the few times we stopped to take a deep breath we also enjoyed the stunning views out over the lake.

The last few winding steps of a ten minute hike took us to almost 4,000 metres above sea level. Musical sounds announced we were close to the main village and plaza. Here with old buildings on three sides it was already a hive of activity. Too much to take in at one glance. In clothing predominantly red and white, traditionally dressed islanders were waving flags and banners of similar colours, dancing, banging drums, blowing horns. Possibly a festival but more likely for the benefit of us camera happy tourists.

We recognised some of our group rallying to the guide so joined them. Taking more pathways and steps everyone walks to a building a short distance from the square. This place can't be described as a restaurant, it's more a family home. Here we'd take lunch seated at tables in the shade on an outside terrace. A choice of two meals only, fish or omelette both with rice. We hadn't had much interaction with any of our fellow passengers but had noted that there were some Europeans. Chris and I shared a table with a mother and her two teenage daughters. A limited conversation took place, because, as our food arrived and the Cooke name was called, their surname was Koch the German equivalent!

After eating we're directed to take a different path of steep slopes and some five hundred steps leading down to the other side of the island where the boat was now moored. By 2.45pm we're all aboard and motoring back to Puno. The sun setting as we arrived in the harbour. A wonderful but tiring day.

Friday 29th May. Day 106. Puno.

After the excursion yesterday, an early night and good sleep. This morning it looks like we're to be locally entertained! From the room balcony, groups of people can be seen forming in the Plaza. Big speaker amplifiers are being set up on the Cathedral steps and lots of banners are on show. It's the last day of the general strike. With the police headquarters two buildings along from our hotel and an army barracks on the opposite side of the square, things could get very interesting!

After breakfast Jamie called in with Saturdays bus tickets and told us the time the taxi would pick us up. In our room, online, I booked a hotel in La Paz. We went out early and bought post cards. Enjoying the bright sunny morning, wrote them while sat in the Plaza, then walked into town to send them at the Post Office.

On the way back there were several marching parades with banners and flags, escorted and monitored by armed police, all heading to the Plaza de Armes. Exciting. It was time for us to go with the flow, all the way to the square now thronging with people. We took lunch at a first floor restaurant, its small terrace overlooking the scenes. The situation became even more complicated as protesters were joined by a funereal parade, a trumpet blowing band led by mourners holding photographs of the deceased. In addition to the crazy sights and cacophony of sound, a large dog barked incessantly, its head and front legs hung over a shop roof parapet.

From the vantage of the hotel room balcony we continued to watch the rally. Trade Union groups marched in, out and around. From the steps of the Cathedral, leaders using loud hailers addressed the crowd. Suddenly a small convoy of military vehicles arrived and parked in front of them. Was it going to get hectic? How would this all end?

In the centre of the Plaza, soldiers climbed the statue of the Warrior. A radio communication wire was hung and connected to one of the Jeeps. At about 3.00pm to the left of our view point a large exclusion zone was marked out the ground, within it actors played the role of casualties being treated. The hotel staff were now outside, saw and beckoned us down. Government and other buildings around the square had been evacuated. Fire, ambulance and other emergency vehicles arrived.

Cleverly, the authorities had organised a civil defence disaster simulation, effectively taking control and possession of the area. Within an hour normality had been restored. The Plaza now populated by tourists, families, children playing, folk sat on benches and everybody enjoying the late afternoon sun.

Early start for exit day tomorrow, so lots to do. Paid the hotel account, bought snacks and best part packed before going to our last dinner in Peru. Afterwards, relaxing and putting MTV on before going to bed early was a good idea, the last song being Hosier's 'Take me to the Church.' Somewhere in town, pipes and drums were still being played, accompanied by the noise of a JCB loading rubble from a demolished building into a bulk lorry in the corner of the Plaza. It's midnight don't these people realise I need to sleep?

273

Bolivia, a tale of two cities

Saturday 30th May. Day 107. Puno, Peru to La Paz, Bolivia. 245km. First land border crossing.

Slept in fits and starts, fully awake before the alarm, got up and on the balcony had a nerve calming smoke. Cleared the room after breakfast. Waited at reception for the 7.00am cab transfer to the bus station. It hadn't arrived by ten past so took one from outside the hotel. A bit of a rush, arrived and bought the station access ticket and located the terminal for Titicaca Travel and joined the queue for the coach. Our names and passports are checked against the passenger list, we and others are boarded quickly.

The vehicle has seen better days and has an anti-hijack internal door, separating passengers from the driver and staff. Off we went, more mountain roads and super views of the lake. I took every possible opportunity to catch up on sleep. There were occasional call of nature stops, the last one included a chance to exchange Peruvian Sols into Bolivianos, although at a very poor rate.

10.30am, we're parked at the border crossing and everyone is out of the coach. Chris and I were first into the immigration building. The last thing needed is to be stuck in a queue if someone else has a problem. Uniformed officers exit stamp our passports. There aren't any bag checks because they're still on the bus! Goodbye Peru.

Walk about thirty metres, we're in Bolivia and present ourselves at the Control Office to get our passports entry stamped. We are extremely pleased that it all went so smoothly, have time to scan the area and enjoy the moment before going to the coach which has been driven over.

Next stop Copacabana, a Lake Titicaca Harbour town and very popular tourist destination. We have over an hour here while waiting for our next bus. Took a walk in bright sunshine then had coffee sat outside a café. Clocks are put forward an hour. In the new time zone it's 10.45am when we and our luggage board a bus to La Paz. Chris woke me as we approached the lake crossing at the Straight of Tiquina. All passengers disembark, have to buy tokens for a motor boat and are taken over with about six people to a vessel. The coach makes the trip on a floating pontoon raft. If it sank, so would all the baggage!

Back on the coach. About an hour later we're in the outskirts of La Paz, dirt roads, scruffy construction sites and industrial areas. We meet heavy traffic. Road works and the street stalls of a Saturday market coming to a close make the scene frenetic and we're not in the city yet!

Seeing La Paz from high up in the mountains is a shock. A sprawling mass of buildings and roads sited in a gigantic misshapen canyon.

Down into the city. The bus station is the usual Latin American chaos, diesel fumes, people milling, busses coming and going. Luggage is out of the coach and on the tarmac and it's a bit of a scrum to get our three bags. Chris keeps close to me as I lead us out. We're soon touted by cab drivers, pick one and agree a fixed price of 30 Bolivianos, about £3, for quite a long drive to the Hotel Castellon, Avenue Argentina 2145 Miraflores. Checked in, we're offered a choice of rooms, taking one that overlooks the road. Its night by the time we have cleaned up and get out for food. The only place we can find open locally is a 'Chicharrone' restaurant. Here we eat deep fried pork taken with a couple of satisfying beers. Back at our room by 9.00pm, wrote diaries and watched some of the FA Cup final, Arsenal v Villa on TV. For us by any standard, this has been a very big day!

Sunday 31st May. Day 108. La Paz.

Seems I picked the wrong room, a very noisy night and early morning, car alarms being the most annoying. Opposite in the San Martin Plaza a small market being set up at 5.30am wasn't helpful. Go to breakfast in a cold, large, ground floor room. Foodstuffs are limited and eggs scrambled or omelettes have to be ordered. We're alone, and counting the tables that have been used, it seems there aren't many other guests.

Afterwards, tourist map in hand we've decided to find the city centre, look for travel agencies and the Plaza Murillo. First we try our Ice travel cards at a nearby ATM, annoyingly they're not working. The walk is long and upward. We soon learn that there aren't many roads or streets here that don't have an incline.

On the way, a fairly large crowd, balloons, banners, flag waving and some heavyweight four wheel drive vehicles with CD plates took our attention, so we stopped to watch. From the crowded balcony of an old palatial building a speech was being delivered by a dignitary. By 10.30am we're in the Plaza, a beautiful place. Buildings include the Cathedral and Presidential Palace. This square has been a rally point for many violent coups during Bolivia's short history. Before moving on we had coffee and pies in a very small café and tried the ICE cards in two bank ATM's, no luck, so got cash with a debit card. Just off the plaza, found a travel agents and picked up some leaflets.

The most popular trips are to Uyuni Salt Flats and as seen on countless TV shows, for adrenalin junkies, the cycle ride down the Death Road. Chris is not interested in the latter and we'd already discounted Uyuni while planning in England. I'd have probably done the bike ride so I'm a little disappointed. It's a long walk back to the hotel, worth it because we start to understand our way around.

Spent most of the afternoon on the web and sent angry messages to the ICE card company. After comparing overland travel times and coach costs, booked an exit flight from here to Santa Cruz for Thursday.

About 7.00pm, out for dinner. Locally there aren't many eateries and f**k all is open anyway! Earlier we'd noted a Burger King about a kilometre up the road, went there as a last resort, but the food was awful. On the way back to the hotel we went into a supermarket and bought some consolation beers to have in the room. Walking, talking and thinking, I've been sold a pup, the hotel is not in Centro as advertised. It doesn't get better when we get to the room and check the web, no flight confirmation or replies from ICE. I'm moody, we could be in Brazil a lot earlier than I planned. Chris noted in her diary, 'nothing much going on in this part of town.' Summed it perfectly.

Monday 1st June. Day 109. La Paz.

This morning we're out to explore the Central district. Had a look online, it's the place to be, so plan to find the 'British Pub' and check out a couple of hostels. Walked across a bridge spanning the deep gorge, there's even a road and a park down there! Then up a steep gradient and onto a busy street. Traffic fumes are horrid, both of us find breathing difficult, so take a cab to the town centre and get the driver to let us out near the San Francisco Church.

We're in the tourist mix here, have a wander then take a walk up one of the steeply inclined roads that intersect lanes full of buildings and shops. There's no rhyme nor reason to the layout, no grid pattern. Construction is simply governed by the topography.

Take our time wandering through the amazing 'Witches Market.' Here a plethora of substances and objects are on display, hanging mummified baby llama carcasses, other animals so dry that identification is impossible, bones, meats, leaf, petals, powder's, potions, boxed and loose. Jewellery shops are abundant, silver is very cheap. Chris buys some pendant necklaces and earrings as gifts. One route to and from the main road is too steep for vehicles and formed in stepped terraces with shops, businesses and cafes either side. Here we sit, buy coffee and take in the ambience. At the top of this pedestrian lane is the hostel I'm thinking of moving to, close by are several others and the 'English Pub,' a St George's cross hanging proudly. It would be an insult not to indulge in a few beers and a traditional 'fry up,' so we did!

Afterwards, on the way down the steps we spotted a tailor's shop, a really old fashioned place, no windows just two large open doors. Stepping inside was as if going back in time, the contents and machinery would grace any museum or antique shop. The owner certainly wouldn't have been out of place either! Having lost so much weight I'm having to tightly synch up my belt to prevent my trousers falling down. Using my best sign language the problem was explained, the old tailor knew exactly what was required, a few nips and tucks. An opportunity not be wasted, no pun intended!

On the main road, Chris and I tried to get a taxi. Unfortunately it's rush hour pandemonium and a strange phenomenon takes place in the city at this time. Along with smoke belching old public service buses, every other vehicle, van or car seems to become a cab of sorts. Obscuring the vision from almost of all the front windscreens, handmade signs indicate the districts they will deliver fare paying passengers. Traffic is basically crawling, locals with coins in hand know the drill. I need to find a vehicle showing San Martin or Miraflores, and do!

Back at the hotel, we quickly showered, I put on a spare pair of trousers then we took a taxi back into town. At the tailor shop, all agreed, the alterations are to be completed by tomorrow. We deserve extra beers!

Tuesday 2nd June. Day 110. La Paz.

Got up late, too many beverages, just managed to get breakfast, such as it was. Before going out to explore more of the city I did some online work, posted some pictures to Facebook, sent another message to the ICE travel card company and arranged a five star hotel in Santa Cruz through Booking.com at a bargain half price!

Midday. Get a taxi into town. At Murillo Plaza tried our ICE cards in two bank ATM's, still no good, so used other cards to get cash. Had an English pub breakfast for lunch then went up further into the central markets. Bought t shirts and sandals for pennies and a nice Trilobite fossil from a street vendor. Paid the 20 Bolivianos, (£2) and collected my altered trousers from the tailors. Met his Grandson and took some memorable photos.

At the hotel. I set about researching and setting dates to places for the last few weeks of the trip. Using Skyscanner arranged some flights in Brazil, Iguassu to Rio, then onto Recife. Still no replies from the ICE card company. At reception using sign language, pictures and a watch, I just about managed to book a taxi to the airport. The staff here do not grasp any English words and my limited Spanish certainly *isn't* understood!

Wednesday 3rd June. Day 111. La Paz.

7.00am, woken by noisy voices from the Plaza. Soldiers and civilians of all ages are doing physical jerks, star jumps, push ups and running on the spot. We're told later that it's national exercise day!

I seem to be welded to the ipad by problems. Latest message, Booking.com needs a new credit card registered to my account. It's my turn to create a few irritations so I text and phone the ICE card company and had a right pop at them. I'm being told that there is a technical difficulty, the cards aren't blocked. We're not going to take a chance on getting another card cloned so a target for today is to visit ATM's and get cash to pay the hotel account.

Took a cab to Murillo Plaza. Went to visit the folk museum but it's closed until 3.00pm, so crossed the Via Balcón, a pedestrian footbridge that spans the main road and leads into the market area.

Went to the pub. I suppose it had to happen, a quiet drink and chat turned into an afternoon session. A New Zealand chap spilt a pint down his crotch, plenty of nappy jokes! Talking and smoke breaks outside the pub. The fun always starts when it's time to leave!

Took a cab back to hotel, paid the account and confirmed they'd booked us a taxi for tomorrow. Stepped out and had dinner, burgers from a street vendor! To bed early at 9.30pm, it's a travel day tomorrow.

Thursday 4th June. Day 112. La Paz to Santa Cruz.

Out of bed at 7.00am. Checked for messages then sent more texts and emails. By 9.15am we're riding in another vintage Toyota taxi. In England, this poor old vehicle would have been picked over as spares at a recycling yard twenty years ago. A steep winding mountain road takes us high up on to the plateau and La Paz's sister city 'El Alto' and its namesake airport. We've allowed plenty of time for check in and security, these go smoothly. I was even permitted to take photographs of a glass sided cabinet containing confiscated items. Pride of place a firework about 60cm long, sat on a bed of enough edged weapons to start a hunting shop. There being only one 'gate' we sit and wait. Free wifi means I can do some online research while drinking coffee!

Flight called, we walked to the Amazonas CR200 jet. It's a small aeroplane and our backpacks have to go under the seats, they're too big for the overhead lockers! At take-off seeing La Paz from the air is a bonus. After only fifty five minutes we landed in Santa Cruz, Bolivia's second city. We're no longer in the Andes Mountains and only a few hundred metres above sea level. Chris will get withdrawal symptoms!

I've time for a smoke. No touts for taxis! It's all properly ordered here. Take the first one from the queuing rank of modern, clean cars and agree a price of 90 Bolivianos to the Senses Hotel Boutique, Sucre 5, Esquina 24 de Septembre. Very chic, modern styling. Looks to have been plenty of investment here, commensurate with the fact that the city has fast growing economies, one suspiciously being non-prescription drugs. We're here slightly early, so a delay on room allocation but are made very welcome and given a computer driven virtual city tour by the reception staff. Leave our baggage here and take coffee in the open plan ground floor café. Checked in for five nights and allocated a plush third floor room. Took a look at the two restaurants and decide we'll take dinner at the roof top one. Settled in and cleaned up. Online, I find a travel agent in town who may be able to help with some local tours and possibly a stay in the Pantanal wetlands, send a message and make an appointment for tomorrow. Text messages between me and Thiago of the ICE Company have continued, our cards are being monitored. I want them working!

As night fell we took a walk around the busy Plaza, found a bank ATM and using the cards got cash, about time! Later, there's a candle lit Church Parade celebrating

Corpus Christie. From the hotel roof, while taking dinner and a few beers, we watched a firework display. On retiring to our room for coffee, found the bed sheets turned back and on the side table a nice slice of chocolate cake. We're definitely going to like it here!

Friday 5th June. Day 113. Santa Cruz.

After a good buffet breakfast, took a taxi across town to 'Nicks Adventures.' An ex-pat Australian, naturalist and photographer with a passion for tracking panthers, who runs a low key tour company from a residential address. We had a good chat, he couldn't help arranging a Pantanal tour but did suggest places for local visits. One being the Parque Lomas de Arena, good for sand dunes and bird watching. Another is the Botanical Gardens on the edge of town. We'd book the former for Sunday and make our own way to the second later today.

Taxis with good honest drivers are readily available outside the hotel, so at 3.30pm I arranged a round trip to the gardens.

Although the ground was wet we had a long pleasant walk, saw cacti and many strange trees, some with spiked trunks, big and sharp enough to take an eye out. There were lots of butterflies, birds and fishing eagles over the lake, spotted a tortoise but no sloths or monkeys, probably because the place was quite busy.

6.00pm, as arranged, our cabbie was waiting for us at the main entrance. Seems he's on child minding duties, a young boy is asleep in the front passenger seat. Traffic is heavy and slow going back into the city. The lad woke up and had to take a leak at road side. A strange situation, there's no standing on ceremony in South America!

At the hotel. Did some research for exit travel to our next destination, across the border into Corumba, Brazil. A journey that seems best made on the 'Ferrobus,' other choices being mini-bus, coach or the supposed death train, as noted in 'Lonely Planet.'

After showering, find I've been insect bitten on my face! Medicine for that, a few beers, a mixed grill and also being able to buy twenty cigarettes for 15 bolivianos!

Being Friday, this evening the Plaza is well populated by the better off Santa Cruz locals, young and old. Many parading in some very expensive luxury SUV's.

Saturday 6th June. Day 114. Santa Cruz.

Some extremely important missions today. The first is to obtain tickets for the Ferrobus. An overnight two carriage train to the Bolivian border town of Quijarro. It only runs from here once a week, on Thursdays. A young receptionist has taught me the Spanish translation for that day. Martes! We take a taxi to the 'Bimodel,' a station hub serving both road and rail transport, a sprawling mix of buildings. In and out it's a mass of milling humanity. The cabbie walked with us, we found the ticket booth and requested tickets. Things then became very confused and we're very lucky to have the driver with us.

The lad at the hotel had mistakenly taught me the word for Tuesday not Thursday, which is Jeuves! It should have been obvious, but our driver helped out. Chris as usual remained calm while I almost had a seizure. Cash cost £70, leaving holding the tickets, absolutely priceless!

At our room. Online, I book a hotel in Corumba, send some emails to the web based 'Gil's Pantanal Discovery Tour Company' and book the 'Lomas de Arena' trip with Nick's Adventures for tomorrow. We then catch up on our diaries. All targets met before midday and there's a good reason! At 2.30pm the hotel has organised a private bar and big TV screen viewing of the European Champions football league final, Barcelona v Juventus. Our seat costs include food and some drinks. For cheap pre-match beers we walked to a bar off the square. Unfortunately and uninvited we're joined by Carlos, a middle aged divorcee with issues. Enough said, he was crackers!

Back at the hotel. Took our seats to watch the game. Beer flowed! Afterwards in the plaza we mingled with supporters celebrating the Spanish team's victory. At about 6.30pm we went to the room for a nap.

Sunday 7th June. Day 115. Santa Cruz. Lomas de Arena

The 'nap' lasted thirteen hours! We're up this morning at 7.30am. After breakfast I continued the email and text conversation with Gils Tours about an organised visit to a part of the Brazilian Pantanal. His firm has mixed internet revues but without making any upfront payment I confirmed arrangements. These include collecting us from the hotel in Corumba, and our delivery to a lodge complex on the banks of the River Miranda for a three day two night stay. Price inclusive of events, excursions and afterwards, an outbound bus journey to Bonito.

This meant all we had to do until the 15th of June was enjoy ourselves and on travel days be in the right place at the right time. To say I wasn't pleased with myself would be an understatement!

After lunch we're met by Nick's tour guide Miriam and we got in an old American four wheel drive vehicle for the afternoon Lomas de Arena trip. On the way, collecting a lone English male and a Dutch couple from a local hostel.

The drive out of the city is through far less salubrious areas. Past the town rubbish dump, replete with circling vultures and the Prison which looked exactly as a scary South American jail should be imagined, mould stained high walls, watch towers and a small village of vendors' shacks close by.

Soon we were off road, the vehicle slipping and sliding but the driver expertly and slowly eased it through ruts, ditches and sometimes wheel arch deep pools of muddy water. A couple of times Miriam had to get out and into them, checking the depth before the wagon could be taken across.

Parked as we arrived at the marshes and windblown sand dunes. Very strange topography, a mix of Arabian Desert and wetlands. Me, Chris and Miriam walked around the dunes hoping to see some birds, some in the distance but hardly identifiable. So we joined a group of young thrill seekers high up and taking turns to board down the big dune. No demarcation for age here, we were invited to partake and did so as a pair. It was good fun, Chris noted that 'she shipped sand in places never thought possible.' Less said about that the better!

Before taking dinner at the hotel, in the opposite corner of the Plaza, we had drinks in Marguerita's Pizza Bar. This place has a covered courtyard and its outside tables are the unofficial offices of the Plaza based money changers. Here, they, their minions, runners and body guards congregate, exchanging and counting wads of bank notes. Euros, US dollars, British pounds, Bolivianos etcetera, get neatly folded into handy bundles, some is piled on tables. Calculators are always at the ready. There is a distinct pecking order, some men with big bags just sit and make transactions. Others with small bags come and go, dealing with their main man. Even the body guards get a piece of the action. Lesser mortals bring them coins and low denomination paper money. Such a very watchable experience.

Monday 8th June. Day 116. Santa Cruz.

I should have known better, climbing the sand and dune boarding gave me thigh cramps during the night. After breakfast, using web mapping I located and wrote down the addresses of local farmacia. With the jungle trip coming up some powerful insect repellent is needed. Took a very long walk to the Central Park and then strolled through the market complex. We'd been to others but this one is an absolutely amazing place. The buildings, roads, streets and lanes are mostly themed. Sections selling used car spares, clothing, shoes, furniture, food stuffs, cheaper than cheap, so I bought Chris a nice safari hat!

Mid-afternoon back to the square, re-visited Margueritas for a late lunch of beer and pizza. Watched the money men for a while through the window before going back to our room for a siesta. A big travel day tomorrow, but we're still eager to enjoy our last night here in Santa Cruz, so later went out and about, finishing off in an Irish themed bar close to the hotel.

Tuesday 9th June. Day 117. Santa Cruz to Quijarro. Ferrobus rail journey. 640km.

The train doesn't leave until 6.00pm, but checking out has to be done and the account needs paying. Our luggage is put in a locked storage cupboard behind reception. This hotel has been good, it remains so and we're allowed the use of all ground floor facilities including the wifi.

In town, at a proper Bureau de Change, did money changing, getting Brazilian Real banknotes. Bought and sent some post cards, also got sweets and snacks for later. Pachamama must know we're leaving, it started raining, heavily!

At the hotel. We hand wrote details of all new flights and hotel addresses into our diaries. Also photographed all of the relevant emails and booking forms then loaded them into the ipad. Triple fail safes!

After a light lunch we visited the Cathedral. Sat for a while and had a thoughtful word. By 4.00pm we're in a taxi to the Bimodel. By now my stress level is nearly off the scale. We're dropped off in the carpark. Inside, obtained directions and went to the area containing the Ferrobus gateway. Full of beggars, touts and vendors, it's not open and I'm not totally convinced we're in the right place so I went back and double checked at the station information booth.

It was only when an old Brazilian chap sat next to us and I saw that his voucher was the same as ours that I calmed and bought the station access tickets.

5.30pm. The Ferrobus arrived at the platform. We queued at the gate. Passports and tickets are checked as people go through. In the allocated carriage found our seats, nice padded recliners with built in leg calf supports. The guard inspected documentation again, just before the train started rolling.

Sat back and enjoyed is the phrase that should be used, but no, it was hot, noisy and rattling, with constant hooting. Narrow gauge rail tracks make the wide carriages sway uncomfortably from side to side. I wondered how bad the 'death train' might have been. The attendant eventually got the TV working, playing a DVD, 'God is not dead,' USA made, in Spanish with English sub-titles.

The on screen entertainment was over at about 11.00pm just as we came to a station stop. I went and stood at the exit door, indicated to the guard by using my cigarette packet and lighter that I'd like to step off and smoke. He pointed to a bench seat opposite the carriage toilets and with typical Latin American tolerance gave a thumbs up sign. I sat close to the open window and indulged!

Wednesday 10th June. Day 118. Santa Cruz to Quijarro, onto Corumba, Brazil. 9km.

I visited my personal smoking zone on several occasions as the journey continued, at one time being joined by another passenger. Kate, an Irish woman, divorcee, sixty plus years old and with tales of woe, now travelling alone because she'd had her passport stolen. Her group had moved on while she visited an Embassy to arrange temporary documents.

5.00am, sunrise imminent. 7.00am, the train arrived at Quijarro. Not much of a station, a concrete platform and one small building, high up on the embankment. It was hot already as Chris and I walked out and down steps to a dusty car park. Bolivians in this border town are entrepreneurial. A young chap pointed to a very old vehicle, most of its interior was missing but it had seats, it looked like a taxi, so must be one or we're being kidnapped!

We're driven at little cost through a town that would pass for a spaghetti western film set then dropped off at the ramshackle village that had grown alongside the border outpost.

The office isn't open, but a couple of uniformed guards are sat on wooden chairs with the backs lent against walls.

So, in early morning sunshine we joined the long queue and stood waiting with fellow travellers. Among them a rowdy group of Brazilian young men who'd obviously just enjoyed a 'lads' weekend somewhere in Bolivia, some migrant workers, a poor couple and infant child with a horrid cough and runny nose, but still being fed crisps for breakfast. My new 'friend' Kate also arrived, as did youths on motor cycles. Nothing untoward, just selling water and other refreshments. All the while, trucks of all types were raising clouds of dust and crossing the bridge unimpeded.

Just after 8.30am the immigration and customs office opened. Chris and I eventually got to stand in front of one of the two operational desks. Here, a woman officer worked at a computer key board. How I don't know, it had so many missing keys. Our documentation all in order, we obtained passport 'exit' stamps, then walked the short distance over the bridge to Brazil.

Brazil!

In the heat, outside the border office it's another long wait. More heavy trucks pass and make dust clouds. By about 10.00am, after convincing the control officer that we're British, not Irish or American and don't have to pay a visa fee, we got our entry stamps and left the office.

A five minute walk took us to a canopied taxi rank, bizarrely, here, the cars are all like new. Showing the intended hotel address to a driver, he says in Portuguese and some broken English that it's no longer in business.

Is this a scam? We're going into town anyway, so I ask him to show me. He parks up outside and sure enough it's boarded up. I ask him to take me to another. A couple of blocks later he dropped us at the National Palace Hotel, Rua America 936, Corumba.

No one at reception speaks a word of English, so paper and pen are used. The room rate is more than we'd normally pay, I don't care, somewhere to stay is all important. Checked in for three nights and the lovely, smiling lady at the desk gives me a discount!

Importantly, by text I inform Gil's Pantanal Discovery of our new address and get a reply that all will be fine for our collection Saturday. We cleaned up then went for a walk to explore, find places that we can get food tonight and then took lunch of soft drinks and sandwiches in a local cafe.

During the evening enjoyed some beer and a good steak in a fine restaurant. Chris noted that 'we'd watched the sunrise in Bolivia and the sunset in Brazil.' Apt for such a hectic time spread over two days.

Thursday 11th June. Day 119. Corumba.

Too much beer, heat and yesterday's tension had me up at 3.00am.

8.00am, this hotel lays out an exceptional buffet breakfast. Not surprising, there are plenty of well off clients. The carpark is full of sports and utility vehicles, very expensive marques, registration plates from many states and cities including Belo Horizonte, Rio de Janeiro. Lots of people come here for sport fishing on the River Paraguay.

It's a beautiful day, we walked down, through and beyond the town then took a steep slope which drops to an even lower elevation, the harbour promenade. The navigable river flows fast, clumps of vegetation float on the surface. A mixture of boats are moored. Large, tall touring types with double decked cabins and small punts with canopies. We negotiated a one hour trip in one of the latter, our first in the Pantanal wetlands. The boatman pointing out giant lily pads, dragonflies, butterflies, tree lizards, birds and some of the people who actually live on the many small islands.

Back in town we took lunch in a 'weight' restaurant. These are particular to Brazil. I'd used similar during my 2014 visit and I enjoyed introducing Chris to the experience. After making self-service selections from a diverse hot or cold buffet, meats, vegetables and salads, the plate is scaled and priced by how much is taken. Payment is made on leaving. After shopping and buying a small battery powered torch we sat at pavement set tables of a corner café bar, had a couple beers, relaxed and 'people watched.'

In our room watching TV, we caught a little of the opening soccer game for the 'Copa de Americas,' the home nation Chile losing 2-0 to Ecuador. Afterwards, went out for dinner.

Friday 12th June. Day 120. Corumba.

Got up late, 9.00am. We'll need to do better for tomorrow's early start! I've noticed that reception is unattended first thing in the morning, to avoid delay on leaving I'm paying the hotel account today. Using 'Google translate,' I copied the Portuguese words to explain my reasons. It worked a treat, the lady receptionist was all smiles.

We haven't got a paper map and need something to do today, so while having internet access use mapping to locate the Pantanal Museum near the river and also note an old 'Fort' on the edge of town.

We walked for ages to find that, when we did, it was 'old' but still active and serving as operational barracks for the Army border battalion!

In the heat we trudged a guessed route back towards town, fortunately intersecting a road we recognised. From here we went back down to the harbour. A large boat had just disgorged both anglers and catch. A one metre long catfish among other species laid out for viewing on a plastic tarpaulin.

Free entry to the museum and quite interesting mixed exhibits, actual and natural history set out on three floors, just had to avoid the noisy un-attentive school children doing a tour.

Back to the 'weight' restaurant for lunch, selected snack foods with fresh green skinned oranges squeezed for our juice!

I'm struggling to find cigarettes in town, don't want run out in the jungle! Eventually get several packs, water and snacks at a garage shop. Not knowing what may or not be available in the Pantanal lodge we bought some cans of beer at a supermarket.

Later, went to the classy restaurant Dolca Café for our third and last night's meal. Being Friday it was extremely busy, a band played and there's a visit by a 'female celebrity' with camera and lighting crew in tow. We're almost definitely the only Brits in town so didn't have a clue who she was!

Saturday 13th June. Day 121. Corumba to the Pantanal. Lontra Pantanal Hotel

Had a good sleep. By 5.30am we're fully packed. While leaning from the window, watching the town wake up, I smoked two pre-match nerve calming cigarettes. Had just enough time to drink coffee and eat some cereals in the breakfast room as our transport is due at 6.15am.

It arrives an hour late. The driver didn't have any idea who we were but I'd written 'Gil's Discovery Tours' in my note book and he recognised that. We're then treated to almost two hours of local driving as the mini-bus is filled with passengers. Stops made in small villages and townships collecting people going to the city of Campo Grande. Several are very fat, big women, so large that they can barely squeezed into the seats!

Still being cautious, once aboard the van I'd texted Gil to get confirmation that all was as arranged. He hadn't replied. My query was resolved in an odd way. The driver asked me for fare money, I refused and again pointed to Gil's name and number, so '*he*' called him! After the payment situation was sorted the phone was handed to me for a brief conversation. All OK, so quite a relief.

I dozed until 10.20am when Chris and I are dropped off at a fairly isolated highway junction. This situation being the cause of some poor reviews on the web. I could understand why, it's slightly unnerving to be left standing in the middle of what seems nowhere! Signs only indicate the next city, Campo Grande and the other direction, back to Corumba. A few heavy trucks rumbled by.

At one side of the road is a building. As a police car is parked outside I presume it to be a traffic control office. On the 'island' where we stand is a large old shack, it looks like living accommodation. A couple of chickens wander about pecking at the ground. In the shade of a tree we talked, joking that we wouldn't want to be here at night! I ate a banana, smoked a few cigarettes and took a leak against a lamppost.

Thirty minutes pass, then a large, rough old pick-up truck arrives, the driver introduces himself as 'Netto' from the lodge. Our baggage thrown in the back and us seated in the cab, we're off down the only other track leading from the junction. Very rough, bumpy, rutted, boulder strewn with marshland, trees and bushes either side. There are quite a few heavy wood plank bridges over streams and pools. Stopping the truck on one of these structures. Netto pointed out small caiman in the water. We're definitely in the Pantanal!

Turned off the track and head over a high arched concrete road bridge. From this vantage point the river and a collection of buildings can be seen, we're soon in amongst them. Fairly shanty and artisan construction, lots of ply wood and corrugated iron sheeting, most of the shacks are on stilts. Entering the grounds of the Lontra Pantanal Hotel we find a more organised cluster of better constructed cabin style buildings. The truck is parked on a central grassed area and we're taken to the restaurant. This place serves as reception, bar, meeting place and breakfast room. Here we meet Louis, one of the guides. A charming man, late thirties, quietly spoken and not too far from being a young Morgan Freeman lookalike! He gives us the run down, whys and wherefores, times of meals, activities and took payment for our stay. Bonus. We never knew that meals were inclusive!

Key in hand, Chris and I walked across the green to a terrace of cabins with veranda, these are also on posts. One of these is ours for the duration. It's good, insect mesh screen over the windows, shower room and a fridge to store the beer and snack foods. We have until 3.00pm to relax and sort ourselves out before the first group event of the day.

We're ready, as Louis suggested, dressed appropriately, hats, long sleeved safari shirts, trousers to match and insect repellent applied by the litre. Walking to the meeting point it's impossible not to notice the plentiful wild birds. So many different colourful species I'm likely to get a bad neck!

The river bank is supplemented by wooden steps down to the water's edge, moored here are many three metre long aluminium river dinghies and other motorised craft. Louis hands out sleeveless life jackets to the gathered group. Introductions are minimal before boarding a multi seated, flat bottomed, canopied punt and take a short ride to where several canoes are laid up. The venture is explained, select one, go out on the river and look for wild life. Considering that our nearest experience to using a canoe was kayaking in the gentle sea off of Mana Island, this should be fun!

Within minutes we're in a two person canoe and paddling up the river. Going with the fast flow it was easy. Lots of verbal banter between boat crews and mini races seemed in order, bumping into the reed banks then having to turn the canoe back to face the correct way. I even found time to sing 'Rule Britannia' much to the annoyance of the only Argentine in the flotilla!

We saw water fowl, some birds fishing, others nesting and took lots of photographs. No one knew how this event was to end.

After two hours of fast current we were all several kilometres away from the lodge. The sun was dropping, there'd be no way any of us could paddle back against the strong current but there in the distance was Louis and the motor boat.

Time to see how this worked and let someone else be first. The trick is to forget health and safety! Aim the canoe at the boat, Louis will grab it. Make a climbing transfer from one vessel to another! All safely aboard, empty canoes now in tow and we're heading back up river.

Darkness is coming by the second and as it does the scenario changes completely. In the blackness a new set of nature's creatures rule above and near the river surface. As our boat motors along we see fireflies twinkling like

Christmas tree lights nestled in the reeds and bushes. Louis pans the small boat lamp, the beam picks up and reflects the eerie red eyes of caiman lurking in and around the water's edge. He points out a monkey carrying a baby high in a tree top.

All of a sudden there are insects by the thousands forming a swirling maelstrom being preyed upon by birds and bats. We're hit all over, including the face, by all manner of bugs, hard shelled beetles, flies and mosquitos, something even has time to bite my finger!

Back at the lodge we showered, put on more insect spray then had a good dinner, dessert and several beers. Discussed the day's events with some of the group. Notwithstanding that we'd been up and about since 5.00am, had a hectic day and were primed for a similar start time in the morning, it should have been early to bed. Not to be!

Chris and I sat talking and drinking late into the night with three Brazilian men here on a privately organised fishing trip. We'd exchanged greetings earlier in the day. Now, using their broken English and my fragmented Portuguese we exchanged anecdotal stories, discussed tax, politics, religion, commerce and education. Name it, we talked it! Each man had a career and were all of European ancestry, one a farmer of German extraction living near Bonito, a lawyer with Spanish heritage and a civil engineer from an Italian family. Great fun, we laughed a lot and got very tipsy. It would have been unsociable not to!

Our last test of the day was back at the cabin. Simple, up the steps and put the key in the door, open and go in. Not quite! An outside light attracts hundreds of bugs, they whiz around the lamp and others arrive in a suicidal manner. Big ones fly in so fast that they hit the door and walls like shrapnel then drop to the floor spinning and reeling in death throws. Opening, entry and closing must be made within a micro second! Otherwise our sleeping companions will be less than welcome. Only once inside can a light can be turned on, a quick double check made for interlopers, plug in and turn on the electric mozzie repellents. Good night campers!

Sunday 14th June. Day 122. Pantanal.

Up at 5.30am. After a fine buffet breakfast by 7.00am we're sat on benches in the back of a safari truck bouncing down a rough track. An eight kilometre drive into wetland jungle. Plenty of rickety wooden bridges crossed with random stops made for scenic views and photo shoots when anything interesting is spotted. Louis and Netto are in the cab, the rules are, if they don't see something and you do, bang on the roof! They obviously had the eyes for the job, on route we saw plenty. In water holes, caiman and wild boar. Elsewhere, birds, nesting, feeding and flying, eagle, stork, toucan, heron and many others.

The truck is pulled into a clearing and parked. Louis leads us for a walk through long grasses over two metres tall. Staying on the trail and keeping up with the group is essential, disappearing being the only other option! In the forest the ground is a soft carpet of dry and decaying vegetation. Among many things he points out are different tree species.

One is a parasite that grows up and around palms, suffocating and using the victim as nourishment. We stopped to view red and blue feathered macaws, saw and heard howler monkeys moving through high branches.

Standing well away from the group I smoked a cigarette, this upset the Argentine who berated me and said I was annoying the 'bears!' I was about to retort but Chris sensibly stopped me.

Back at the lodge we all had lunch.

3.00pm, the afternoon activity is piranha fishing in the river just in front of the restaurant building. Louis hands out three metre long bamboo poles, a similar length of nylon line is already attached and has a tied on hook. The bait is raw meat!

The sun is shining, it's shorts on, shirts off. We make ourselves comfortable, one person to each of the punts tied along the riverbank. Chris is in the one next to me. There's plenty of fisherman's banter, she didn't catch, it was two nil to me. Not very big fish but their teeth need carefully avoiding when un-hooking!

5.00pm. Louis has us all in the canopied boat for a night trip, lamping for caiman. It's been a sunny day but cloudy skies then heavy rain causes quite a temperature drop. We're out for about an hour and half. Before sunset we saw a large capybara feeding in the reed beds and some noisy howler monkeys. At nightfall, more firefly lights and another insect, bat and bird storm!

At dinner Chris and I talked at length with three Swedes, two brothers, one with a girlfriend. They are travelling across South America in the opposite direction to us. We shared information about places we'd stayed, using the Ferrobus and the vagaries of land border crossings. I also sold them the last of my Bolivianos at exchange rate. Louis came to the table and informed us of tomorrow's early start and hill walk plans. I took the opportunity to ask him about our afternoon departure details. There is absolutely no wifi internet access here. Fortunately while in Corumba I'd researched and written down several hostel addresses in Bonito. We'll make a choice on arrival.

Although using plenty of repellent we'd still suffered a few bites. In the cabin Chris cleared the uninvited bugs that had come in on our clothes and her hair. I stood on the veranda and had a late smoke. Bats flitted in and out taking insects just inches from my face. Here in the Pantanal, I have no doubt that even as human beings we are somewhere on the food chain!

Monday 15th June. Day 123   Pantanal, Lontra Hotel to Bonito. 185km.

Up at 5.30am. After breakfast. Gathered as a group in anticipation of the hill climb. Louis arrives declaring that after such heavy overnight and this morning's continuing rain the ground will be too dangerous. He hands out, and we put on, yellow polythene ponchos. Chris reckons we look like the 'Banana Gang.' We're going on another boat ride. During which, the rain became heavier, so bad that we were all soaked and quite shivery. In just over two hours we'd seen more birds, a capybara and an otter but it's a wet end to our stay. At the cabin we changed into dry clothes then had lunch before leaving. At 2.00pm, gave our thanks and goodbye to Louis.

Netto drove us and the Swedish trio out of camp, we're all dropped off at the road junction collection point. There are other folks here, probably from another lodge.

We didn't have to wait long, a mini-bus arrived, sign written Catalina Tours. The transport to Bonito and already has some passengers aboard. Our baggage is loaded into the rear by the driver. His cohort, an older man, asked how many people did or didn't have accommodation arranged. Obviously intent on selling places at the Catalina tour hostel. I almost agreed a stay but Chris correctly and discretely reminded me that Gil had said to avoid the place. Good girl! I said that we'd booked the Sao Jorge.

On route by 2.45pm. The young driver had some worryingly bad habits, hands through the steering wheel resting on the dash and constantly texting or making phone calls.

6.00pm. Arrived at Bonito in darkness. After several other drop offs, we're disembarked outside the Hostel Pousada Sao Jorge, Rebua 1605. At reception we introduced ourselves to the manager, Nicolas, I apologised for not making an advanced booking and asked if we could be accommodated, requiring a minimum of three nights with an option to extend once we'd sorted out plans. He's a nice chap and agreed to everything. We're allocated a very small room with double bed, toilet and shower. There's a shared kitchen with fridge facilities in the courtyard. Wifi access is free. We're very pleased. After washing we did some web based research, sent some messages to family letting them know where we are and that we're safe.

The night time temperature drop is significant enough to wear a top coat. Went out, found a local pizza restaurant and ate a simple meal.

In bed by 9.20pm. Chris's diary note, 'a long but very enjoyable day.'

Tuesday 16th June. Day 124. Bonito.

The hostel lays on a continental style buffet breakfast, Chris and I had cornflakes, toast and coffee. Wifi is good in this area so we checked for messages then wrote our diaries. Last night we'd been given a good tourist map with street plan and lots of advertisements for tours, trips and local attractions. After studying it we decided to explore, walk and talk about what else to do with our time here.

Visited the Aquarium, multiple exhibits, excellently presented, fish and other water creatures, great and small that dwell in the Pantanal. An artificial pond contains freshwater rays, a species I never knew existed. They're about forty centimetres across and similar to the seawater variety. Amusingly they like to be petted and present themselves for smoothing by hand when a person goes to the edge of the pool.

Bonito is tourism oriented, a growing town without high rise buildings. We walked the busy but far from frenetic high street looking at clothing and souvenir shops, cafes, bars and restaurants. Took lunch at one of them while continuing discussions. In the surrounding area there are river beach resorts but we won't have time to stay at any of these. Back at the hostel we met with Nicolas to discuss trips. He can make all of the arrangements. After some advice given and deliberation taken, Chris and I are booked to swim in the River Prata tomorrow, visit two 'grottos' on Friday and have arranged Saturday's overnight transportation to Iguassu, our next destination. Our stay here is extended to allow for that.

During the afternoon Chris and I undertake some long overdue personal grooming and make some loose plans for Iguassu.

Later, we indulged in a few beers and a burger for dinner in a café, while watching football on TV. Uruguay v Argentina in the Copa de Americas. With an early start looming, took to our bed at 9.30pm.

Wednesday 17th June. Day 125. Rio Prata.

Up at 5.30am. Chris and I grab toast and coffee as breakfast is being set out. Shouldn't have, but also made some cheese & ham rolls as snacks for later. Little did we know that it was going to be a day full of surprises!

7.00am, a Mercedes mini-bus collected us and two others, then went around town making more pickups until there were about twelve passengers. Singles and couples of several nationalities but predominantly Brazilian.

On leaving town the route became rough, mainly sand or gravel track. After some 50 kilometres, at about 10.00am, arrived at Recanto Ecologico Rio de Prata. An eco-centre based within a working ranch. It's immaculately laid out with flower and tree planted landscaped gardens. We're not sure what to expect but get signed in, allocated to a group and booked to the 11.30am slot for our river swim. We indulge the waiting time resting, enjoying the sunshine and watching wild birds, including beautiful blue and red Macaws that come here for the free feeding session.

11.00am we're called for an induction talk. Difficult because 'Maximo,' the guide, doesn't speak a word of English but we get the general gist, plus, that insect repellent or lotions are not to be applied. A large sign is much easier to understand, stating that it's your own fault if bitten, stung, eaten alive by snakes, spiders or some other jungle monster. The disclaimer profoundly confirms my food chain theory!

The group is gathered to be fitted for swimming attire, our discarded day clothes and possessions are individually bagged. All of us, now bizarrely wearing knee length semi floatation suits, neoprene bootees, carrying snorkels and goggles, are led to a flatbed bench seated safari truck.

After a short ride Maximo leads us onto a chipped bark forest path with sign posts. We walk for forty minutes. He talks about trees and their uses until arriving at a small lake sized pool with a short wood built pier.

Here he gives the option to wear a life jacket and precisely demonstrates to each and everyone how to wear a snorkel and mask. To test facemasks and breathing tubes we all step down into the water and for the first and only time are allowed to stand on the vegetation strewn pool bed. Communication now is hand signals. It's hard to concentrate! There are fish everywhere in the crystal clear water. We're signalled to swim in single file following Maximo around the pool then out into the stream that flows to the River Prata.

This pool is created by water percolating from underground. Swimming across the supply is eerie, a little scary and noticeably cold. I feel as if I am in a tank, surrounded by hundreds if not thousands of small fish, some are caught in the underwater swirl, which is powerful enough to spin me full circle as I use the camera on video setting. Looking up, I'm the last swimmer and long way from Chris. Attempting to catch up, I excitedly and foolishly call her and swallow a lot of water.

As the stream is entered there is no need to swim, the water is very fast. Taking pictures of fish, single, shoals and of so many colours is difficult, they seem unaffected by the flow. Obstacles are plentiful, overhanging branches, rocks and fallen trees. Some lie deep enough to glide over, others have had sections cut out. Aiming for and making the gap is essential!

Suddenly, there's bend in the stream, it narrows and the current is even faster, the surface rapid, rolling and breaking over sharp rocks. I saw Chris hit one, so twist my body sideways to the current and only avoid the same fate by kicking off the boulder with my feet. Nearby and stood chest deep backed up against a rope spanning the stream, Maximo is acting like a hook on an aircraft carrier deck, catching each person and ensuring they can use the rope to pull themselves to the steps of a fixed wooden pontoon.

Everyone is now out of the water. From a first aid box on a post fixed to the pontoon, Maximo took out some ointment. It was applied to Chris shin where she'd sustained a small but deep puncture. The stream had washed it clean but it was still weeping watery blood. A sticking plaster completed the treatment.

In case of shock I jested that she was now likely to be attacked and eaten by a shoal of piranha. "In your dreams fat boy," if I remember her reply correctly. Evidently she was mentally unaffected!

From here Maximo led us a short distance through some thick forest to another pool. Quite deep, again crystal clear and the bottom is sandy gravel. He pointed out the hole from the underground spring that fed it, sand swirled around. We all got in and took a closer look at another of Mother Nature's wonders.

From here we swim out into the actual River Prata. A very different situation, its banks overgrown with trees and bushes, the water isn't clear but still flowed quickly. We all swam about half a kilometre, finally reaching and boarding a motorised flat bottomed boat that took us to a purpose built dressing station where our bagged clothes were waiting.

A truck ride across open range passing herds of cattle got us back to the ranch house at 3.00pm. Here we ate, selecting food from the excellent cost included buffet. We bought beers and talked with Linda, a bubbly middle aged fellow Brit also staying at the hostel and she'd been in our swim group. Without doubt we were all in some awe and amazement at what we'd seen and not less, just done, agreeing several things. The least being that if we'd been previously informed of the danger levels and physical requirements we may not have signed up to it! Nevertheless a fantastic experience that will be a conversation subject for many years.

Chris later noted in her diary, '...........from start to finish about three hours in the river, it was probably the biggest adrenalin rush I've ever had, thought it was going to be a gentle swim, how wrong I was!'

6.00pm, back at the hostel. Chris is carrying one more jungle souvenir other than her cut leg. She's been insect bitten, a nasty swelling now apparent between the eyebrow and lid of her right eye. If we were at home I can imagine the wife beater jokes!

Showered and about to go out for dinner when Nicolas intercepts us at reception, says he is having a BBQ at his home and we're invited. Who'd turn down such a kind offer? He drives us. We meet his wife and baby son, get the guided tour of his house and are soon mingling with other guests, mostly family and friends. A short time later he has been back and forth to the hostel and collected Linda and Uli, a young German lad of twenty years old. (He'd also been in the swim group). We discuss many things. He doesn't understand why England football fans are still using the Hitler Nazi salute at games between our countries, I defer from too much explanation, not even mentioning the old phrase, 'the sins of the father are oft visited upon their children.'

Other conversations flow. There's plenty of beer, food on the griddle is meat and sausage, no Tesco's burgers here. A small TV shows football, Brazil losing to

Columbia in the Copa. Nicolas doesn't mind, he's an Argentinian! Not only that, he and a friend are trying to set up a computer module to show a feature film on a giant screen. Tonight has been the perfect way to end a special day!

Thursday 18th June. Day 126. Bonito.

After last night's event we're up a little late at 8.45am, still tired and slightly fuzzy! The swelling near Chris's eye is more inflamed so she took an antihistamine tablet. At reception we confirmed tomorrow's trip to the grottos then shopped for insect bite cream. In the farmacia, a 'basket and pay' method is in use. Another Brazilian quirk! Self-selected items are presented to one shop assistant, another bags them, the next takes the cash. Rain started to drizzle just after we bought some post cards and cans of lager.

Later, sat in the hostel garden, relaxing, drinking coffee, wrote the postcards and up-dated our diaries. Online, I booked a place to stay in Iguassu. Nicolas joined us and we had a good chat. Uli also put in an appearance, we talked at length about the Pantanal, his next destination.

Early evening. Chris and I treated ourselves to a steak dinner at the 'Italy Grill.' Afterwards in our room, using a flash drive we watched a sci-fi film titled 'Lucy.' We're both tired. This travelling lark does take it out of you!

Friday 19th June. Day 127. Bonito. Grotto visits.

So glad we went to bed early last night. Apart from the disruption I caused having another attack of thigh cramp, both of us slept well and were ready for the 5.30am alarm.

The tour bus arrived at 7.00am. Again we're the first of the pick-ups. The grotto visits, although in different locations are extremely well organised with visitor centres at which guides give induction talks, issue hard hats and any other safety equipment deemed necessary.

'San Miguel' is accessed by a rope and timber bridge, then a short forest walk. It's a massive natural cave with stalactite and stalagmite formations. It's good exploring the nooks and crannies.

'Lago Arul' is reached by a forest walk up a gentle hill slope. After entry, steep winding concrete steps are taken down to several viewing platforms. A guide points out rock and calcite formations that have similarities to statues, some animal other human. Deep at the very bottom is a wide, azure blue, alkaline pool.

Both tours made for some good photographic opportunities.

Back in town by 1.00pm. Went to the 'take a ticket' post office. A staff member licked and stuck stamps on our postcards. During the afternoon, while sat in the pousada's garden we had coffee and the breakfast rolls made earlier. Using the hostel laptop and a few cables I successfully uploaded the River Prata video to Facebook. Very pleased with myself! Later indulged in another steak dinner at the Italy Grill. Intended to relax and watch a film on TV but were both asleep by 9.00pm. The trip is telling on us now.

Saturday 20th June. Day 128. Bonito to Iguassu. 650 km.

Up at 8.20am. Albeit later, it's leaving day! Uli our young German friend departed this morning, we spoke at length before saying goodbye.

In the garden, Chris and I talk about many subjects with Nicolas and the hostel owner Phillipe. In a very kindly gesture he invites us to join him for lunch at 'Juanita's' a popular 'all you can eat for one price' buffet restaurant. I agree as long as I can pay for beverages. We're joined by his girlfriend and an associate and have a good conversation.

Afterwards, shopped for souvenir t shirts. During the afternoon did our final packing, relinquished the room and paid the hostel account which included costs all of the trips and todays bus fare.

To say this has been a pleasant stay is too simple, the kindness shown, trust and friendliness received has been second to none.

7.00pm, the overnight midi-coach to Iguassu arrived, with driver and a relief aboard. Us and our luggage loaded it did the usual round of pick-ups. We had a choice of seats, all padded and reclining and they were comfy. Once we were rolling it became apparent that the vehicle had suffered a hard life, the suspension and springs are worn, so it's a jolty ride. Most of the sixteen passengers are South American. Sat behind us is a group of four young Asian origin British, we had no interaction or acknowledgements.

At about 7.45pm, we eventually left town, soon travelling on unknown roads. Chris and I snacked and or dozed. Shortly before midnight the coach stopped at a café, enabling a toilet break, refreshment purchases and change of driver. I have no idea which town!

Sunday 21st June. Day 129. Iguassu.

During fitful sleep, on my watch I had noted one o'clock, three then five! At 6.00am the coach arrived outside the 'Hotel Foz,' the designated drop off point. Passengers disembark and luggage is unloaded. Chris and I bumped our kit to the opposite side of the road where a taxi cab happened to be parked. Nobody had a booking at the hotel or a map. Odd that people wanted to talk now, one of the Brits who had been so into themselves came across asking if we knew the route to the Argentine side of the falls. I suggested he spoke to someone in the hotel. It being stupid o'clock in the morning I wasn't fully functional nor in any panic to go anywhere, so had a smoke and bounced some ideas around with Chris. The cab was there, so decided to show him the address of our accommodation, take a chance and go there. Knew we'd be far too early for a room, but in the hope of using some facilities.

6.45am, at Pousada Caroline, Irlan Kalichewski, 231, Vila Yolanda. The leather trouser wearing bag of bones female receptionist isn't the usual welcoming Brazilian type, her morning mood as glum as she looked, but does allow us to use the WC and leave our bags.

Hoping to find an open café or shop, we walked down the long hill slope of Avenue das Cataratas to the edge of the city. On a major road junction there's a 'Shell' petrol station. At least here we could get a snack with coffee and kill some time. I wrote my diary and opened a phone text, a Father's Day greeting from my son Charles. Afterwards we wandered about the locality for a while, then walked back up the avenue and sat on a bench outside the hotel for couple of hours. At noon, checked in for six nights, a comfortable room ensuite with a fridge, kettle and cups. We showered and rested. During the afternoon I met with the tour rep and booked a trip to the Brazilian side of Iguassu Falls.

The hotel is spread about, here in two buildings and over the road, some self-catering units. It advertises a restaurant as part of the facilities so by 6.30pm we're ready to indulge. Unfortunately after wasting some time looking for it found that it doesn't operate on Sundays! So went down the avenue again and patronised the first place that had f*****g lights on! Ate curried chicken drumsticks and shared a deserved five large bottles of beer. 8.30pm, back at our room, the reward was being sound asleep within seconds.

Monday 22nd June. Day 130. Iguassu to Foz du Iguassu, Brazil side.

Up at 7.30am. Or so we thought! Breakfast is a good buffet spread. 8.00am on the way back to the room I checked the trip schedule at reception, turns out that it's actually 9.00am. This Brazilian city is on Argentinian time! There's been a lack of understanding and communication. The mini-bus driver is waiting on us!

We organise quickly and are soon on the road for the 12 kilometre ride to the falls.

At the drop off we're given a return trip meeting time by the driver. The visitor centre and reception is in a beautiful landscaped area. Having bought tickets and a tour map, we made our way past the café to the bus station. An open top double decker delivers us to a stop opposite the Hotel Cataratas. Here we select our first walking trail. It's a superb sunny day, the first views of the waterfalls were good. They just got better and better. My camera worked overtime. The trails are long and meandering but we stopped at every view point. Using a metal balcony bridge walkway gets as close as is possible to the major fall called the 'Devils Throat.' Here the noise is loud and spray rises. We got very wet, but the photographs of rainbows are worth the soaking. Nearby is Naipi spot, a high level viewing platform, also having refreshment facilities, we had coffee at this place. Fluttering around are hundreds of pretty butterflies, numerous species. Some even settle on people. Abundant signs warn of the danger from 'Quatis or Coatis' a small omnivorous, sharp toothed and clawed, opportunistic animal. These beasts climb everywhere and in the blink of an eye will snatch away your lunch, coffee cup or handbag. Four and a half hours had passed by the time we'd returned to the main visitor centre to indulge in a beer and a filled bread roll.

Collected and returned to the hotel. Uploaded pictures to the ipad, then booked a visit to the Argentine side of the falls for tomorrow. We sat in the garden for a while, enjoying the late afternoon sun. In the room, I took a nap while Chris had a Whatsapp chat with daughter Mary.

At about 6.30pm went out and visited 'Ouvidoria,' a restaurant on the avenue, bought beers only, because we couldn't understand the menu, so took one on leaving for 'google translation.' At 'Pacova,' the place we went yesterday, had a nice dinner of barbequed pork ribs, quails eggs and salad.

Tuesday 23rd June. Day 131. Iguassu to Foz do Iguassu, Argentina side.

Breakfast taken, laundry dropped at reception and ready to travel in good time! At the tour desk I changed some Brazilian Reals into Argentinian Pesos. Chris and I are the only passengers in the mini-bus and are driven to the Brazilian customs post at the border crossing. Emigration forms have already been completed by the hotel staff. We don't even leave the van, just hand our passports to the driver. He is in and out of the control building within a few minutes then it's over the Tancredo Neves Bridge to Argentinian Border control. The same thing happens, now our documents are complete with exit and entry stamps. Hey ho, same day, another country!

At Iguazu Park we agree the return journey collection time. Pay for entrance tickets, get a tour map then follow the crowd to Central Station and board a miniature train. This trundles along very slowly and eventually arrives at Garganta del Diablo Station. From here we join many others for a long walk on metal bridging that has clanking mesh foot plates. Its structural supports span the waters of the plateau that flow towards the many waterfalls and main attraction. The remains of collapsed and redundant walkways stand or lay as and where they were abandoned.

The 'Devils Throat' viewing platform is small, sign posted and supposedly operates a two way pedestrian system. Unfortunately, here in Argentina this translates as 'Bun Fight.' Even a professional 'photographer,' using a step ladder is taking paid for pictures of visitors in a prime and crowded spot.

We're English and far from shy. Using elbows, a few strategic shoves we edged and eased ourselves to some good vantage points. Took some fantastic video and still shots of the giant waterfall. Birds flitting behind the curtain of spray, the thundering noise of billions of litres pouring hundreds of metres down into the River Iguassu will forever be etched in our memories. On the platform, taking any picture was fraught with the possibility of being bumped and losing a device. Not only that, I was angered by being unable to read my phone screen in the bright sunlight, almost to the point of losing the plot and launching it. Chris emphatically reminded me that it would be a costly and stupid thing to do!

At the intermediate Cataratas station. Had lunch of pizza and beer while being amused by the antics of the thieving Coatis and the sometimes hysterical reactions of people encountering them for the first time. From here we trekked all of the upper and lower trails. Many of these walkways are steep and winding, some with timber steps, deck and balustrades. Stopped at every good view point for the other waterfalls, all very impressive at close proximity, especially on the crossings built over the cascades. The forest walks gave the added bonus of seeing monkeys, lizards, butterflies and birds. After almost seven hours on our feet we were back at the visitor centre, sat outside a café in bright sunshine and treating ourselves to a beer.

By 9.00pm we'd showered and were eating at the Pacova café and bar, seeing off two towers of beer in the process. Bed and asleep by 10.00pm.

Wednesday 24th June. Day 132. Iguassu. Day of rest!

We'd been privileged to have spent time in two countries and seeing of one of Mother Nature's creations up close and personal. Our next excursion is to visit one of man's great engineering wonders. After breakfast I booked a trip to the 'Itaipu Dam' for Thursday. In the meantime we're going to attempt to relax, but first, shopping at a supermarket, getting snacks, toilet roll, beer and cigarettes. Purely essentials!

The sun is shining so lotions applied, dozed on reclining beds in the hotel garden, indulge in a couple of beers and repeat the process until late afternoon. Our clean laundry is back in the room. I took a pill for back pain and rested. Later, while listening to music and being determined to take dinner at the stylish café bar Ouvidoria, I used online translation to decode the menu. There later we shared two different steak based meals, both served in small terracotta dishes. Back in our room we had coffee. Were in bed by 10.00pm.

Thursday 25th June. Day 133. Iguassu to Itaipu Dam.

The hotel mini-bus takes us to the 'State of Itaipu.' In this semi-autonomous region, a joint venture between the border sharing nations of Paraguay, Brazil and Argentina, a massive reservoir and hydro-electric dam has been constructed. The power generated being used by all three countries. An arrangement exists that the two major users financially compensate the poorer Paraguayans. An excellent example of what can be achieved with sensible international cooperation.

Tickets bought and a slot booked for the comprehensive tour, Chris and I attend an educational film. After which we're allocated to a visitor group, introduced to our guide, issued hard hats, ear defenders and board a bus that takes us to the structure. The tour is very informative, nowhere is off limits, unless danger outweighs sensibility. We're led over the concrete built dam itself, taken into the bowels of the noisy complex and see the spinning turbines. Country border lines are marked in yellow tape on the floor of the viewing balcony, from where the control room is seen through glass windows.

Returned to the hotel and decide to explore further up the Cataratas Avenue. A busy hill route leading all the way to Argentina. At the crest went into a café for a lunch of pastries and coffee. From here, strolled back towards the city through side streets and happened upon a very quaint bar. Obviously an old place, patronised by locals and the signage offering Brahma lager cheaper than we'd seen anywhere. As usual we're made very welcome, so we sat, drank beer, people watching, reminiscing about recent events and discussing plans for the last month of our trip. Which is definitely to be made in 'holiday mode.' After so many days of culture and history we're looking forward to some beach time.

Later took dinner at the Pacova, talked and watched Copa Football, Bolivia v Peru. Rounded off the night with our first 'Caipirinhas.' Been here in Brazil for two weeks, we'd definitely been remiss!

Friday 26th June. Day 134. Iguassu.

Nothing planned for today. Did some online research about Recife and had look for more to do in Iguassu, seems we've done it all! Checked google mapping, found a river nearby and in my note book drew a route. Walked for ages but couldn't find it. Fate decreed that we'd end up in the friendly family run bar at the end of our road, and we did!

Today the man of the house is on show, proudly wearing traditional 'Gaucho' clothing, puff sleeved white shirt with tight cuffs, a waistcoat and a wide belt around high waist, baggy, pleated black trousers tucked into cowboy boots. He looked a picture. Chris and I sat and talked. Words not heard for quite a while started to creep into the conversation, missing, nearly at an end, home, Marmite!

Our chat continued while having lunch at a 'weight' restaurant on Cataratas Avenue. Afterwards we went back to the little bar, continued talking and people watching. The man riding a moped delivering a 'multi-pack' of cigarettes to a house opposite, another walking up the street with a massive tray of pastry and bread items balanced on his head. We won't see things or events like this back in Pompey.

After dinner at the Ouvidoria, we part packed ready for tomorrow's travel day.

Saturday 27th June. Day 135. Iguassu to Rio de Janeiro. Linhas Aeras JJ3186 Dep. 12.53pm. Arr. 14.45pm. 1,400km.

Up at 7.40am, after breakfast at reception I confirmed our ride to the airport. In the room, checked messages on the ipad, one from Booking.com says that my card payment for the hotel in Rio has not gone through. Seems it has been blocked again, so I sent texts and emails to the ICE card company, hoping this will be quickly resolved. Chris paid our account and checked out.

11.00am, the mini-bus arrives at the airport. A strange arrangement here, having to pass through a security zone before checking in and another afterwards.

1.00pm. Departure is on time. From the plane we get a superb aerial view of the waterfalls. Spray rises like a cloud of steam, surreal, almost as if there's a hole in the planet. I slept most of the flight. Arrived in Rio on time. Having been here less than a year ago, for me it was 'Déjà vu.' Remembering the basic rules, I organised a taxi at an authorised booth, this time booking a return journey and getting a good discount. The ride into the city took thirty minutes, our cabbie moaning about roadworks as he turned into the sea front drive.

3.30pm, not far from the beach promenade, he parked outside the Copacabana Sol Hotel, Rua Santa Clara 141. Quite a plush place and no doubt would have cost triple during the 2014 World Cup. Checked in, we're allocated a 5th floor room with all facilities and a view over the street.

5.30pm, out and about. Less than 300 metres down the road is the 'Café Bar Santa Clara.' Wall hung televisions, chairs and tables on the pavement, just my sort of place! Had dinner here with copious beers. Watched Brazil go out of the Copa, losing to Paraguay on penalties.

Camera at the ready, hand in hand, we walked the short distance onto the spot lit sands of night time Copacabana beach. Flight to Rio paid by credit card, beers and meals, cash Brazilian Reals, Chris's smile. You know!

Sunday 28th June. Day 136. Rio de Janeiro, Sugar loaf Mountain.

Had a good early buffet breakfast. To avoid potential crowds or queueing we wasted no time and took a taxi to the cable car station. I'd promised Chris she would see everything that I had during my World Cup trip. So this is my second visit. Using passports as proof of age I obtained concessional fares again! Riding in the scenic windowed gondolas we were at the very top by 9.30am. The man upstairs has given us a clear, bright, warm, sunny day. Views over the bays and city are fantastic, even the Statue of Chris the Redeemer is easily seen in the distance. In 2014 the weather was cloudy, dismal and overcast, similar to the demeanour of England manager Roy Bodgson. Spelling intended!

After a couple of hours went back down to street level. Took a cab to the beach promenade and strolled to Fort Copacabana. Constructed on a headland to defend the harbour and completed 1914. Giant German engineered 'Krupp' naval guns point out to sea from the concrete cupolas. Standing on these the view of Rio and backdrop of mountainside favelas is awesome. The Fortress is still an active military barracks but can be explored inside and out. There are several museum buildings, restaurants and bars.

Walking back along the beach. It's Sunday, so very busy with people sun bathing, partying and partaking in sports activities, volley ball, heading tennis and six-a-side football. There are men, women, children, long legs, short legs. Beauties and not so beautiful wear bikinis. It all happens here, as seen on TV travel programmes! We sat, had a beer, a hot dog snack and watched.

At the hotel I checked online for the best way to get to the 'Redeemer.' A few blocks from the hotel we ate an average dinner in the posh 'Aquero' restaurant. Afterwards had a night cap beer or two in the Café Santa Clara. Not a bad first day in Rio!

Monday 29th June. Day 137. Rio de Janeiro, Statue of Christ the Redeemer.

No hanging about for the same reasons as yesterday. Out and in a taxi by 9.30am to the 'Corcado' mountain station. Plenty of touts vie for punters to take a mini-bus drive to the top but I'd read that the ride on the vernacular railway is spectacular. Bought tickets for the 10.30am train. Had coffee while waiting. An enjoyable thirty minute trip. The steep track winds gently through thick forest passing abandoned buildings to the top station. From here on we use steps, climbing to several levels, each with cafeterias, souvenir shopping and viewing platforms.

At one we stood admiring the city view, buildings so far below us they looked like tiny models. A man standing next to me spoke, describing a feeling that he could reach down and pick them up. I laughed and agreed. He introduced his eighty year old wife, she could have been a Diana Ross double. We four then engaged in an impromptu chat. He a tall, handsome, eighty one year old Afro-American, speaking impeccable English, had served in the USAF and been stationed at Upper Heyford in Oxfordshire in 1955, the year Chris was born! It was lovely to hear the language spoken without 'like' being used every third word.

We eventually joined the milling throng of tourists at the base of the tall statue. The jostling for best picture position is frustrating, some folks lay on the floor, others imitate Christ's pose and selfie sticks are brandished as if swords. Nevertheless I shot video and stills of the impressive Redeemer and some magnificent panoramic views. Charles and I never managed this visit in 2014, so I was extremely pleased to have done so on my return. After almost two hours we went down to ground level. Close to the station we had a simple lunch sat outside a fast food café. I kid you not, called 'Bob's!'

Took a taxi back to the hotel then went and sat on the beach for an hour. The weather has been wonderful, blessed all day with sunshine and bright blue skies.

In the evening we went out. Locating a 'Havaianas' shop on the way to our 'local,' for beer and food. Had too much of both while watching a Copa de America semi-final. Chile beat Peru 2-1. We rounded off the night with Caipirinhas. Holiday mode has kicked in completely. More and more hand drawn 'smiley faces' are appearing in the pages of Chris's diary!

Tuesday 30th June. Day 138. Rio de Janeiro. Copacabana Beach.

Had a late breakfast, then dressed for the beach. It's our last day in winter time Rio, we're going to try and have an easy one! On the sands by 11.00am. I hired a folding chair, Chris relaxed on a towel. As new arrivals we're immediately targeted by the strolling vendors that sell everything from food to clothing. The list of items '*not*' on offer would be very short. Having said "Nao por favour" and declined purchasing anything from his racked array of sunglasses, oils and requisites. One persistent smiling fellow then asked. "Anything?"

I presumed he was joking when he suggested that a woman, weed or cocaine maybe my need?

3.30pm, left the beach and the crashing waves. On the way back to the hotel Chris bought a souvenir sarong and t shirt. At the Havaianas shop we had a special request to fill. Here last year, I'd bought Susie a pair of 'tiger print' flip flops, she'd worn these to extent that sticking plasters are now being used to close holes in the soles. I'd found replacements, she'd be a very happy daughter!

At reception, staff were kind enough to telephone the taxi company and book tomorrows return journey to the airport. In the room we part packed and posted some pictures to Facebook. Went out early for our last dinner at the 'café.' The second Copa semi-final, Argentina v Paraguay, was on television but we left shortly after kick off, the Argies were already 2-0 up.

Bags totally packed, alarm set for 4.15am, we were asleep by 9.00pm.

Wednesday 1st July. Day 139. Rio de Janeiro to Recife. Gol Airlines G31470. Dep. 07.43am Arr. 10.44am. 1,875km.

Out of bed at 4.40am. Double check the room. Last personal items such as toothbrushes put into the day bags. 5.05am, at the reception lobby, our account paid and the taxi is waiting outside.

Hardly any traffic, we're at the airport by 5.30am, find the 'Gol' desk and check in. Waiting at the gate bought croissants and coffee for breakfast. Depart on time. Arrive Recife on schedule at the North East Coast Guararapes Airport. Having used it twice before I'm pretty familiar with the layout.

Took a 'priced' fare taxi to the Hotel Aconchego, Felix de Brito e Melo 382, Boa Viagem. We're early at 11.30am but able to check in. Allocated a 3rd floor ensuite room with fridge, TV and a small balcony in one of the several two storey buildings. The place itself looks quite good. There's a little swimming pool in front of the terrace restaurant area, above that is a small canopied games patio.

It's a strange situation, we're surrounded by high rise apartment blocks!

The weather is not so good, grey cloudy sky and very humid. Had lunch here and while sat at the table Chris was insect bitten. Being early afternoon went to explore, it's only a ten minute walk to the beach and promenade. Unfortunately, by 2.00pm the many very tall buildings at road side block any sun and cast shadows on the sands. The 'No swimming' and 'Beware of Sharks' signs bode badly! Walked several blocks along and then back through the locality looking for shops bars or restaurants, there's not much on offer in this area. At the hotel, search the web using mapping and it just proves the point. We'll explore more tomorrow. Accepting that for dinner tonight we'll probably have to use the hotel facilities, so we take a menu to the room for online translation. I took a nap. Woken at 4.30pm by heavy rain! After dinner we're in bed by 9.30pm. Have I made an error in coming here?

Thursday 2nd July Day 140. Recife.

8.30am, still raining heavily, hardly a break all night but it's not cold. We partake the buffet breakfast. This place has an 'omelette' chef so I order a couple of plain ones. Water is running off of roofs and canopies, splashing and sloshing. We tuck back in at a table away from the drips and use the internet. The weather forecast is grim. I've found a restaurant-cum-bar, but it looks like a cab ride distance away.

10.30am, mooching about the room and balcony, we've written diaries but not come to any decision about what to do. Even read the hotel rules, supposedly while on the premises, guests are only allowed to consume drinks from the bar or room fridge. Who sticks to that rule anywhere in the world?

Midday. Bored now, so I totalled the kilometres travelled for diary purposes. Double checked the web for local bars. It's not Rio!

1.30pm, the rain has stopped, but the sky is still very grey and threatening. Online I found a Carrefour supermarket. Thought that was clever until Chris pointed out the sign for the multi storey car park at the back of the hotel complex! Went there, big place, very busy, sells everything, fridges to food, tyres to TV's. To save cash on lunches we bought butter, cheese, sardines, rolls, yoghurts, water and of course, some beers. On the way back the heavens opened, p****d down is the phrase.

At our balcony table, using the never discarded airline issue plastic cutlery, made and had lunch. Rain continued, so we sat talking most of the afternoon and decided to find the 'Praca' tomorrow.

This is the first real time we've lost to bad weather and we're finding it hard to deal with. We'd promised ourselves some quiet and easy last days, but them being forced on us is weird. Probably because this is a beach resort!

6.30pm, the afternoon has gone, wasted, sat on the balcony or laying on the bed. Chris has been reading and I've smoked too much. It's still raining. Had a couple of beers before going to dinner. At one time we're the only people in the bar area.

Bed by 10.00pm. Chris summed it perfectly in her diary 'the hotel is a bit dull, no one around at all.'

Friday 3rd July. Day 141. Recife. Boa Viagem beach.

Had breakfast, ready to explore by 10.30am. Head south, walking about four of the fifteen kilometre long beach promenade. On the other side of the very busy four lane road is one multi-storey high rise block after another, some have thirty floors! These are mostly self-contained gated communities, classy mini-towns many with their own built in social centres, some a restaurant, a few have gymnasiums. They reminded me of the cities of Sau Paulo and Belo Horizonte.

Arrived at the 'Praca de Boa Viagem,' supposed centre and site of the original village established in 1740. Not much here bar the old church, which unfortunately is closed and being worked on. Walked towards town, stumbled upon a farmacia, so topped up our stock of ointments, insect sprays, Paracetamol and anti-histamine pills. The latter because I've definitely got swimmers ear again. Close by is a 'Walmart,' obviously where the locals shop, very busy. People beg for small change at the exit doors. Bought some pre-packed sandwiches and a couple of beers for lunch. In the same area we found the restaurants mapped on the web. Getting to them would definitely mean an expensive night time return cab ride, and there's no guarantee they'd be any good either.

The weather brightened, the rain forecast hasn't arrived. On the beach we selected a place to sit among the rocks and had our picnic lunch.

During the late afternoon, rested in our room, Chris read, ipod music played, I dozed. Later we dined in the restaurant, very poorly patronised. Even on a Friday it seems that around here Recife shuts down at 9.30pm. From our balcony the many lights visible in the towers suggested where the people were.

Saturday 4th July. Day 142. Recife.

Being hot and humid we had a broken night's sleep, even the air conditioning seemed to struggle, until 2.00am, when a proper noisy tropical downpour cooled the atmosphere. I'd left my day clothes on the balcony so they all got wet. At breakfast I asked if today's Copa final was being shown in the games area, the friendly waiter confirmed that it was. He was also adamant that Argentina would win, 6-0 his forecast. I suggested that Chile would be the victors. We'll find out later.

10.00am, still raining heavily. 11.00am, shopped for beer and food at Carrefour. Vehicles driving through big puddles in the road gutters sent water splashing everywhere. After making and having lunch, the rain stopped. We decided to walk southwards along the promenade. Not many people about, some joggers and one four a side football match going on. It's windy, the sea is very rough, big waves breaking over the exposed reefs. It started raining again. We went back to the hotel. In our room drank a few beers and watched the first half of the game. For the second half we joined the few folks that were interested, viewing the big screen TV on the upper terrace. Chile eventually won on penalties. I was very pleased considering they had been cheated out of the 2014 World Cup quarter final against Brazil. Chi-Chi-Chi, Ley-Ley-Ley! Had Burgers for dinner and went to bed. Slightly beery!

Sunday 5th July. Day 143. Recife. Boa Viagem Prias.

There is a God, the sun is shining and it's hot! Wouldn't want to cause a hotel incident, so I crushed and bagged the empty beer cans, dumping them in a bin on the way to the beach.

We're soon spotted by a fellow offering places in chairs and sunbeds, took a couple and joined other folks under parasols. There's no charge but you are expected to buy a beverage. Cristina, a barrel shaped woman sets a polystyrene cool box on our table, inside cans of lager are floating in iced water.

The sea is very rough again, but people are paddling in the shallows between the reefs and waterline. Similar to Rio, it's busy with vendors selling an array of hats, beachwear and oils but here there are lots of differing foodstuffs on offer, oysters, prawns, hot cheese, Black beans in sauce. Others rent out and fill children's paddling pools.

We have our own private window on the scenes. On his own, an old chap is sat in front of us quaffing beer, the empty cans below his chair are kept for tally purposes, he buys peanuts to feed numerous pigeons and they climb all over him. Later, he has a henna tattoo put on his chest by a one armed woman using a cocktail stick!

We watched and chilled. Excitement came when a rescue took place, a helicopter hovered as people pointed and waved. Lifeguards entered the sea and pulled in two men from way beyond the dangerous reef. Too much "bebe" (drink) Cristina said and indicated by jerking her thumb at her open mouth!

2.30pm, the sun dropping behind the tower blocks, we went back to the hotel. Still hot and humid. Showered, then slept for an hour. Drank a couple lagers before taking dinner by the pool. It's still in use by a couple of new arrivals, two plump bikini clad girls drinking cocktails. Holiday makers!

Monday 6th July. Day 144. Recife. Boa Viagem Prias.

On every flight or shared transport we've used 'First Defence' nasal spray as a preventative against picking up an infection. Unfortunately my chest has a rattle and I have a horrid sinus discharge, so last night I started a course of anti-biotics in the hope of not having my last trip days spoilt by illness. Everywhere is wet, it must have rained last night but I didn't hear it. The sky was cloudy earlier but cleared while we had breakfast.

11.30am we're back in the care of Cristina and sat in beach chairs. Today we've brought a 'home made' lunch of sardine and tomato filled rolls. With slightly tender tummies it's coke and water for liquid starters! A good breeze blows, it's still hot but not so busy on the sands. We watched volley ball football style, the women's one touch control would embarrass some British players. Henna tattoo man is here, continuing his enjoyment, plenty of beer for him and peanuts for the flying vermin. Sat nearby a group of Oriental's fed on Oysters and prawns for nearly an hour, the vendor had a big smile.

2.30pm, paid the small cash bill to our beach host Cristina. These folks are so trusting, caring and friendly.

She asks if we're back here tomorrow. Sadly not, we explain that we're leaving the city. We know they want custom but her goodbye hugs are no less genuine for that!

Went to Carrefour, bought some extra insect repellent, sun tan lotion and cigarettes. All of these items cost a premium rate at our next destination the Island of Fernando de Noronha. Online I double check our 'Condor' flight to London, having not received e tickets I've some concerns, so send an email. While I had internet it was prudent to send a note to the Portsmouth based Airport Taxi firm. Sad really but it's the stark reality of the situation. We'll be going home soon, very soon!

Tuesday 7th July. Day 145. Recife to Fernando de Noronha. Gol Airlines G31798 Dep. 2.00pm. Arr. 4.05pm. 562km.

Up at 7.30am, travel day, edgy as usual and I'm smoking too much. Pack bags and clear up the room after breakfast. 10.30am, check out, Chris pays. Reception staff organise a taxi to the airport. We're going a little early. I want to find the Condor desk and do. It's closed and only opens on flight days. Had coffee and tried to access one of the many free wifi sites offered, but logging on requires so much info I gave up! Boarded by 1.45pm, there are a few seat's vacant, very unusual as the island with limited accommodation operates an almost one tourist in, one out policy. Managed a nap, even on such a short flight.

Clocks are put one hour forward on landing. It's a messy operation at immigration. Fortunately I've done this before. Forms need to be filled, duration, place of stay given. At the desk an Eco tax is calculated and paid, ours for six days totals 700 Reals. Outside the small terminal building shuttle mini-buses are waiting. Ours found, luggage loaded, we're soon dropped off at the Pousada Leao Marinho, Alameda do Sol Nascente 538. The site is nowhere near the location shown on google mapping. The same as in 2014 for the place Charles and I stayed at. No complaints though, we're here on a tropical paradise island!

Our room is bigger and better than I'd had hoped, two beds, fridge and a TV. It's ensuite, but with only cold water feed for the shower and basin. The breakfast room is just outside. We meet the owner, Marie, who informs us of the home 'rules,' breakfast timings etcetera and because of business on the mainland tells us that she won't be here for our stay duration. She speaks good English but her 'houseman' doesn't, nor understands a word of it.

5.15pm, I think it's best to give Chris a limited guided tour of our new location so out we go and make a sweaty fifteen minute downhill walk, past the rusting German built World War One era howitzer and into the main square, which is little more than a long oval shaped grassy area. The roads either side are dotted with a few pousada's, cafes, restaurants and small shops. Bought water and beer then made the uphill walk back.

In our room tried the free wifi, it's very intermittent. Afterwards, readied to go out. A dinner of steak meals with beers at the 'Flamboyant' restaurant. One of the few places I'd used before. Now certainly more expensive and not as good as last year. The day's exertion has taken a toll, we took to bed at 9.00pm.

Wednesday 8th July. Day 146. The Island of Fernando de Noronha.

We're situated at about 300 metres above sea level on the north side, the declared inhabited zone and it's environmentally protected. To access other areas with stricter preservation controls a further expensive fee is payable. Everywhere can be explored by hiking on the many published trails. To get about, some tourists hire fibre glass bodied buggies with fat tyres, mostly powered by air cooled Volkswagen engines. The stink of petrol, exhaust fumes and noise pollution belies the stated ecological principles.

Many visitors come here for scuba diving. Organised trips are frequent. Collecting and depositing those that indulge, early morning and evening, sign written mini-buses towing trailers rumble through the village, bouncing along the potholed, cratered and crumbling roads.

It's also apparent to me that many of the shacks and domestic buildings have been or are being converted to holiday accommodation, even more so than last year.

Established in the 16th century, fortified against invasion, over the years the island has been used for many purposes. Among them a political prison and US Airforce base. A small museum in the village has a good historical display and geological explanations of how the Island was formed.

7.30am, slept well, the air conditioning being unusually quiet. The buffet breakfast is good, scrambled egg, melon, ham, breads, juice and coffee available.

10.00am, the sun is blazing. It's time to show Chris the beaches on this side of the Island. Plenty of tanning lotion applied and swimwear on. Towels and shirts looped in the shoulder strap of a day bag packed with snacks, water, camera, hats and other essentials. Out we go!

Pass the square and beyond the tarmacked roads we start the steep downhill walking on very large cobbles. These once neatly bedded into the hill side, now in many places uneven and loose, having been disturbed by sewerage pipe excavation and motorised traffic. To our left is the old Town Hall, in front of it sat on rough concrete platforms are two more slowly rusting vintage Howitzers. Down further and to our right is a 17th Century Church, doors closed. Fortunately I was able to visit and enjoy the simple interior a year ago.

The slope becomes gentle, we're still at a good elevation, on part of the old fortifications. Accessing the grounds of a restaurant a patio with walled parapet allows stunning views, down to the small cove of Cochorro Beach, up to the fort and way out over the Atlantic Ocean horizon. I think Chris was pleased. The smile on her face I captured on camera.

I knew my way from here. Staying close to the crumbling rampart walls, across the vegetation strewn redoubt parade ground, then through a thick, cool, tropical forest glade. This allows the crossing of a headland. A path leads out and downwards. Sharp tall plants and bushes encroach either side but steps formed by tree roots, stones and boulders goes down to the sea lapped rocks of the shoreline.

Its high tide, sandals are off, our feet are going to get wet before we reach the sands of 'Melo' and 'Conceicao' beach.

With at least three other people dotted along the length it was far from crowded! We picked a large rock to lay our towels then sat and talked while watching sea birds, especially the large Frigates with their pterodactyl like appearance.

Behind us, tumbled rocks and boulders are benched against the vegetation that grows up the steep rise of the Island. On occasions, Skinks, black and grey skinned lizards can be seen scuttling about.

From here and eastwards a ten minute barefoot stroll, then over another headland to the longest beach, strangely named in four sections, Boldre, Americano, Bode and Cacimba de Padre.

Pico Mountain is nearby. One of nature's oddities, it seems as if a gargantuan pointed boulder has been dropped from a great height and embedded into the island. Of course the reverse has happened, movement of tectonic plates and volcanic activity millions of years ago forced it upwards.

Further on we approach an impassable high rocky promontory. Here giant black boulders are being crashed into by a far more excited sea, a powerful swell washes and foams between the rocks. This distance away from the village the only footprints in the soft sand are ours! I took some touristy photographs.

We retraced our steps back towards Pico and close by lay out our towels, sun bathed and had a swim. The surf and undertow quite strong but still an enjoyable dip.

Continuing our return stroll we stopped at a beach café. This serves a few isolated pousadas hidden from sight in the forest. We sat in the shade of reed canopies. Ordered some fried potato chips as a snack and a couple of expensive bottled beers, which were at least delivered with iced glasses. Unfortunately the chips never arrived. They must have been lost in translation! Fortunately we carried biscuits and ate them while sat at another spot further along the walk. Although having re-applied lotion, by now we were wearing long sleeved shirts as additional protection against the merciless sun.

By 4.00pm, we'd taken cold water showers and applied insect repellent. Chris lay on the bed reading, I dozed in the hammock slung across the area outside our room that served as a balcony. Later, went for dinner at the 'San Miguel,' had beers and a nice pizza. While there I helped a young Swedish boy and his slightly elder sister with menu translation.

Thursday 9th July. Day 147. Fernando de Noronha. Remedios Fort and Cochorro beach.

Made up a couple of filled luncheon rolls while having breakfast. Shouldn't have, but as others were doing so, we didn't feel guilty. Checked the web, annoyingly no reply from Condor airlines. Readied for the beach but first we're going up to Remedios Fort.

The route similar to yesterday, except at the redoubt rampart level, turn east for a few paces and walk up a steep cobbled track. A barely legible collapsed sign indicates that the fort has had some restoration. Unfortunately Mother Nature and the weather have been very unkind to both. Almost a year exactly since my last visit, obvious to me, it's even more tumbled down and overgrown.

Cattle graze quietly within the grounds, building materials and roof tiles lay around. Walked up to the highest point where three flags flutter on a staff. Quite a distance from Pico but almost level with its peak. Views to all compass points are virtually uninterrupted, Remedios village, beaches, San Antonio North harbour and the far distant horizon on the Atlantic Ocean.

Although in poor condition, sentry post cupolas still stand in three corners at this level. On the ramparts, their carriages long rotted, are large bore iron cannon. Many have the 18th century cypher of England's George III. I take some photographs, intending to investigate why they are here. Fascinating because Britain has never had a political or military interest in or on the Island.

We sat, ate some of our picnic lunch before walking back down the cobbled path. Then used the steep steps that drop fifteen or more metres onto the small cove of Cochorro Beach. Here we laid our towels on the sand and had a swim. When a table and parasol became available we took to the chairs, ordered beers and watched the scenes. Children and adults climbing rocks then jumping into a hidden pool. A man swam from point to point, his dog following, in deeper water when he rested on rocks the brilliant animal climbed up as well. We did more swimming, took touristy selfies, underwater pictures of fish and the rays that lie sunning themselves in the shallows.

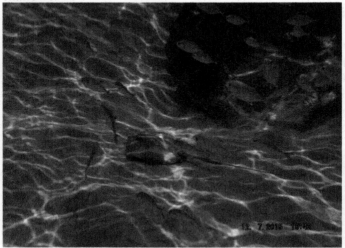

3.00pm, having been more in the sun than out, we paid our bill and left. At the pousada partook in 'afternoon coffee and biscuits,' a nice touch organised by the owner. Today is our daughter Susie's 29th birthday. I managed to get a good wifi connection and placed messages on Facebook indicating that she was 30. Her friends posted confused questions, unsure that they *'actually'* knew her properly. I'd stitched her completely!

Drank a few beers in our room while relaxing to music, before going to dinner at the very busy San Miguel's. We shared a steak meal, it should have been two but one didn't arrive. Translation blamed again or possibly the waiter being amused by my freshly sunned complexion and chuckling that I was, "pink, like a shrimp!"

Our ice cream dessert and account took ages to arrive. As I paid, the two young Swedes turned up, this time with parents. The father thanked me for my assistance to his children, he and the boy giving me genuine handshakes. The simplest of events in life can endow you so much pride.

10.15pm, back at the pousada. A couple with a baby have moved into the room next door, the child cries a lot. Online, no reply from Condor but Bob from Airport taxis messaged, giving me the name and telephone number of the driver who will be collecting us at Heathrow on the 15th. I noted both in my diary. More reality creeping in!

Friday 10th July. Day 148. Fernando de Noronha.

Had a bad night and woke with a sore throat. I've been taking antibiotics but other symptoms all point to a full blown chest and sinus infection, f**k it! To cap it all, it seems it's going to be the hottest day yet.

We visited the museum then walked to Melo beach. Far too hot to sit without shade, so stayed in the sea for quite a while. At low tide, negotiated the walk through the rocks and slippery plateau at the bottom of the headland to Cochorro cove. There must have been a cruise ship arrive at the port, the beach is crammed with people. Not a chair or parasol to be had, so we walked up the steps to rampart level and had lunch at 'Cochorros bar.'

3.00pm. Arrived at our room. I was breathless and crashed onto the bed. Went out to dinner later, but so desperate to sleep I was in bed very early.

Saturday 11th July. Day 149. Fernando de Noronha

Had a bad night, coughing, spluttering and I'm no better at breakfast time, in fact quite tetchy. It didn't help that people seemed to be shouting their conversations across the tables. Chris made up some rolls for lunch. I've taken so many pills I rattle. Feel very weary, so caved back into bed. I'm feeling sorry for myself and worse for Chris. She has no one else to talk to and nowhere to go on her lonesome. A day like this is horrid, no real home to go to, no tea or coffee making facilities. A hot Oxo drink would have done me the world of good. In the room, me dozing, Chris read and listened to music until about 6.00pm, when I felt well enough to go out and get dinner.

Back at the pousada we relaxed in chairs on the communal patio deck and got involved in conversation with a Brazilian family from Sao Paulo. We'd briefly met them yesterday. They spoke excellent English. The eldest son, a very grown up fourteen year old is soon off to Taiwan to further study Chinese language. His step mother a teacher, Chris got on well with her. Here for the diving, the father an engineer. He's quite opinionated, thought that Maggie Thatcher was a good example of a politician. I hated to disagree, my views about the Witch Queen were given as full explanation!

Sunday 12th July. Day 150. Fernando de Noronha.

Had a reasonable night's sleep. Still coughing and clearing this morning. Horrid. Had to have another nap after breakfast, but decided to make a supreme effort and not to lose the day. With more pills in me than a drug mule, walked, albeit slowly to the small cove. Sat on our towels until a light shower of rain. It could have been worse. Last year in almost the same calendar week, Charles and I experienced several tropical downpours.

We managed to get chairs, table and a parasol. Ordered beers and ate the luncheon rolls Chris made earlier. Went for a swim, afterwards topped up lunch with a dish of skewered roast chicken hearts. Chewy!

Watched some American new arrivals embarrass themselves by clicking their fingers at the beach waiters for table service.

3.30pm, made the slow walk back. Up the slopes I struggled to breathe deeply. Showered then dozed for an hour. The houseman has let us down, no afternoon coffee or biscuits laid on! In the kitchen I found a flask with stored hot water, used some of our sachet supplies and made a drink. Stood on the 'balcony,' I watched a large lizard stalking bees that hovered about a nest entrance high in a timber frame. Its success rate was good, snatching several victims.

For second time this trip I trimmed Chris's fringe using a comb and my electric shaver. Necessity the mother of invention and cheaper than a visit to a hairdresser. Later, had dinner and caipirinha night caps. In bed by 9.00pm. Not such a bad day in paradise after all!

Monday 13th July. Day 151. Fernando de Noronha.

Up at 7.30am. Rattling or not this piece of s**t that I call a body is going to the beach! Made ourselves ready. Went to the small cove, got chairs, table and parasol immediately. Today there's a very low tide. I'd mentioned to Chris that on my last visit Charles and I spotted a blow hole in the headland volcanic rock, so went and found it again. While there I saw a sea snake in one of the pools, damn, I never had the camera! Chris with me now, standing close to the hole. An amazing phenomenon, the sea floods over the plateau but must also be under it, the hole acts like a sink waste, water spirals down making a sucking noise, within seconds it spouts upwards. I'm sure that there is enough width and power to swallow a child.

Stayed on the beach until 3.45pm, our conversation turning more and more to the facts and details of leaving tomorrow. This talk continued most of the evening and during dinner and created a strange emotional paradox. Deflation and exhilaration at the same time.

Chris's diary note says it all. '....had a Whatsapp with Susie, she's home for a week, so getting a Tesco shop in for me, Angela's there for a couple of days but will be gone by Wednesday when we get back. It's all starting to feel so final now......Looking forward to seeing the kids, will be giving them big hugs.......'

Going home

Tuesday 14th July. Day 152. Fernando de Noronha to Recife. Gol Airlines. G31799. Dep. 4.35pm. Arr. 4.40pm. Recife to London via Frankfurt. 1st Leg, Condor Airlines. DE2075 Dep. 7.05pm. Arr. 15th July 10.05am. 2nd Leg, Lufthansa LH906. Dep. 12 noon. Arr. 12.40pm. 9,000km.

Chris's dairy note, 'Well here it is, last day. Very mixed emotions, have had a great time. Done and seen things I never knew imagined in my wildest dreams.......'

Heavy rain woke us at 7.15am, I jumped out of bed to get our towels from the balcony rail. The last thing needed is heavy wet gear to pack. Tidied the room before breakfast, lifting bed sheets to make sure there were no hidden personal items. When I moved my pillow it became apparent that the green lizard that was in the room last night had slept comfortably, with me! Laid everything out on the beds, loaded day bags and backpacks, carefully sifting through and discarding unnecessary items. Half empty lotions, the stash of sachet condiments, paper work, tickets and leaflets. Sadly, both sets of airline plastic cutlery had to go! There was some confusion about the account payment with the houseman, he couldn't work the credit card terminal. After a struggle I eventually settled with my debit card. More importantly using pen and paper I managed to explain we needed a taxi for 2.00pm. He made the phone call.

We had some time to waste, the beach was definitely a no go, so went for a walk. Afterwards sat in the patio chairs and waited. The taxi arrived and there wasn't a person here to say goodbye to!

The airport terminal is extremely busy, but we're eventually checked in. Hand luggage only still surprising some attendants!

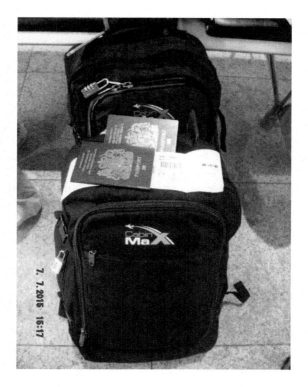

The gate waiting room is rammed, hot and not a seat to be had. Boarded and soon off the tarmac. The Island looked very small from the air.

It's one of those weird flights, only an hour but with the clock going back it lands the same time as take off!

4.15pm, arrive at Recife Airport three hours before the 'Condor' flight departure. My planned timings of six months past had been perfect. Didn't go outside for a smoke because the check in desk had a very long queue. I only have the booking print out but we're processed and pleased to be issued boarding cards both to Germany and the second leg to London and also told we should go to the gate immediately.

All targets have been met but for some reason a female Ge***po security officer decided to empty my bags and give them a proper tossing! I'm now grumpy and sweaty, desperate for a smoke and probably a mite terse with Chris. She did in fact make a note in her diary to the effect! Went to the toilets and stuck a nicotine patch on my buttock. At the shopping area bought coffee and duty free cigarettes using as many Reals as possible.

Boarded at 7.00pm, it's a pay for movies and headphones flight. We won't spend a penny! Meals I'd booked and paid for ages ago. Very pleased I had because dinner at 9.00pm comes with complimentary drinks. Normally I sleep easily but can't, a combination of uncomfortable seat, noisy plane and anxiety.

Wednesday 15th July. Day 153. Frankfurt to London.

Must have dozed eventually. My unadjusted wristwatch shows 3.00am and breakfast is served. It's actually 8.00am, German time. I still struggle with the differences.

10.15am, local time in Frankfurt. Landed and disembarked after a nine and a half hour flight. A bus ride takes us from one part of the airport to the building for European flight connections. Checked in at the Lufthansa desk, passed through security. On the way to the gate I used the bathroom and cleaned my teeth initiating a nasty coughing fit. Took more pills!

Blighty! The London bound flight is more comfortable than the first leg and we quickly clear Heathrow customs and immigration. A couple of phone calls located the taxi driver and a two hour drive by way of the M25 and A3 to Portsmouth completes an almost 80,000 kilometre, one hundred and fifty three day around the world trip!

By 4.00pm we're looking at welcome home banners hung on our own front door and being met by a smiling daughter Susie.

Later Chris made a chilli con carne and with a few beers we three did a lot of catching up, well into the night!

New reality

It's definite that we'd never again be the same two people that boarded the aeroplane to Delhi. Our levels of self-reliance, confidence and diligence increased daily. We'd expected to meet unknown difficulties and challenges but probably underestimated how many and the types. Especially those that if encountered at home would be accepted as mundane, possibly irritating, maybe involve cost but easy to overcome or simply resolved by a meeting, telephone call or email. Unfortunately while abroad these problems become gargantuan, sometimes all consuming, raising a mood of annoyance to that of anger, even vengeance when Microsoft is thought of. Nevertheless, every situation or obstacle that came at us was resolved or at least bypassed and I am rightly proud of that.

Several discussions with fellow travellers led to a couple of topical subjects that we'd not even thought of. Two cropped up with regularity. One was that as husband and wife the stresses and problems would search out any weakness in a relationship and tear it apart. Fortunately we disproved that. The other was that males lose weight and females gain it. In this we became living proof of the statement. Chris put on almost a stone, (7 kilograms). I lost the equivalent!

Chris also came to realise that she didn't need to be a painted lady for presentation anywhere in the world. She'd only taken limited 'make up' and noted that during the trip she'd only used mascara and eyeshadow twice, nail varnish once!

It was certainly strange to be back but reality started to creep in almost at once. A large pile of mail needed sifting through. Mostly mundane, but to test my sense of humour there was a replacement credit card!

Having the facility to make a hot drink at any time was good. As was reacquainting with Marmite on toast for breakfast. Days later Chris made a roast dinner, her cooking skills hadn't been diminished while we were away!

It was very odd being back in a house, having responsible for closing so many doors and locking up front and back when leaving. It would take a while to get used to normality but during the next few weeks we did.

Loose ends

Having prioritised a 'to do' list, during the coming days I contacted Thiago of the ICE travel card company. He'd been a good man and very helpful while we were away. I'd detailed most of my complaints on paper to make explanation easier. The nuisance of the card being blocked in South America, expense of having to use other forms of payment, the cost of telephone calls and text messages. I accepted a £50 gratuity for the inconveniences caused.

Lloyds bank credit card department were on the receiving end of a polite but firm call. I explained the situation and registered a complaint, because before leaving the UK I had informed them of every country that I would be visiting along with most of the dates. When my card was blocked without notice, this so called international company had been as much use as chocolate hammer. I listed the costs of communicating using my mobile phone while abroad and also requested a financial penalty for a late payment be refunded. I was reimbursed in all respects and closed the account forthwith. Unfortunately, I imagined that behind the polite reply and apology was the usual 'we don't really give toss,' corporate attitude.

Air Asia was a more difficult nut to crack. This airline company doesn't reply to emails and contact telephone numbers are all based in the Far East. However it does have a refund policy. This is very difficult to negotiate, even when in possession of an email that states that you are correctly entitled! Nevertheless I persisted. After several attempts I succeeded in converting the correspondence into an acceptable format and attaching it to the online electronic claim form. Thirty one working days later the cancelled flight fare was returned to my bank account. Albeit, I would have liked an apology, but there is no chance of that. To understand why, one only has to read any of the many angry statements on AirAsia internet forums!

It's been suggested that travelling with 'hand luggage' only we will have saved a small fortune. No!

Airlines, international and domestic. As a whole these companies provide proficient and practiced services. After all, without them our around the World trip could not have possibly been undertaken in its timescale. Leaving aside the possibility or probability of a late departure, being uncomfortable on an aeroplane or being charged for extras, a major criticism is management of baggage. Not handling, but size, weight and costs. There isn't a unified system! Every time a booking is made it becomes imperative to double check individual company policy, especially with hand luggage. Extremely frustrating is their sly practice of advertising an online ticket price and automatically adding the cost of hold luggage 'for your convenience' at check out. This becomes even more of a rip off when there is no way or facility to uncheck the requirement. Almost all of the major players are guilty of this. Less so, many of the budget and small airlines, they are strict but at least honest.

Postscript

Please don't let anything I've written be perceived as negative. Anything that seems such becomes trivial because we'd met and enjoyed the company of so many people in different countries, seen historic buildings, been overawed at the planet's power, felt insignificant in the shadow of Mother Nature's wonders. At times we'd been fraught, our nerves raw but for certain had never before felt so much alive!

Check the expiry date in your passport and start planning!

Lightning Source UK Ltd.
Milton Keynes UK
UKOW04f1817260717
306110UK00001B/152/P